THE LEADERS
BIRMINGHAM CITY

The official publication for the 140th
Anniversary of the formation of BCFC

First published 2015 by DB Publishing, an imprint of JMD Media Ltd, Nottingham, United Kingdom.

ISBN 9781780914534

THE LEADERS
BIRMINGHAM CITY

The official publication for the 140th Anniversary of
the formation of BCFC

Keith Dixon

Foreword by PAUL ROBINSON
– captain of Birmingham City Football Club

Contents

INTRODUCTION

The Leaders is a history of the successful captains of Birmingham City Football Club from 1930 to 2015. Success is defined as appearances in FA Cup Finals, Football League Cup Final victories and appearances, Wembley Final victories and successful promotion campaigns.

The Leaders was never intended to be a definitive record of every player who has captained The Blues, as it would be impossible to track the number of times a player has being given the responsibility (in recent times the armband) because the formally appointed skipper has not been selected, been substituted or suffered an in-game injury.

This is my seventh book on Birmingham City Football Club and its players:

1. *THE BLUES – GREAT GAMES – GREAT TEAMS – GREAT PLAYERS* – self-published in 2006.
2. *GIL MERRICK* – published by Breedon Books in 2009.
3. *50 GREATEST MATCHES* – published by Breedon Books in 2009.
4. *MODERN DAY HEROES* – published by DB Publishing in 2011.
5. *BAD BLOOD* – published by DB Publishing in 2013.
6. *ROBBO – UNSUNG HERO* – published by DB Publishing in 2015.

As with my previous books I have tried with *The Leaders* to give my readers new interesting material rather than regurgitate the same facts under a different format.

Each captain/leader section will include: Personal Information, Career Overview, Details of the success being recognised in the book and their Blues career.

Note: Unless otherwise stated the statistics in 'Career Overview' are for senior club appearances and goals counted for the domestic league only.

At the start of writing this book in July 2014, we Bluenoses, were looking expectantly at the new season, an unbeaten pre-season campaign involving non-league, League Two and Scottish League opposition plus what seemed to be a settled squad gathered together by manager, Lee Clark boded well for at least mid-table security in the Championship, certain in the knowledge that the players were committed to the club for the 2014–15 season. No longer did we have the huge salary commitments of Nikola Zigic and Chris Burke as the squad had been amassed with a salary cap of £5,000 per week. Guess What?

By the end of October 2014 Lee Clark had been sacked as manager initially to be replaced for one game by Scout Malcolm Crosby and development coach Richard Beale and then eventually ex-Blues player Gary Rowett was appointed, making the step up from managing League Two team Burton Albion. We had suffered a record-breaking home defeat of 0–8 against Bournemouth and were languishing in the relegation zone with 11 points. Massive swings from optimism to near despair are just part of the way of life for Bluenoses.

The Leaders chronicles only the good times as we celebrate the 140th Anniversary of the formation of the football club now known as Birmingham City.

PREFACE

Before I decided to write *The Leaders* I needed to consider what the structure of the book would be, and what the content might be for each section.

As with my previous books I needed someone to write a Foreword, someone with connectivity to the subject plus being well-known to the readers. Previous writers of Forewords for my books were Malcolm Page (*Gil Merrick*), Peter McParland (for my biography of *Jackie Sewell*), Ian Clarkson (*50 Greatest Matches*), Mike Wiseman – Honorary Life President Football Club (Modern Day Heroes) and Malcolm Stent – Entertainer (*Bad Blood*).

My preference was obvious, could I persuade Paul Robinson the existing Blues club and team captain to write the Foreword for *The Leaders*?

Thanks to the efforts of Andy Walker (Media and Communications Manager – Birmingham City Football Club) who organised for me to meet with Paul on Tuesday 22 July 2014 at the Wast Hills Training Ground to discuss my idea.

I discussed with Robbo the proposed format of the book and he was sufficiently interested in the idea to agree to contribute the Foreword plus add some personal insights and thoughts for his chapter. After more discussions it became evident that although he had rejected the idea of having a biography written previously – now could be the time. The initial idea was just to expand the planned chapter devoted to him in *The Leaders* book, but it soon became obvious that to fully document his extensive career would require a stand-alone volume. My publishers, JMD Media agreed to support a second book and *ROBBO – UNSUNG HERO* was published at the same time as *The Leaders* with Paul getting a joint author credit alongside myself.

Paul had been appointed Team and Club Captain for the 2014–15 season, which left Lee Clark with the decision as to who would be Paul's vice-captain, an important role which had been shared during season

2013–14 between Paul Caddis, Jonathan Spector and Chris Burke when Paul was absent. Clark's choice was Tom Adeyemi who had impressed everyone with his midfield performances during the pre-season campaign such that Lee Clark's decision was fully endorsed by Paul. This was a chance for Tom to learn the role of a leader alongside Robbo.

The headlines on the back page of the Birmingham Mail dated 25 July 2014 claimed 'TOM HAS RIGHT STUFF TO LEAD – Blues youngster named vice-captain'.

Colin Tattum's article went on:

'Tom Adeyemi has been handed a significant responsibility at Blues. The midfielder has been formally named as the new vice-captain. And manager Lee Clark described the 22-year-old as a skipper-in-waiting – and potentially even managerial material. Paul Robinson stays as Blues' captain and last season Jonathan Spector was his deputy, while Paul Caddis and Chris Burke also stepped into the vice-captain breach on occasions. As Robinson has not yet recovered from a knee niggle, Ademeyi will therefore lead the Blues in tomorrow's friendly at Kidderminster Harriers. "Tom Ademeyi will be our vice-captain, officially," revealed Clark. "I have spoken to the board, Paul Robinson and Tom about it. I just think he is future captain/managerial material within his career. He is a very intelligent boy, he is our PFA club representative at such a young age and usually, when he is fit he is going to play. So if anything happens to Paul, Tom will take over the armband. He was taken aback when I spoke to him about it yesterday but delighted also. It's something you enjoy seeing when you tell a player some good news like that. His reaction was really heartfelt and honest. So I've made the right choice and, going forward, he's a potential leader, without a doubt."

Adeyemi was plucked on a Bosman by Clark from Norwich City last summer. He knew Adeyemi from his days as a Carrow Road assistant. Adeyemi's powerful midfield performances were a highlight before back and hamstring injuries around the turn of the year affected his rhythm. Nonetheless, Adeyemi received Blues' young player-of-the season award and Cardiff City have him on their radar. "Blues shooed away the Bluebirds and their interest has not affected Adeyemi," said Clark – only added an extra spring to his step. "It has been in my thoughts for a while, to make him vice-captain, but I didn't want to put that pressure on him last year," the manager added. "It was his first season at the club, it was his first in the Championship and he was tremendous. He has come back in pre-season and the speculation about Cardiff has given him even more confidence and kicked him on. I just think this is another way of telling him how important he is to us and to me as the manager." Adeyemi's tender years was not a factor for Clark when it came to making the decision. "Steve Watson was telling me that when he played with Curtis Davies at West Bromwich Albion, Bryan Robson made Curtis captain at 19 or 20," he said. "As I keep saying, age doesn't matter. It's about responsibility and Tom is looked upon by the other players in the way he delivers himself. Not only is he a good player, he's a very intelligent young man and he has the ability to lead by example in any walk of life, in any situation."

After the Notts County pre-season friendly game I spoke with Adeyemi to ask him for an interview for this book, he agreed subject to my agreeing dates etc. with Andy Walker. Andy kindly proposed an interview on 14 August 2014 but when I chased Andy for a time, he said in light of the announcement my interview was at least postponed. The announcement was Ademeyi asking for a transfer on 5 August 2014!!

Lee Clark was 'gutted' by Tom Adeyemi's move to Cardiff even though the club did everything to try and keep the midfielder. The 22-year-old was sold to Cardiff City on Thursday 7 August 2014, two days before the Blues' opening match of the Championship campaign away at Middlesbrough.

He joined Blues in June 2013 having been released by Norwich City and played 40 games scoring three goals in 2013–14 season.

"I'm gutted that we've lost one of the most powerful, talented midfielders in this league. We tried everything to keep him within our means," said Clark. "But he wanted to leave, so the club got the best deal we could – it's a very, very good deal for a player with only a year left on his contract."

Birmingham's Championship rivals Cardiff moved for Adeyemi shortly after the sale of Jordon Mutch to Queens Park Rangers for £6m – another player the Bluebirds signed from St Andrew's. Born in Norwich, Adeymi progressed through his hometown clubs' academy and later worked with Clark during the Birmingham boss' time on the coaching staff at Carrow Road. Tom started his career with The Canaries as a trainee making 17 first-team appearances for the club. Most of his career in East Anglia was spent out on loan making over 100 starts for Bradford, Oldham and Brentford. "I have known Tom since he was a 14-year-old and I brought him here as an unknown quantity," said Clark. "I think there's a potential Premier League player in there, but now we move on. Other players will get an opportunity, and I've got targets in mind should we need to bring someone in."

Before the Capital One Cup First Round match at home to Cambridge United, Clark signed David Davis from Wolverhampton Wanderers for an estimated fee of £100,000.

How times have changed? Probably up to the start of the 21st century to be given the chance to be part of the on-the-field management team of a professional football club would have meant the world to a young footballer embarking on his career. Some of the captains featured in this book were given that opportunity and took it with both hands, others had to wait until much later in their careers before the opportunity to be a captain or vice-captain was presented to them. However in 2014 things had changed dramatically resulting in this disappointing event. Tom had obviously been in conversation with Lee Clark and Paul Robinson about his prospects at the football club; as well as being a first-choice in the midfield area; he would be playing every game and would have the opportunity to learn the art of captaincy alongside a true Blue hero. None of this meant anything to him when the lure of more money came into his life. To value so lowly this opportunity was to show a lack of respect for the previous captains of St Andrew's. Many of the captains featured in this book would have given everything to be appointed as vice-captain to a club of the stature of Birmingham City Football Club at the age of 22 years of age. A move to a Premier League club might have been understandable but to move to another Championship club it has to be about money rather than ambition. How is Tom's career to date? At 23 January 2015 he had made only 12 appearances for Cardiff City and was not a regular first choice to start matches.

FOREWORD BY PAUL ROBINSON

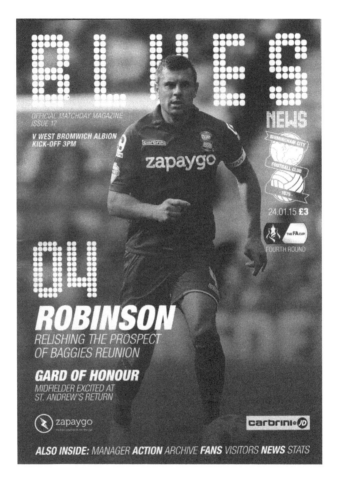

Paul Robinson on front of Blues News on 24 January 2015
v West Bromwich Albion in FA Cup Fourth Round

I am delighted to be writing the Foreword for *THE LEADERS – BIRMING-HAM CITY.*

When Keith asked me if I was prepared to write a few words, there was not a moment of hesitation on my part because I wanted to be associated, even in just a small way with some of the great captains that have become part of the history of The Blues.

I can't believe that I am following on after some great personalities who have been given the honour of leading the men in Royal Blue; Stephen Carr – a personal friend and we share the same representation, Lee Carsley, who helped me when I was out of contract following my spell at Bolton Wanderers, Martin O'Connor, Ian Clarkson and Michael Johnson who are still involved in the club either with the Blues Former Players' Association or featuring as 'Star of The Day' at home games, plus those leaders who appeared in FA Cup Finals. Won the League Cup and gained Promotions in the 30s, 40s, 50s and 60s. What a responsibility to be listed alongside such legends of Birmingham City.

When Lee Clark appointed me as Team and Club Captain at the beginning of the 2013–14 season I was immensely pleased and proud to be given the joint roles of a club with such a history (140 years in 2015) and reputation in the world of football.

Lee was thoughtful in his appointment of me saying: "I've confirmed to Paul that he will be team and club captain next season. He knows as well as I do that that doesn't guarantee him a starting position. But I think he ticks all the boxes in terms of what I'm looking for in a leader both on and off the field. He knows when the time is right to give someone an arm around the shoulder and some encouragement and also when the time is right to give someone a kick up the backside. He also leads by example as well in terms of his performances. Allied to his dressing room presence, he played a big part in Blues climbing away from the wrong end of the Championship to even briefly flirt as outside play-off contenders before an ultimately respectable top-half finish. And the work he has done in helping young Mitch Hancox along has hinted at a role on the touchline when his playing days finally come to an end."

For me as captain I do not play the game any differently, but I am conscious of the fact that I'm leading by example. You can't be caught out not putting in full effort as a captain – the number one thing is to be leading by example. You have to practice what you preach – otherwise the other players won't respect you when you ask them for things. The other main element is communication. You're the manager's right arm on the pitch and you need to make sure that your team are all getting the message. I've got quite a loud voice and I've worked hard on being more vocal – it doesn't come naturally to everyone. Captains don't have to scream and shout but sometimes you need to get information across during a game. You also have to change your attitude. It's not just you and your game that you have to concentrate on any more. You can't let leadership distract you from your main job – defending in my case – but you need to have more of an eye on what's going on around the pitch. Make sure you're on good terms with all the other players, and let them know that they can come to you with any problems. I feel the need to be a consistently good performer, getting scores in the newspapers of six or seven out of ten in match after match. If I had to describe the qualities of a good captain or leader outside of consistent good performance they would be talkative – command respect – seen as part of the club as well as the team – level headed and fair. Hopefully I tick all those boxes.

I am very conscious of what the fans expect from me as a captain. In October 2014 we suffered a home defeat to Bournemouth of 0–8. This defeat went down in the history of Birmingham City Football Club as the biggest home defeat in its 139-year history and I was captain. I believe and hope that I showed the qualities of a captain in two ways:

a.   I ensured the players remained on the pitch after the final whistle to applaud the fans, who had been defiant and sang *Keep Right On to The End of the Road* even when the fifth goal went in! Although as the goals continued to go in, a section of the crowd turned on the players with chants of 'you're not fit to wear the shirt'. I made sure they did not hide and faced the boos of criticism. My action drew some criticism from Kevan Broadhurst who was commentating on the match alongside Tom Ross on Free Radio 80. 'Broads' a previous captain of the Blues, said that he would have been too ashamed to go and applaud the fans after such a performance and would have left the pitch in a hurry.

Obviously I do not agree but an Interestingly different approach to the role of a captain.

b.   I made a post-match apology via video on the Blues' web site saying I vowed that the players would work hard to make amends. What I said was; "I can only apologise to the fans for that shambles of a game. We're all very disappointed, the fans will be even more disappointed paying lot of money to come and watch – that is not acceptable. We all know we have got to knuckle down as a team and work hard. When you lose 8–0 you don't forget it, but I'm not going to stand here and throw the towel in because I'm not that kind of person. I'm going to get the lads together and we're going to put this right together. This group can recover, because they're a good bunch of lads. They're going to take full responsibility, like I have. They are going to get on the training ground on Monday and get ourselves ready for Wolves. If the new manager does come in, then I think he has had a bit of a wake-up call with players he has got to work with. But when he sees the players he will know they are a good group of lads."

For me it was also important not to hide away immediately after the game although there was a part of me that wanted to, but I had some corporate activities to fulfil as captain. I do not wish to seem arrogant but this is how it was reported in the match day programme for the next home game against Cardiff City:

'DAVE'S EZE WISH COMES TRUE!

A chance to meet Paul Robinson eased the disappointment of Blues' hefty home defeat by AFC Bournemouth for fan and cancer sufferer Dave Roberts.

Thanks to an EZE Wish granted by Blues diamond partner EZE Group. Dave, from Solihull, had a post-match chat with the club captain. The 66-year-old lifelong Blues fan, who has incurable bowel cancer, had just witnessed the club's eight-goal thrashing at St Andrew's, but his spirits were boosted by his encounter with the amiable defender. "Meeting Paul did lift my mood somewhat," said Dave, "And I thought it was very brave of him to come and face everyone like that after such a heavy defeat. It takes someone like the club captain to do that. We had a good chat, and I reminded him that we had met some years ago when he played for Watford. I used to be a season ticket holder, but this was the first game I have been to this season, and would you believe it – it was an 8–0 drubbing! It was a great day in the EZE Group box though – the hospitality shown by Blues was superb."

EZE Group's Dave Smith said, "The last thing many players would want to do after a result like that, especially at home, is chat to fans. But Paul's such a great guy; he was only too happy to meet Dave, and after having heard about his battle with cancer certainly put the match in to perspective for him."

Being a captain is not about having the title it is about doing the right things for the team, the management, the club, the fans and the game.

In September 2014 the *FourFourTwo* football magazine's special supplement entitled 'Season Preview 2014–15' reviewed each club in the Premier League and Football League regarding its prospects for the season. Each club was designated a 'Key Player' and for Blues it was me and they very succinctly identified the task ahead for me and the club stating: 'The "heart-on-sleeve" captain and defender, now 35, is a model of the graft and determination needed to survive in this division (Championship), and will need to help galvanise a much-changed squad quickly to do it again.'

I cannot explain to you the immense feeling of pride I get when I lead the team out onto the St Andrew's pitch and witness the passion of the Bluenoses. Those readers who go to the matches will know that after the coin toss and the formalities are completed I spin off towards the Tilton Road end and applaud the crowd – this is not just for show but to say thank you to the fans for being there and supporting the club and the team.

When the fans start singing the anthem *Keep Right On To The End Of The Road* it means a lot to the players and me.

KEEP RIGHT ON!

Lee Clark and Robbo

ACKNOWLEDGEMENTS

My thanks go to a number of people: Andy Walker and Colin Tattum who have both served as 'Head of Media and Communications – BCFC' (Note: Andy moved in to a similar communications role within The Football Association in December 2014) during the writing of the book.

Steve Caron and his team at DB Publishing and JMD Media for getting the book edited, proofread, printed and published.

My Bluenose friends – Mike O'Brien for the use of his archives and Mick Sherry for his meticulous proofreading skills.

My appreciation to all the Blues' former players/captains for answering my questions and thereby providing lots of new material for my readers.

Special thanks go to Paul 'Robbo' Robinson for writing the foreword and contributing to the 'Art of Captaincy' chapter.

Thanks to my family for supporting me: Julie, Holly and Harry; Matt, Caleb and Amy; and Ben.

1.

THE ART OF CAPTAINCY

For many of us the thought of being a professional footballer is beyond our wildest dreams, but to captain the team would be amazing. This chapter hopes to chronicle some of the recent attitudes to football captaincy and at the same time clarifying some of the roles of a captain whilst de-mystifying some of the widely held beliefs of what a captain can and cannot do.

Prior to the start of the 2014–2015 football season Wayne Rooney was confirmed as captain of Manchester United and England. In terms of captaincy, to be given that responsibility for England (the birthplace of Association Football) and for the most famous football club in the world there can be no greater accolade in a footballer's career. Apparently not everyone in football thinks so, Gary Lineker (purveyor of Walker's Crisps and host of Saturday's *Match of The Day* on BBC television) wrote in *The Guardian* on 28 August 2014: 'Do we give the captaincy too much importance? Well I rather doubt it alters events dramatically…on the field of play at least. A skipper has no say in selection, he has no say in tactics, he has no say in substitutions. Football ain't cricket.' Is this a true statement about the art of captaincy or Lineker's opinion of Rooney (or how Lineker carried out his duties as a skipper with Leicester, Everton and Spurs?)

After Rooney's captaincy debut in a friendly 1–0 victory over Norway at Wembley on Wednesday 3 September 2014 Patrick Collins wrote in *The Mail On Sunday* on 7 September under the headline 'Don't worry Wayne, it's just a strip of cloth':

'The choice of Wayne Rooney as England captain was not universally popular. Some worried that the responsibility might prove inhibiting and that his form might suffer. In the event, the armband made not a scrap of difference. Rooney worked as hard as ever in the match against

Norway but his touch was wayward, his efforts unproductive and a game which once came so easily to him now seemed a murky mystery. When he departed, in the 69th minute, he appeared uncertain what to do with the armband. He looked around, spotted Gary Cahill nearby and hastily passed it on. It would be good to report that Cahill was inspired by his call to the colours. In truth, he simply carried on making the same mistakes he had been making all evening, before thrusting the armband at Joe Hart with six minutes remaining. The transactions evoked images of harassed mothers handing over a screeching infant. There are those who cling to the caricature of captaincy, the peculiarly English myth of the fist-shaking skipper rallying his troops by the force of his personality. That delusion perished when Roy Race hung up his boots at Melchester Rovers. We now accept that the captain is required to predict the toss of a coin and make a choice of ends. But we resist pretentious attempts to mystify the office. For we know that the reality of football captaincy can be quite different. And that it can involve three embarrassed young men, hurriedly exchanging a shabby bauble. Because convention insists that somebody has to be nominally "in charge", his authority signified by a strip of cloth.'

Whether Patrick Collins is right or not here are some ideas/facts surrounding the art of captaincy:

- The role of captain is often under appreciated in the world of football. But the man wearing the coveted armband can often prove the difference between a good team and one that has the ability to take on all comers and become remembered as one of the greats.
- The team captain of an association football team, sometimes known as the skipper is a team member chosen to be the on-the-pitch leader of the team: it is often one of the older or more experienced members of the squad, or a player that can heavily influence a game. The team captain is usually identified by the wearing of an armband.

- A great captain does not need to be the best player on any given team; nor, indeed, a footballer of spectacular talent. But this individual needs something special to drive his companions on to glory. It could be an unbreakable spirit, unyielding commitment or the ability to lead by example, which inspires the best from those who surround them on the pitch.

- A *vice-captain* (or *assistant captain*) is a player that is expected to captain the side when the club's captain is not included in the starting eleven, or if, during a game, the captain is substituted or sent off. Often the vice-captain is appointed the new club captain upon the departure of the incumbent.

- A club may appoint two distinct captaincy roles: a *club captain* to represent the players in a public relations role, and correspondent on the pitch. He is usually appointed for a season. If he is unavailable or not selected for a particular game, then the club vice-captain will be appointed to perform a similar role – a *team or match captain* is the first player to lift a trophy should the team win one, even if he was not the club captain.

- The only official responsibility of a captain specified by the Laws of the Game is to participate in the coin toss prior to kick off for choice of ends and prior to a penalty shootout.

- Contrary to what is sometimes claimed, captains have no special authority under the laws to challenge a decision by the referee. However, referees may talk to the captain of a side about the side's general behaviour when necessary.

- At an award-giving ceremony after a fixture like a cup competition final, the captain usually leads the team up to collect their medals. Any trophy won by a team will be received by the captain who will also be the first one to hoist it.

- The captain generally provides a rallying point for the team: if morale is low, it is the captain who will be looked upon to boost their team's spirits.

- Captains may join the manager in deciding the first team for a certain game. In youth or recreational football, the captain often takes on duties that would, at a higher level, be delegated to the manager.
- The captain is usually a midfielder or defender, and less often the goalkeeper; a striker, due to the more one-dimensional nature of his position up front, is rarely called upon to wear the armband.
- Players who have received the captain's armband during the course of a game are not considered by the Football Association as being official England captains.
- However ex-Birmingham City players, Emile Heskey, Joe Hart and Michael Carrick – who have never officially captained England – have worn the captain's armband during the course of a match when the official captain and vice-captain have been sent off or substituted. The other players on the list are Robbie Fowler, Danny Mills, Phil Neville, Jamie Carragher, David James, Gary Neville, James Milner, Joleon Lescott and Phil Jagielka
- David Seaman (ex-Birmingham City) captained the full England team on one occasion. In the World Cup Qualifying Group Two game against Moldova at Wembley on 10 September 1997 which England won 4–0. Seaman earned 75 caps during the period 1988–2003.

2.

NED BARKAS

– FA CUP FINALISTS 1930–31

FULL NAME: Edward 'Ned' BARKAS.

DATE OF BIRTH: 21 November 1901.

PLACE OF BIRTH: Wardley, near Gateshead, Northumberland.

DATE OF DEATH: 24 April 1962.

PLACE OF DEATH: Little Bromwich, Birmingham at the age of 60.

PLAYING CAREER:

Youth Career:

He started his football career as a full-back with St.Hilda's Old Boys, East Borden, Hebburn Colliery, Bedlington United, South Shields, Wardley Colliery.

Senior Career:

Originally a centre-forward he scored five goals in one game for Bedlington United. After completing his apprenticeship in non-league football as a part-time footballer and full-time miner his senior career had a 'false start' in 1920 with a single appearance for Norwich City, without scoring before returning to Bedlington United for a second spell.

His career took off at the end of 1920–21 season, when he signed for Huddersfield Town as a professional in January 1921. He was for some reason immediately converted into a defender and eventually into a tough tackling, no frills full-back. He went on to make 131 senior appearances scoring four times and achieving back-to-back League Championship winner's medals in 1922–23 and 1923–34 seasons. He also played at Wembley in the 1927–28 FA Cup Final where Huddersfield Town lost to Blackburn Rovers. In the summer of 1928 he toured Canada as a member of the Football Association party. In December 1928 Leslie Knighton signed him for Birmingham for a then club record transfer fee of £4,000. He established a long-standing full-back partnership with Jack Randle playing initially as a right-back before switching to the left. He stayed until 1937 making 288 senior appearances scoring nine goals. He was Leslie Knighton's first signing for Blues and he probably did not make a better signing – what he got was exactly what he wanted a hard-working full-back which was exactly what you would expect from a player brought up in mining communities. He made his Blues league debut against Manchester City on 29 December 1928 at Maine Road winning 2–3 with Pike (2) and Bradford the scorers in front of a crowd of 28,365. He scored his first league goal from the penalty spot on January 5 1929 in a 1–2 defeat at St Andrew's against Huddersfield Town. His last league game for the Blues was on 24 April 1937 at home in a 1–0 victory over Wolverhampton Wanderers in front of a crowd of 22,110, Jennings scoring the only goal from the penalty spot. He had the distinction of being selected as a reserve for England in two Home Internationals. Knighton signed him again, this time for Chelsea in May 1937. After two years at Stamford Bridge where he made 27 appearances without scoring, Ned returned to the Midlands to become player-manager of Solihull Town from 1939 to 1943. He then helped out Willmott Breedon FC in 1943–44 and Nuffield Mechanics in 1944–45 whilst working as a chargehand in a munitions factory. He came from a footballing family: his brother Sam played for and captained England, a cousin, Billy Felton, also played for England, and three other brothers Tommy, James and Harry were professional footballers.

HONOURS:

Huddersfield Town:
First Division champions 1922–23 and 1923–24.
FA Cup finalist 1928.

Birmingham:
FA Cup finalist 1931

DETAILS OF SUCCESS
1931 FA Cup Final Team

Surname	First	Nickname	Appearances	Goals	Seasons
HIBBS	HARRY		388	0	14
LIDDELL	GEORGE		345	6	12
BARKAS	EDWARD	'NED'	288	9	9
CRINGAN	JIMMY		284	12	11
MORRALL	GEORGE	'LOFTY'	266	7	9
LESLIE	ALEC		143	0	6
BRIGGS	GEORGE	'NIPPY'	324	107	10
CROSBIE	JOHNNY		432	72	12
BRADFORD	JOE		445	267	15
GREGG	BOB		75	13	4
CURTIS	ERNIE		182	537	7

1931 FA Cup Final Team – Ned Barkas holding football

The 1931 FA Cup Final team, where did they go?

Surname	First Name	Outcome
HIBBS	HARRY	RETIRED 1940
LIDDELL	GEORGE	RETIRED 1932
BARKAS	NED	CHELSEA 1937
CRINGAN	JIMMY	BOSTON UNITED 1934
MORRALL	GEORGE	SWINDON TOWN 1936
LESLIE	ALEC	RETIRED 1932
BRIGGS	GEORGE	PLYMOUTH ARGYLE 1933
CROSBIE	JOHNNY	CHESTERFIELD 1932
BRADFORD	JOE	BRISTOL CITY 1935
GREGG	BOB	CHELSEA 1933
CURTIS	ERNIE	CARDIFF CITY 1933

FA Cup Appearances for players that did not make the Wembley line-up:

FIRTH 2 appearances 1 goal – HORSMAN 2 appearances 0 goals

MATCH REPORT:

A wet but eager 90,368 crowd packed into Wembley to cheer the first all Midlands Final for 36 years and Birmingham's Final for the first time in 50 years of trying. It was Blues from Division One against promotion chasing Second Division West Bromwich Albion. The rain threatened to spoil the occasion and it was the wettest Cup Final in years, ensuring both sides would be tested on the huge Wembley pitch in the mud. Blues settled to the conditions well and on their first real attack had the ball in the Albion net. A free-kick from Cringan was floated over towards the running Bob Gregg who steered his header past a flat-footed Pearson for a perfect start. However linesman Harold Mee of Nottingham surprised almost everyone in the stadium when he raised his flag to rule it out for offside. Blues, to their credit, put the disappointment to one side and were soon back attacking. Joe Bradford broke clear but Pearson rushed out to smother the Blues forward, then Curtis sent in a dangerous looking cross, which again was clipped away from Bradford this time by centre-half Magee. Albion then countered and Barkas just managed to catch and then clear from Glidden who had raced free from a hopeful long-ball clearance. It was now a good end-to-end game with both teams looking likely to score and after 25 minutes Albion went in front. A fiercely hit Glidden cross struck Barkas on the hand and before the Albion players made any appeal Richardson latched onto the loose ball. His first-time shot was blocked by Hibbs but he followed up to smash in the rebound. Blues came close moments later with Bradford and Crosbie, who should have made more of their chances inside the Albion penalty area. Then with half-time approaching Bradford should surely have equalised when he stubbed his shot and the ball bobbled past Pearson who scrambled across his line, grateful to see it roll wide of the post. Albion were better starters in the second half and Hibbs pulled off a great save from Wood. On their next attack Wood hit the post with a belting shot from 20 yards as Blues held on and tried to settle the game down. As the Albion storm subsided, Blues counter attacked. A long ball from Crosbie found Bradford, as his fellow forwards looked to make space for a return pass he turned sharply and in the same movement shot past Pearson and Blues were level on 56 minutes at 1–1. But with the Blues fans still celebrating the goal, Albion hit back with a sucker punch. After the ball was thumped forward Liddell failed to clear to any great distance and W.G. Richardson pounced to slip it past Hibbs from close range. Albion dominated the final moments of the game and only the brilliant Hibbs kept Blues in with a slight chance with some brave diving saves, which kept the score down to 2–1. Blues will always rue the early disallowed goal, but Albion had earned their win and made it a promotion double when they won their last two league matches of the season.

Albion: Pearson; Shaw, Trentham; Magee, Bill Richardson, Edwards; Glidden, Billy Richardson, Sandford and Wood.
Referee: Mr A. Kingscott (Derby).

19th in Division One with Leslie Knighton as manager – Season Record was: played 42 – won 13 – drew 10 – lost 19 – goals for 55 goals against 70 – points 36.

BLUES CAREER
SEASON BY SEASON

Season	League Appearances	League Goals	FA Cup Appearances	FA Cup Goals
1928–29	18	1	2	0
1929–30	38	3	3	0
1930–31	33	0	7	0
1931–32	19	0	1	0
1932–33	28	0	5	0

1933–34	36	2	3	0
1934–35	30	1	4	0
1935–36	32	2	2	0
1936–37	22	0	1	0

The cover of the programme of the day, including advertising on the cover for the first time. An original would cost in excess of £1,000.

The programme for this match was the first ever to have product advertising on the front cover: 'DRINK BOVRIL ONCE IT'S IN YOU IT'S SINEW' was the slogan, you obviously could not keep a good advertising man down even in those days.

The cost of the programme was sixpence (in today's money 2.5p) or a tanner, and it was 36 pages packed with information and advertisements, which are fascinating now some 84 years later:

OSRAM VALVES – The Public's 'final' choice for Radio – no transistors in those days!

MYATT Daymark BLADES – As supplied for the Third Time under Annual Contract to the whole BRITISH ARMY – product endorsement was around even then!

MADAME TUSSAUD'S announced: 'LOOK! THERE'S BARKAS and THAT'S GLIDDEN'.

'Here they are – at Madame Tussaud's – both rival captains!'

CLASSIC CURLY CUT TOBACCO – 10d per ounce – The 'extra-time' Tobacco.

LOCKWOOD & BRADLEY – Special Cup-Tie Tailoring Offer – All Wool Botany Serge Suits for 50 shillings/

RECKITTS BATH CUBES – FEET, FEET, FEET, YOUR FEET NEVER GET A HOLIDAY.

BEMAX – Whatever your system needs – YOU'RE BOUND TO BENEFIT FROM BEMAX – The Natural Vitamin Tonic Food 2/6d.

TRUE STORY – 100 pages of thrilling real life stories – fully illustrated 6d.

MACKINTOSH'S 'CHEWLETS' – The Great British Chewing Sweet – five for 1d.

ST MARGARET – West Bromwich Albion are playing today in St Margaret Jerseys.

The match day programme was also used to promote other sporting events:

RUGBY LEAGUE FINAL – York v Halifax – best priced seats were 10/6d.

GREYHOUND RACING – Tonight at 8 – 'Public restaurant – Free Parking for Motor Coaches and Dancing Free'.

ROYAL TOURNAMENT – Olympia – May 28 to June 13.

Just like today's programme's it appealed to the statistician with a full page on 'HOW THEY REACHED THE FINAL'.

BIRMINGHAM

		Goals			
		F	A	Gate	Receipts
Third Round.	v Liverpool (A)	2	0	40,500	£2,655
Fourth Round.	v Port Vale (H)	2	0	44,119	£2,763
Fifth Round.	v Watford (H)	3	0	49,757	£3,223
Sixth Round.	v Chelsea (H)	2	2	55,298	£4,298
Replay	v Chelsea (A)	3	0	74,365	£5,147
Semi-Final	v Sunderland	2	0	43,572	£3,939
	(At Leeds)				
	Total	14	2	307,611	£22,025

Goal Scorers:

Bradford	7
Curtis	6
Firth	1
	14

WEST BROMWICH ALBION

		Goals			
		F	A	Gate	Receipts
Third Round.	v Charlton (H)	2	2	25,000	£1,574
First Replay.	v Charlton (A)	1	1	18,700	£1,050
Second Replay.	v Charlton (Villa Park)	3	1	27,700	£1,805
Fourth Round.	v Totten. H (H)	1	0	40,850	£2,402
Fifth Round.	v PortS. (A)	1	0	30,891	£2,410
Sixth Round.	v Wolv. W (H)	1	1	52,300	£3,150
Replay	v Wolv. W (A)	2	1	46,860	£3,410
Semi-Final	v Everton (At Old Trafford)	1	0	69,421	£7,629
	Total	12	6	311,722	£23,430

Goal Scorers:

W.G. Richardson	4
Wood	4
Carter	2
Glidden	1
Sandford	1
	12

So 307,611 fans paid £22,025 to see Blues play in the FA Cup excluding the Final that equates to an approximate average admission charge per person of 1s 6d or 7.5p

Match Entertainment was not forgotten:

PROGRAMME OF MUSIC

1.30 p.m. to 2.15 p.m. THE BAND OF HIS MAJESTY'S IRISH GUARDS (By permission of Colonel H.V. Pollok, C.B.E., D.S.O.)

Director of Music – Lieut. J.L.T. Hurd L.R.A.M., P.S.M.

1.	March	'The Mad Major'	Alford
2.	Selection	'The Student Prince'	Romberg
3.	Valse	'You Will Remember Vienna'	Young
4.	Selection	'The Three Musketeers'	Friml
5.	(a) Tango	'O Donna Clara'	Peterburski
	(b) One Step	'There's a Good Time Coming'	Butler
6.	Selection of Old English Airs		arr. Myddleton

2.15 p.m. to 2.45 p.m. – COMMUNITY SINGING

Arranged by the *Daily Express* National Community Singing Movement

Conductor – Mr T.P. Ratcliff

Accompanied by the Band of H.M. Welsh Guards (By permission of Colonel R.E.K. Leatham D.S.O.)

Director of Music – Capt. Andrew Harris L.R.A.M.

2.50 p.m. to 2.55 p.m. – BANDS OF H.M. IRISH GUARDS & H.M.WELSH GUARDS

GOD SAVE THE KING

3.45 p.m. – MARCHING BY THE COMBINED BANDS

After the Match – THE COMBINED BANDS WILL PLAY

Player Profiles were also included:

PEN PICTURES OF PLAYERS

BIRMINGHAM

H. HIBBS (Goalkeeper) Born: Wilncote. (Height 5ft 9 and half inches; Weight 12 st 2 lb.)

Without doubt the greatest goalkeeper in Great Britain and one of the finest who has ever played for England. There is no aspect of goalkeeping at which Hibbs is not an expert. He has, of course, played many times for England and should continue to do so.

G LIDDELL (Right Full-Back) Born: Durham. (Height 5ft 8 and three quarters of an inch; Weight 11 st 3 lb.)

Originally a half-back, Liddell has developed into a fcarless and safe defender. Throughout the Cup competition Birmingham have been noted for stability and safety in defence, to which Liddell has contributed a fair share.

E. BARKAS (Left Full-Back) Born: Wardley Colliery. (Height 5ft 7 and three quarters of an inch; Weight 12 st 12 lb.)

Barkas has had experience of a Cup Final; he played with the Huddersfield team that lost to Blackburn Rovers in 1927–28. Captain of Birmingham, he inspires his men with his own deeds. He asks no quarter from any man, nor does he give quarter. Dogged and safe is Barkas, certain to fight to the last whether his side is leading or not.

J.A. CRINGAN (Right Half-Back) Born: Douglas Water, Scotland. (Height 5ft 9 inches; Weight 11 st 7 lb.)

Formerly a centre half-back, Cringan is now playing equally well on the wing. He is the type of player to succeed in any position, for he is untiring in action and most difficult to overcome; in fact, he is one of the most stubborn half-backs in the First Division, for he never gives up

G.T. MORRALL (Centre Half-Back) Born: Smethwick. (Height 5ft 11 inches; Weight 12 st.)

Before the England team to meet Scotland was chosen, Morrall was one of the newspaper favourites for the centre-half position. There are few better pivots in the game today. His height is of great advantage with the ball in the air, but wherever it is Morrall is reliable and sure. His tackling is keen and, if defensive play seems his stronger point, attack is not quite forgotten for his passes out to the wing are exceptionally accurate and worrying to the opposition.

A. LESLIE (Left Half-Back) Born: Greenock. (Height 5ft 8 inches; Weight 10 st.)

The lightest player on the field today; yet lack of ounces does not affect his play. With the possible exception of Magee, Leslie is probably the best attacking half-back in the match. His play is typically Scottish, his push passes through to the forwards being ideal for attack.

G.R. BRIGGS (Outside-right) Born: Wombwell, Yorkshire. (Height 5ft 8 inches; Weight 12 st.)

Another personality of the game. Briggs is a match winner; he may appear ordinary for some time, then he will pop up to score a great goal. In fact, there is no branch of forward play in which he does not excel and, as his weight might indicate, once he has the ball he takes some moving off it. It is said that he does not look the part of a footballer, but opposing defences know that appearances, when Briggs is concerned, are highly deceptive.

J. CROSBIE (Inside-right) Born: Glenbuck, Ayr. (Height 5ft 9 inches; Weight 10 st 5 lb.)

The mastermind of the Birmingham attack. Cup Finals have been won by teams who had a star inside-forward, and history may well be repeated today, for Crosbie is really a star. He rarely scores goals, he does not shoot very often; he really makes the openings for others. Without Crosbie the Birmingham team would be sadly handicapped – it is fortunate for this unlucky club that Crosbie has escaped serious injury.

J. BRADFORD (Centre-forward) Born: Pegg's Green. (Height 5ft 9 and three quarters of an inch; Weight 12 st 6 lb.)

A great all-round forward capable of scoring from any angle, Bradford has been for some seasons one of our finest footballers. Some weeks ago he was injured in a League game, and there were fears that he might have to miss to-day's game, it adequately sums up the value of Bradford to Birmingham to say that it would have been a tragedy had he not played.

J. FIRTH (Inside-left) Born: Doncaster. (Height 5ft 8 and half inches; Weight 12 st.)

Originally a right half-back, Firth came into the Birmingham team half way through the Cup competition. He supplied the dash, which had been missing. A most versatile and valuable man.

E. CURTIS (Outside-left) Born: Cardiff. (Height 5ft 7 and half inches; Weight 11 st 4 lb.)

Came from Cardiff City as an inside-left, in which position he has played for Wales. As a winger he has developed strength and his shooting power has become more marked. He scored both goals against Sunderland in the semi-final round. Curtis played for Cardiff City in the Final when the Cup was taken to Wales for the first time; he was then at outside-right.

Again as with current matchday programmes there was a match preview:

TODAY'S GAME By W.F. SANDERSON

SPORTS EDITOR, *SUNDAY NEWS*

This meeting today of two clubs who are neighbours – though it is not strictly correct to call it an all-Birmingham Final – once again brings into prominence the great attraction of the Football Association Cup Competition; anything can happen. Of the hundreds of clubs who have battled through the rounds, two are left whose grounds are but a few miles apart.

There is more in the game, however, than this friendly, but keen rivalry. West Bromwich Albion a few seasons ago were slipping from the high place, which has always been theirs in the game of football. The club saw the danger and acted. They decided upon a policy of rebuilding.

The team of today is the result. Youth was given its chance; young men were found and trained on in the tradition of West Bromwich Albion – to play good football. There was no haste or desire for quick results. Time was allowed to have its effect, and whatever happens this afternoon it is certain the Albion will play good football.

Turning to Birmingham, we see the result of amazing courage. There has been but one previous round when Birmingham were expected by the experts to win; always theirs was a frail chance. Yet they are here today and the others are gone. There is even more than that, I cannot recall a club who have been faced with such misfortune as have Birmingham.

CUP FINAL 1931

Daily Express

COMMUNITY SINGING at WEMBLEY STADIUM, APRIL 25

1
DAISY BELL

Daisy, Daisy,
Give me your answer, do !
I'm half crazy,
All for the love of you !
It won't be a stylish marriage,
I can't afford a carriage,
But you'll look sweet on the seat
Of a bicycle built for two !
(*Reproduced by permission of
Messrs. Francis, Day & Hunter, Ltd.*)

2
JOHN BROWN'S BODY

John Brown's body lies a-mould'ring
in the grave,
John Brown's body lies a-mould'ring
in the grave,
John Brown's body lies a-mould'ring
in the grave,
His soul is marching on !

Chorus—
Glory ! Glory ! Hallelujah !
Glory ! Glory ! Hallelujah !
Glory ! Glory ! Hallelujah !
His soul is marching on !

It isn't any trouble just to s-m-i-l-e,
It isn't any trouble just to s-m-i-l-e,
So smile when you're in trouble,
It will vanish like a bubble
If you s-m-i-l-e.

It isn't any trouble just to ha, ha, ha,
ha, ha,

3
LOCH LOMOND

By yon bonnie banks, and by yon
bonnie braes,
Where the sun shines bright on
Loch Lomon',
Where me and my true love were
ever wont to gae,
On the bonnie, bonnie banks of Loch
Lomon'.

Chorus—
Oh ! ye'll tak' the high road and
I'll tak' the low road,
And I'll be in Scotland afore ye,
But me and my true love will never
meet again,
On the bonnie, bonnie banks of Loch
Lomon'.

4
PACK UP YOUR TROUBLES

Pack up your troubles in your old
kit bag
And smile, smile, smile !
While you've a lucifer to light your
fag,
Smile, boys, that's the style.
What's the use of worrying ?
It never was worth while,
So, pack up your troubles in your old
kit bag,
And smile, smile, smile !
(*Reproduced by permission of
Messrs. Francis, Day & Hunter, Ltd.*)

BIRMINGHAM
v.
W. BROMWICH ALBION

* * *

SINGING CONDUCTED BY
T. P. RATCLIFF
with the Band of H.M. Welsh
Guards under the direction of
Capt. Andrew Harris, L.R.A.M.
By permission of Col. R. E. K. Leatham, D.S.O.

5
LOVE'S OLD SWEET SONG

Just a song at twilight, when the lights
are low,
And the flick'ring shadows softly come
and go,
Though the heart be weary, sad the
day and long,
Still to us at twilight comes Love's old
song,
Comes Love's old sweet song.
(*Reproduced by permission of
Messrs. Boosey & Co., Ltd.*)

6
COCK ROBIN

Who killed Cock Robin ?
" I," said the sparrow,
" With my bow and arrow,
I killed Cock Robin."

Chorus—
All the birds of the air fell a-sighing
and a-sobbing
When they heard of the death of
poor Cock Robin ;
When they heard of the death of
poor Cock Robin.

7
JOHN PEEL

D'ye ken John Peel with his coat so gay,
D'ye ken John Peel at the break of day,
D'ye ken John Peel when he's far, far
away,
With his hounds and his horn in the
morning ?

Chorus—
For the sound of his horn brought me
from my bed,
And the cry of his hounds which he
oft-times led,
For Peel's " View hallo ! " would
awaken the dead,
Or the fox from his lair in the
morning.

8
POOR OLD JOE

Gone are the days when my heart was
young and gay ;
Gone are my friends from the cotton
fields away ;
Gone from the earth to a better land
I know,
I hear their gentle voices calling " Poor
Old Joe ! "

Chorus—
I'm coming, I'm coming,
For my head is bending low,
I hear their gentle voices
Calling " Poor Old Joe ! "

9
THE BRITISH GRENADIERS
(*Whistle*)

10
ANNIE LAURIE

Maxwellton's braes are bonnie,
Where early falls the dew—
And its there that Annie Laurie
Gi'ed me her promise true.
Gi'ed me her promise true,
Which ne'er forgot will be ;
And for bonnie Annie Laurie,
I'd lay me doon and dee.

11
**THE MAN THAT BROKE THE
BANK AT MONTE CARLO**

As I walk along the Bois Boolong with
an independent air,
You can hear the girls declare :
" He must be a millionaire,"
You can hear them sigh, and wish to
die,
You can see them wink the other eye
At the man that broke the Bank at
Monte Carlo.
(*Reproduced by permission of
Messrs. Francis, Day & Hunter, Ltd.*)

12
ABIDE WITH ME

Abide with me ; fast falls the eventide ;
The darkness deepens ; Lord, with me
abide ;
When other helpers fail, and comforts
flee,
Help of the helpless, O abide with me.

Swift to its close ebbs out life's little
day ;
Earth's joys grow dim, its glories pass
away ;
Change and decay in all around I see ;
O Thou, Who changest not, abide with
me.

Hold Thou Thy Cross before my
closing eyes ;
Shine through the gloom, and point me
to the skies ;
Heaven's morning breaks, and earth's
vain shadows flee ;
In life, in death, O Lord, abide with me.

NOTE : Whichever team you support in to-day's great struggle for the Cup, you will be
eagerly interested to compare your impressions with those of the acknowledged experts
in football criticism who will sum up the game in the "Daily Express" on Monday.
Read the "Daily Express" on Monday and it will convince you—as it has already
convinced the great majority of football enthusiasts—that it is far and away the best

Community Singing Song Sheet

Their number of seriously injured players in one season is a record. On the top of this they have had illnesses and setbacks. I think I am right in saying that not once in the Cup Competition this season have they been able to select their team until the morning of the game, and today there is a grave doubt about that great forward, Bradford. Theirs is a triumph over adversity.

Perhaps Birmingham do not play the same scientific game as West Bromwich Albion; it is impossible to do so with a much-changed team. Yet despite these things, Birmingham are effective, and that is what counts.

So the promise of today's game is good. There are no favourites, there can be no logical favourites in a Cup Final, and I am prepared to leave the game with the remark that whoever wins will well deserve the honour.

1930–31 Team Group

3.

FRED HARRIS

– SECOND DIVISION CHAMPIONS 1947– 48

Fred Harris

FULL NAME: Frederick 'Fred' Harris.
DATE OF BIRTH: 2 July 1912.
PLACE OF BIRTH: Solihull.
DATE OF DEATH: 13 October 1998.
PLACE OF DEATH: South Warwickshire at the age of 86.

When his playing career was over he became a chiropodist and physio-therapist in the Solihull, Olton and Acocks Green district of Birmingham. For some time the clinic still operated as a family practice on the Warwick Road in Olton, Solihull.

PLAYING CAREER:

Youth Career:

After enjoying a successful junior and non-league experience with Sparkbrook F.C., Birmingham City Transport and Osborne Athletic he joined Blues as a professional at the age of 20 in March 1933.

Senior Career:

He scored on his debut in a 2–1 home win against local rivals Aston Villa on 25 August 1934 in front of a crowd of 53,930 the other scorer was Billy Guest.

His initial claim to fame was that he was in the team that played in front of the record attendance at St Andrew's – 67,341 for the FA Cup Fifth Round match against Everton. The match was a 2–2 draw against the subsequent League Champions

During World War II he converted to play as a wing-half and played out the rest of his career in that position. His strong tackling and constructive use of the ball impressed manager Harry Storer sufficiently to make him club captain. He is credited with recommending Johnny Berry to Birmingham, having seen him play for an Army team while both were serving in India during the war. He won representative honours for Football League XI against the Scottish League in 1948–49.

He retired from football in 1950, aged nearly 38, having made 312 appearances in all competitions for Birmingham and scored 68 goals. His final game was away at Wolverhampton Wanderers on 6 May 1959 in which Blues lost 1–6 with Cyril Trigg scoring in front of a crowd of 42,935.

HONOURS

As a Player:

- Top goal scorer 1938–39 with 14 League goals and 17 in all competitions.
- Football League South Champions 1946.
- Second Division Champions 1947-48.

The final match of the 1947–48 season was a 0–0 draw against Tottenham Hotspur on 1 May 1948 at St Andrew's in front of crowd of 35,569. The team that day was: Merrick, Green, Jennings, Harris, Duckhouse, Mitchell, Stewart, Dougall, Trigg, Bodle and Edwards.

Blues won their 59th point of the season to reach their best ever total under the two points for a win rule.

DETAILS OF SUCCESS
BLUES 4 WEST BROMWICH ALBION 0

Date: 29 April 1948
Venue: St Andrew's
Attendance: 43,168
Referee: A. Baker (Crewe)
Blues: Merrick, Green, Jennings, Harris, Duckhouse, Mitchell, Stewart, Dorman, Trigg, Bodle, Edwards.
Albion: Heath, Pemberton, Kinsell, Millard, Vernon, A.J. Evans, Elliot, Drury, Walsh, Haines, Rowley

MATCH REPORT:

The 1947–48 season's Second Division Championship title fight had been at the mercy of these two West Midlands teams for most of the campaign. West Bromwich Albion had led the Division since September, only to be pushed out from first place by the Blues in December. Blues played with real class and quality to win this vital clash, which was virtually worth double the points.

Blues were at full-strength and unchanged, whilst the Baggies made one significant change; their kit, wearing white shirts and blue shorts. The morning's deluge of rain had made the pitch a virtual quagmire, making it difficult for all the players but especially the defenders. Blues took an early advantage of the conditions when seven minutes into the game, following a George Edwards' corner, two Albion players slipped in a goalmouth incident to allow Jackie Stewart to score from two yards. After 17 minutes the muddy ground was once again influential in Blues' second. Vernon, under no pressure, played a back pass to Heath, which skidded off the pitch, despite a despairing attempt by goalkeeper Heath, the ball went out for a corner. From Stewart's flag-kick Harold Bodle rose magnificently to head the ball home at the far post.

Blues remained in control throughout the ninety minutes and second half goals from Cyril Trigg and another from Stewart gave Blues an impressive 4–0 victory

1947–48 Team Line-Up – Home Programme

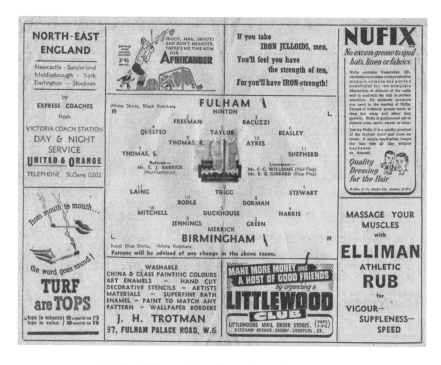

1947–48 Team Line-Up – Away Programme

Champions: Played 42 games – won 22 – drew 15 – lost 5 – goals for 55 - goals against 24 – points 59.

SEASON APPEARANCES

Player	League Appearances	League Goals	FA Cup Appearances	FA Cup Goals
MERRICK	36	0	0	0
GREEN	35	0	1	0
JENNINGS	29	0	1	0
HARRIS	40	0	1	0
DUCKHOUSE	36	0	1	0
MITCHELL	41	4	1	0
STEWART	17	7	0	0
DOUGALL	34	5	1	0
TRIGG	25	6	1	0
BODLE	39	14	0	0
EDWARDS	37	2	1	0
BADHAM	2	0	0	0
LAING	4	2	0	0
DORMAN	8	1	0	0
WHEELER	6	0	1	0
GARRETT	8	1	0	0
OTTEWELL	5	2	0	0
BERRY	3	0	0	0
HUGHES	3	0	0	0
MCDONNELL	13	0	0	0
AVEYARD	7	3	0	0
QUINTON	8	0	0	0
MCINTOSH	9	1	0	0
SOUTHAM	1	0	0	0

BLUES CAREER

PLAYING RECORD – SEASON BY SEASON

Season	League Appearances	League Goals	FA Cup Appearances	FA Cup Goals
1934–35	30	9	4	3
1935–36	42	17	2	1
1936–37	35	11	1	0
1937–38	19	7	1	0
1938–39	37	14	4	3
1939–40 Midland Regional League & League Cup	28	1		
1940–41 League South 1st & 2nd Championship & League (South) Cup	13	2		
1941–42 No Competitions				
1942–43 League North 1st & 2nd Championship & League North Cup	4	1		
1943–44 League North 1st & 2nd Championship – League North and Midland Cup	4	0		
1944–45 League North 1st & 2nd Championship & Midland League Cup	0	0		
1945–46 Football League South	39	2		
1946–47	29	1	4	1
1947–48	40	0	1	0
1948–49	36	2	3	0
1949–50	12	0	0	0

4.

LEN BOYD

– DIVISION TWO CHAMPIONS 1954–55
& FA CUP FINALISTS 1955–56

Len Boyd leads out the team

FULL NAME: Leonard Arthur Miller Boyd.

DATE OF BIRTH: 11 November 1923.

PLACE OF BIRTH: Plaistow London.

DATE OF DEATH: 14 February 2008.

PLACE OF DEATH: Melton Mowbray at the age of 84.

PLAYING CAREER:

Youth Career:

Ilford.

Senior Career:

1945–1949 Plymouth Argyle 78 appearances 5 goals.

1949–56 Blues 255 appearances 14 goals.

1959 Hinckley Athletic.

International:

1952 England 'B' 1 appearance 0 goals,

Len played 333 games in the Football League in the 1940s and 1950s. After serving in the Royal Navy during the Second World War, Boyd signed for Second Division club Plymouth Argyle where he spent two seasons playing as an inside-forward. When he began playing as a wing-half, a position to which he was better suited, he attracted attention, and soon secured a transfer to the First Division with Blues for what was for Plymouth a record fee.

Though his club was soon relegated, Boyd established himself in the first team and was appointed captain. He was an industrious, dynamic player, described by Gil Merrick as "a good player and a bloody good captain". Boyd led the team to the championship of the Second Division in the 1954–55 and to the FA Cup Final and sixth place in the league the following year. Sixth place is still, as of 2015, Birmingham's record league placing. He played only once more for Birmingham, forced to retire by the back injury, which had disrupted his final season with the club.

He played for the West Ham Schools team alongside Ken Green, who was later to be a Birmingham teammate, and as a youth played for Ilford FC. The outbreak of the Second World War when Boyd was 15 delayed his entry into football as a career. He joined the Royal Navy, and while serving in Malta was spotted playing for a Navy team by a Pilgrims supporter, who recommended him to the club. After a trial, Boyd signed professional forms in December 1945.

He made his debut on 12 October 1946, taking over at centre-half from Alf Miller for a Second Division game away at Leicester City which Plymouth lost 4–1. In his first season, Boyd played 16 league games, mainly in the inside-left position, and scored four of his five Plymouth goals. He played regularly on the right side of the forward line in the following season, but failed to score, and was regarded as 'a promising but not exceptional inside-forward'. When manager Jack Tresadern switched him to right-half for the 1948–49 season, it became clear he was better suited to that position. After three consecutive seasons helping the Devon club avoid relegation from the Second Division, Boyd was sold to First Division club Birmingham City in January 1949 for a fee of £17,500, the first five-figure fee ever received by Plymouth for a player. Understandably the Argyle supporters had been incensed at the mere suggestion that one of their favourites might be allowed to depart, so the transfer negotiations were kept secret until the deal could be revealed as a fait accompli.

He went straight into the first team as replacement for Frank Mitchell who had joined Chelsea earlier that month, and made his debut in a goalless draw away at Preston North End In the 1949–50 season, his first full season with Birmingham, he established himself in the first team but was unable to prevent his new team's relegation to the Second Division. When Fred Harris retired at the end of that season, manager Bob Brocklebank appointed Boyd as his successor as club captain, a post that he retained for the remainder of his Birmingham career.

He made his league debut on 22 January 1949 away at Preston North End in a goalless draw in front of a crowd of 31,894. His first league goal was the winner in a 1–0 victory v Manchester United at St Andrew's on 19 March 1949 in front of crowd of 46,819

Under Boyd's captaincy Birmingham reached the semi-finals of the 1950–51 FA Cup, when they were defeated by the powerful Blackpool side of the 'two Stans' – Matthews and Mortensen only after a replay. They twice came close to winning promotion, missing out by three points in the 1950–51 season and then on goal average the following year. Boyd's performances were rewarded with selection for England B against Netherlands B, a match played in front of a crowd of 60,000 at the Olympic Stadium in Amsterdam but this, and a selection as reserve for a Football League representative side in 1954, was as close as he came to full international honours.

Manager Brocklebank significantly strengthened Birmingham's playing staff, but although the club nearly reached another semi-final in the 1952–53 FA Cup, losing in the sixth round to Tottenham Hotspur after two replays, their league results failed to improve. In late 1954, Arthur Turner was appointed manager, and his ability to instil a positive approach in the players transformed a team stagnating in mid-table into one needing to win the last game of the season, away at Doncaster Rovers, in order to be promoted as champions on goal average. Boyd led the team to a 5–1 win, later recalling: "The ground was packed and alive with supporters wearing the colours of Birmingham City. We knew we would win – and so too did those fans – and our performance that day was quite brilliant."

The same squad of players carried their promotion form into the 1955–56 season in the First Division, achieving the club's highest league finish of sixth place, and reaching the FA Cup Final. They became attractive to the media; after the FA Cup semi-final victory, Boyd signed an exclusive contract committing himself and his teammates to appearing only on BBC programmes in the weeks leading up to the Final.

Fellow wing-half Roy Warhurst injured a thigh in the sixth round at Arsenal and played no further part in the season. Boyd himself had for some time been suffering from a debilitating back problem, and relied on injections to keep him playing; he missed five of the last seven games of the season but was passed fit on the Wednesday before the game. In the event, Boyd played, in Warhurst's position at left-half, and the 22-year-old Johnny Newman came in on the right. With Warhurst missing and Boyd out of position and not fully match-fit, Birmingham's strength and balance was disrupted, leaving them particularly vulnerable to Manchester City's unconventional style of play, known as the 'Revie Plan' At half-time, a row erupted between the manager and some of the players, Boyd included, about their fitness; in the second half, whether due to physical and mental exhaustion or the effects of the row, Birmingham were soundly beaten.

On their return to Birmingham, the team received a civic welcome; Boyd told the thousands outside the Council House that the team felt they had let the supporters down. Though the crowd roared 'No!' recriminations followed. Speaking fifty years later, goalkeeper Gil Merrick refused to attribute blame for the loss to Boyd's lack of fitness: "The reason why we lost, in my opinion, was nothing to do with Boydy who some claimed was unfit. Why we didn't perform in the second half was mainly because nothing was said in the dressing room at half-time about stopping the damage caused by Don Revie. He was a good player and ran the game but at half-time we should have talked about stopping him. Tackles should have been talked about, but they weren't. It was a lack of tackles that caused us to fold in the second half, and that's all I'm going to say. Don't put all the onus on Len Boyd. Len was a good player and a bloody good captain."

His final senior appearance was in the FA Cup Final at Wembley on 5 May 1956.

Boyd played only one more game for the club, two weeks after the Cup Final. Not risked in their first game in the Inter-Cities Fairs Cup, against Internazionale on a hard pitch in the San Siro he played in their next, a 1–0 win against a Zagreb Select XI in Yugoslavia on 21 May 1956 in front of an attendance of 12,000, with Brown scoring.

The team was: Merrick, Badham, Allen, Boyd, Newman, Warhurst, Lane (Cox), Finney, Brown, Kinsey, Murphy.

Ivan Ponting said: "As a footballer the tall, long-striding Londoner was a fiendishly industrious wing-half, passably skilful on the ball as might be expected of a former inside-forward, and courageously combative, too, capable of dishing out physical punishment implacably and taking it without a whimper. Yet for all his intrepid, sometimes frenetic efforts in the midfield trenches, there was an aura of composure about him, and perhaps the most abiding image of captain Boyd is of his majestic bearing as he ploughed forward in support of his attack like some stately galleon in full sail, waving imperiously to direct the men ahead of him, the very heartbeat of his team."

Following a favourable specialist's report during the close season, Boyd took part in pre-season training, but his back still troubled him. On 17 August 1956, the day before Birmingham were to open their 1956–57 League campaign, Boyd's contract with the club was terminated at his own request.

Boyd was a tall man with a long stride. He was hard-working, combining industry with composure and skill on the ball. His dynamism was regularly mentioned; *The Times* match report of the 1953 FA Cup sixth round replay against Tottenham Hotspur, a 2–2 draw, in which Boyd scored the equalising goal and had his name taken, attributed Birmingham's second-half comeback to their captain's performance:

And behind it all there was the constant driving force of Boyd, their captain, at right-half. Boyd, in fact, one would say, was the final hero of a desperate day. Up in attack and back in defence he played a magnificent game to inspire and keep his colleagues going.

Against Arsenal in the 1956 cup run he was, 'a champion who covered every inch of Highbury's mud, a dynamo and a man of steel,' and, later the same season, *The Times* correspondent wondered rhetorically 'was there ever such a human dynamo at wing-half?'

Birmingham based their success of the 1950s on 'their acutely drilled and disciplined defence – founded upon the authority of their half-backs Boyd, Smith and Warhurst though these three did much more than protect their defenders.

... the towering young Smith, centre-half in the England Intermediate

(Under 23) XI, is flanked by two men, Boyd and Warhurst, who keep the ball flowing forward quickly all the time. There are no superfluous frills about them. Their accent is on a quick release along the lines of longitude. They are the real driving force

They acquired a fearsome reputation: Boyd himself once played four matches carrying an injury, which turned out to be a hairline fracture of his leg. Team-mate Alex Govan, preferring to describe Boyd as 'hard, very hard' rather than a 'dirty player', recalled: "I used to think thank God I'm playing in front of them and not against them! Birmingham probably had the hardest defenders in the First Division in those days, with Len, Trevor Smith, Roy Warhurst, Jeff Hall and Ken Green – no one liked the idea of playing against them."

Boyd was married to Dolly, and had two children. He enjoyed oil-painting as a hobby. According to Govan, 'Len was a typical Cockney really. He was hard on the pitch but soft off the field, he wouldn't do anybody a bad turn.'

Boyd suffered from a fear of flying, which had on occasion caused difficulties in his football career. Chosen by the Birmingham County Football Association for a representative match in Hamburg in 1953, the players were already at the airport when he requested to be omitted from the side. While his teammates flew to Birmingham's Fairs Cup match in Milan, Boyd travelled across the English Channel by boat and then across France and into Italy by train.

When Boyd retired from professional football, the Birmingham City directors 'had stated their readiness to help him in any venture he decided to take up'. He chose to enter the licensed trade and kept a public house in Birmingham. Having once said that "if I can't play in first-class football, I don't want to play any football at all," after two-and-a-half years out of the game he changed his mind. In early 1959 he attempted a comeback with Leicestershire side Hinckley Athletic, but found himself unable to play a full game. He remained involved with football for a few more years, acting as coach and scout for Redditch of the West Midlands (Regional) League between 1960 and 1965. Settling in Melton Mowbray, Leicestershire, he went on to become one of the town's first traffic wardens. In later life he moved into a care home in Melton, where he died in February 2008 at the age of 84

BLUES CAREER
PLAYING CAREER FOR BLUES

Season	League Appearances	League Goals	FA Cup Appearances	FA Cup Goals
1948–49	9	1	0	0
1949–50	27	0	6	0
1950–51	36	3	0	0
1951–52	37	0	0	0
1952–53	40	4	7	1
1953–54	35	2	2	0
1954–55	39	1	4	0
1955–56	32	3	6	0

Plymouth Argyle

1946–47 16 League Appearances 4 goals.

1947–48 37 League Appearances 1 FA Cup Appearance.

1948–49 25 League Appearances 1 goal 1 FA Cup Appearance.

TOTAL 78 League Appearances 5 goals 2 FA Cup Appearances equalling 80 appearances 5 goals.

Blues Total 255 League Appearances 14 goals 25 FA Cup Appearances 1 goal 1 Fairs Cup equalling 281 appearances 15 goals

Career Total 333 League Appearances 19 goals 27 FA Cup Appearances 1 goal 1 Fairs Cup equalling 361 appearances 20 goals.

Ex-Blues favourite Alex Govan started his career at the same time as Boyd in Plymouth before moving north to join Blues and recalls: "I look at some of the games now and I get annoyed when I see Blues have conceded a goal with two minutes to go or in injury time. No way in those days would we have lost so late in the game. They would have been kicked over the stand, kicked into the Railway, anywhere to kill the time! It may not have been nice for the supporters but it got the points. I remember Len played about four games with a hairline fracture, which is a broken leg really, before they realised what it was. But that was the type of player he was."

DETAILS OF SUCCESS
PROMOTION 1954–55

4 May 1955 v. Doncaster Rovers won 5–1 (away).

> **Attendance:** 21,303
>
> **Score Times:** Astall (38 minutes), J. Walker (44 minutes), Murphy (55 minutes), Brown (65 minutes), Astall (73 minutes), Govan (90 minutes).
>
> **Team:** Schofield, Hall, Badham, Boyd, Smith, Warhurst, Astall, Kinsey, Brown, Murphy, Govan.

Celebrating promotion with mugs of tea?

The Blues are back! 54–55 Promotion Souvenir Brochure

HOW WE CAME FROM NOWHERE TO WIN IT

Skipper LEN BOYD tells the story :

Len Boyd programme article

Football League Division II 1954-55

ROVERS
v
BIRMINGHAM CITY

WEDNESDAY, MAY 4th

MR. JACK HODGSON

OFFICIAL PROGRAMME   3d

Programme Cover – Doncaster Rovers 4 May 1955

Season Appearances

PLAYER	LEAGUE APPEARANCES	LEAGUE GOALS	FA CUP APPEARANCES	FA CUP GOALS
SCHOFIELD	15	0	0	0
HALL	32	0	4	0
BADHAM	11	0	0	0
BOYD	39	1	4	0
SMITH	24	0	4	0
WARHURST	34	4	3	0
ASTALL	33	11	4	0
KINSEY	35	13	4	1
BROWN	28	14	4	3
MURPHY	37	20	4	0
GOVAN	37	15	4	1
MERRICK	27	0	4	0
GREEN	29	0	4	0
ALLEN	13	0	0	0
NEWMAN	17	0	0	0
LANE	22	8	0	0
ROWLEY	4	1	0	0
WARMINGTON	4	0	0	0
COX	4	0	0	0
HILL	2	0	0	0
WATTS	10	0	0	0
MARTIN	1	0	0	0
STEWART	1	0	0	0
BRADBURY	2	2	0	0
JONES	0	0	1	0

Blues finally did it! Promotion at last to the First Division where they have not been since they were relegated in 1950. In a double bonus they also secured the Second Division Championship, pipping Luton. A crowd of 21,305 watched the match, including many travelling Blues fans, and also followers of Rotherham, who would have benefited from a slip-up by Blues. Blues had to win this game, and they did so with an emphatic four goal burst in a one-sided second half, which eventually ended with a 5–1 scoreline.

The opening minutes were a typical tense clash of biting tackles and goalmouth excitement, Blues taking advantage of a strong wind by loading high crosses with which Hardwick often had difficulty. However he kept them out with an array of improvised goalkeeping manoeuvres. The importance of the first goal was such that Blues allowed gaps in defence to appear. Doncaster took advantage of these, and Schofield did well to keep out a Jimmy Walker attempt. Moments later the 'keeper again pulled out a spectacular save from Geoff Walker which had been deflected on its way towards him. On 38 minutes however, the pressure from Blues paid off when Astall scored. Latching onto a pass from Murphy he outclassed the Rovers' defence, and although his shot was blocked by Hardwick, Astall followed up to hammer in the rebound. This brought about more pressure from Blues as they pushed for another goal to wrap up the game. However, despite forcing three quick corners, it was Doncaster on a breakaway who got the game's second goal just a minute before half time. Jimmy Walker rose to plant his header past Schofield from only the second corner of the game. So typically Blues, after dominating and needing to win were now level at the break and needing another goal. Again they would have to do it the difficult way.

The second half started much in the manner as the first; only this time Blues put their chances away. The first came after 55 minutes. Hardwick again only half saving a shot by Murphy, who picked up the rebound to score via the inside of the post. Just ten minutes later Brown controlled a cross from Hall skilfully enough to turn and fire past Hardwick. There was no restraining Blues now, and after 73 minutes Brown went through on a weaving run, which opened up Rovers' defence again. He then waited at the edge of the area and lobbed a pass to Astall, to volley in Blues' fourth. A memorable night ended perfectly when, right on the final whistle, Govan scored a fifth goal, and the championship celebrations started in earnest.

Doncaster: Hardwick; Makepeace, Gavin; Hunt, Williams, Herbert; Mooney, Jeffrey, Jimmy Walker, Mcmorran, Geoff Walker.

Roy Fairhurst, Arthur Turner, John Newman, Jack Lane,
Albert Linnecor and Gil Merrick cheer on the team

BLUES DIVISION TWO CHAMPIONSHIP WINNING SQUAD 1954/55
Eddie is seated on the front row sixth from left, next to manager Arthur Turner

Home Programme Cover 1955–56

FA CUP FINAL 5 MAY 1956

1956 FA Cup Final Team

SURNAME	FIRST	APPEARANCES	GOALS	SEASONS
MERRICK	GIL	551	0	15
HALL	JEFF	265	1	9
GREEN	KEN	442	3	12
NEWMAN	JOHN	65	0	7
SMITH	TREVOR	430	3	12
BOYD	LEN	281	15	8
ASTALL	GORDON	271	67	8
KINSEY	NOEL	173/1	56	5
BROWN	EDDIE	185	90	5
MURPHY	PETER	278	127	9
GOVAN	ALEX	186	60	5

Jeff Hall shakes hands with the Duke of Edinburgh

The 1956 FA Cup Final team, where did they go?

Surname	First Name	Outcome
MERRICK	GIL	RETIRED 1960
HALL	JEFF	DIED 1959
GREEN	KEN	RETIRED 1959
NEWMAN	JOHN	WORCESTER CITY 1957
SMITH	TREVOR	WALSALL 1964
BOYD	LEN	RETIRED 1956
ASTALL	GORDON	TORQUAY UNITED 1961
KINSEY	NOEL	PORT VALE 1958
BROWN	EDDIE	LEYTON ORIENT 1959
MURPHY	PETER	RETIRED 1961
GOVAN	ALEX	PORTSMOUTH 1958

On Saturday evening commemorative banquets were held for the players of FA Cup finalists Manchester City and Birmingham City in two London nightspots no more than a stone's throw apart. Disappointingly this was as near to the trophy as Blues got all day. Blues lost their fighting spirit, an early goal, the battle in the Wembley cauldron, and most importantly, they lost their chance of a major trophy. The day seemed so promising; with the teams coming out to a huge roar from the 100,000 fans crammed into the home of English football, Wembley Stadium. On a lovely hot day, after the introduction to the Queen, the game kicked-off, and everything seemed perfect until the third minute, Revie starting the move 10 yards from his penalty area, swung over a long pass which cleared the head of Hall. Clarke raced in from behind to deliver a return ball to Revie who had made ground quickly. The ball was back-heeled square to Hayes inside the area, and he hit a crisp first time shot past Merrick. Even then this was viewed as a stimulant – something to get Blues quickly into top gear. Unfortunately it simply did not, and this was the day's biggest disappointment. Although Blues hit back with a Kinsey shot, which went in off the post to equalise 11 minutes later, there was still something lacking in their overall performance. Their spirit, prominent in other rounds, simply wasn't there when needed. When the Blues' famous battle cry *'Keep Right on'* failed to raise the tempo after the goal, things began to look ominous. Blues held on until half time with the scores remaining level, but they were clearly frustrated by the astute offside trap employed by Revie's men. Manchester City started off the better team in the second half, and were 2–1 up after 65 minutes, Johnstone, running at Green on the right, was presented with an opportunity to feed Dyson, who had run diagonally across the field to the edge of the area. A perfectly timed pass allowed Dyson to take the ball in his stride and fire past Merrick as he came out to narrow the angle. The winning team then put the game well beyond Blues' reach with a sucker-punch goal three minutes later. It came from a Blues attack, Trautmann dived bravely at the feet of Brown, took the ball from him and kicked long upfield. It was flicked on by Hayes into the path of Johnstone, who had sprinted clear of the static defence. He finished with a lovely strike into the bottom corner. Moments later Trautmann received treatment after a collision with Murphy whilst saving Brown's header at goal. The goalkeeper played on despite holding his head in agony for 20 minutes. Any shot on target would have made a save impossible in his condition, but Blues failed to trouble him further. The game, and Blues FA Cup dream withered for another year.

MANCHESTER CITY: Trautmann; Leivers, Little; Barnes, Ewing, Paul; Johnstone, Hayes, Revie, Dyson, Clarke.
Referee: Mr A. Bond (Middlesex)

THE ROAD TO WEMBLEY

Round 3: 7 January 1956 v Torquay United (A) won 1–7 Astall, Brown (3), Kinsey, Murphy (2).
Crowd: 18,730.

Round 4: 28 January 1956 v Leyton Orient (A) Won 0–4 Brown (2) Murphy Finney.

Crowd: 24,727.

Oriental Chatter

By " FORESTER "

GREETINGS one and all to Leyton Stadium.

* * *

A special welcome is extended to Birmingham F.C.—officials, players and supporters—for this afternoon's F.A. Challenge Cup fourth round tie.

It was in the corresponding round in January, 1952 that Orient scored a sensational 1—0 victory over Birmingham, at St. Andrew's, and thereby earned the right to a fifth round meeting with Arsenal, at Leyton Stadium. Orient lost that game by 3—0, but like today's clash with First Division Birmingham, the O's had everything to win and really nothing to lose in soccer prestige. They had already earned the label of " Giant Killers " for that season, and in their triumphant progress showed the utmost disregard for soccer reputations and fame. Such then is the F.A. Cup.

Our friends from Birmingham, perhaps, will hardly need reminding of that magnificent conquest of four years ago, but for Orient it is a cherished record. The winning goal was scored by little Tommy Harris, playing at centre-forward, but the man of the match

AN EPIC

CUP-TIE

MEMORY

was the other Tommy in the Orient's side—Tommy Brown, who skippered and inspired the team at inside-left. On his day, Tommy Brown was the ideal soccer artist, and this was his day at St. Andrew's. Of the occasion I wrote in " Oriental Chatter " . . . " Brown gave a showing that was talked of for long afterwards. He was the perfect artist and architect, and when he is playing well there is none to better him. As a captain, too, he was " an inspiration."

Three members of that successful Orient team are playing today, Pat Welton, Les Blizzard and Stan Aldous. The side was : Welton ; Evans, Banner ; Blizzard, Aldous, Deverall ; Woan, Pacey, Harris, Brown, Blatchford. The same eleven played against the Arsenal afterwards.

Birmingham have, no doubt, planned to try to avenge that beating, and, believe me, Orient do not underestimate the magnitude of their own task this afternoon. As champions of the Second Division last season, Birmingham have more than demonstrated their power and talents and, indeed, have they not been tipped in many quarters as likely winners of the coveted F.A. trophy this season ?

If beaten fairly and squarely, Orient will not squeal. They will be the first to congratulate their conquerors, and wish them well in future battles to reach Wembley. However, Orient are determined fighters and on their own ground can usually produce their best against the best. Under the guidance of Manager Alec Stock, Orient players give their " all " all the time, and Mr. Stock has a fine cup record—Yeovil Town (5th round), then, Orient (fifth and sixth rounds). It is said he has a knack of manœuvring " little ships " into harbours " safe from violent storms and raging seas." But, Mr. Stock says, the Orient cannot win matches alone, they must have the help of their supporters. And on that note I want to make an appeal to all loyal O's fans this afternoon. For goodness sake let your " hair down " and give the players encouragement. Let's have a Leyton roar. Please help the boys to achieve, and if things are going badly for them don't just give up the ghost, but exercise your vocal chords and shout ! The players will just love it.

* * *

Concensus of opinion is that Orient's 2—1 win over Brentford in last Saturday's league game here was just about one of their best successes. There were eleven heroes on the field from Pat Welton to unlucky Jack

STINGING

" THE BEES "

AGAIN

Gregory, whose dislocated knee cap, forced him to switch from right-back to outside-left. It was truly a wonderful team effort, the sort of stuff which surely must make Orient followers very proud of the team and club they support. Gregory was an inspiration to his colleagues. His injury received in most unfortunate circumstances when the game was only four minutes old was enough to knock the life out of most sides, but not Orient. That old fighting spirit just had to come out. Trainer Les Gore told me that Gregory was in great pain, and after tending to the injury and

TODAY'S MATCH — K.O. 2.45 p.m.

BIRMINGHAM

(Fourth Round—F.A. Cup)

Round 5: 18 February 1956 v West Bromwich Albion (A) won 0–1 Murphy.
Crowd: 57,213.

Round 6: 3 March 1956 v Arsenal (A) won 1–3 Astall Murphy Brown.
Crowd: 67,872.

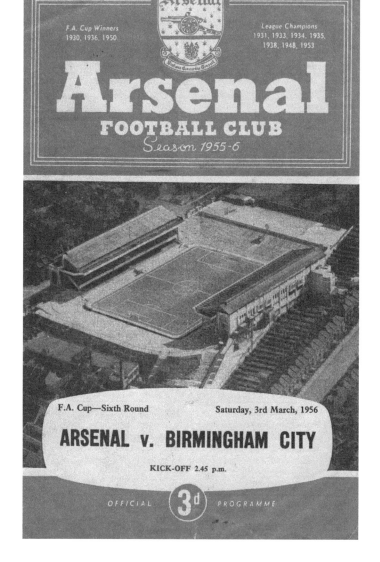

Semi-Final: 17 March 1956 v Sunderland (at Hilsborough) won 0–3 Kinsey Astall Brown.

Crowd: 65,107.

It's Over – Blues on the way to Wembley

Final: 5 May 1956 v Manchester City (at Wembley) lost 3–1 Kinsey.
Crowd: 98,982.

Jack Peart – Sunday Pictorial commented:

'…..and what wide-open spaces there were! Birmingham's covering was shocking and they played without fight or bite except for the fifteen minutes after their equaliser. The only star in defence was centre-half Trevor Smith. He had a thankless task trying to cover all the gaps in a defence as leaky as a colander. I didn't blame Gil Merrick for any of the goals but I thought Jeff Hall, England's right-back against Brazil next Wednesday, had a nightmare of a game. Skipper Len Boyd looked like a fish out of water at left-half. Far better to have taken a chance with Jack Badham there and kept Boyd on his favourite right flank.'

In the Daily Mirror on Monday 7May 1956, Bill Holden reported:

'SKIPPER BOYD WINS MEDAL FOR COURAGE'

'Now it can be told…the inspiring story of the courage and determination of Len Boyd, Birmingham's left-half and captain, who went through two weeks of torture to win a Cup finalists medal.

For two weeks before the Final Len was encased in a plaster cast.

It was his one chance of getting fit enough to play…And the cast was taken off only one hour before the match began.

On 19 April, with the final sixteen days away, a specialist discovered that Boyd was developing a slipped disc.

This caused a pressure on his spinal nerves and produced intense pain.

The only way to correct the trouble and remove the pain, was for Boyd's body to be held rigid in a cast. From then on Len slept, trained and actually played in practice games while wearing the cast.

"It was uncomfortable, and Dave Fairhurst, our physiotherapist, regularly added strong adhesive bandage to it to make sure it kept in place," Len said.

"When it was finally taken off we discovered it was ten pounds in weight. Often it felt heavier when I began to sweat while training, but it was more than worth it. I was able to play and never once felt a twinge of pain during the match. Some people thought I might still be suffering from fibrositis. I wasn't. I never have. But we thought it best to let everyone go on thinking it was that."

Only Boyd's wife, Doreen, Birmingham City officials and *Mirror Sport* knew just how close Len came to having to take a seat on the sidelines.

That fight for fitness was as tense as any encounter on the field, and we pledged to keep it secret until Len had collected his finalist's medal.'

Gil Merrick spoke to me in my biography *GIL MERRICK* about his recollections of the 1956 Final:

"Everyone wants to know why we lost the 1956 FA Cup Final as we were red-hot favourites to win. There have been many stories about why we lost;

1. Len Boyd played in a back brace.
2. Trevor Smith had been out late drinking the night before the Final.
3. The shirts were too thick and made of the wrong material, which became heavier as it absorbed sweat.
4. There was resentment in the team that Johnny Newman had been chosen ahead of Jack Badham.
5. None of these factors were true except the thing about the shirts, Manchester City's shirts were short-sleeved, V-necked and made of a lightweight fabric, our shirts were the complete opposite; long-sleeved so everyone rolled them up, they had collars and were made of typical football shirt cloth that was heavy, retained the heat and sweat and was generally unsuitable for the hot conditions on the day.

But the real reason we lost was down to poor man management!

At half-time we were 1–1 and we knew we were a team that was stronger in the second half, however instead of using the 10 minutes at half-time positively, a huge row broke out between Arthur Turner and Len Boyd. Arthur came storming in and laid into Len about getting hold of Revie, who had been playing in a deep position for a centre-forward. Len gave as good as he got and the language was disgusting but it took up the whole of the half-time break. Len was really upset and turned to me and asked 'Am I really playing that bad, Gil?' and that was it we had lost the opportunity to turn the half-time team talk into one that could have helped us to win the Cup and it was a de-motivated side that left the Wembley dressing room."

The relationship between Len and Arthur was never healed and then Len did an article for *The People* newspaper for which he got paid and that was tantamount to handing in his resignation. Len never played another senior game for Birmingham City Football Club.

Gil adds:
"Regarding who should have played instead of Roy Warhurst my choice would have been Johnny Watts because we played Manchester City at Maine Road on 31st March 1956 and John had frightened Revie such that he did not get a kick We drew the game 1-1, Spud Murphy scoring"

Gil recalls:
"We travelled up to a small hotel outside Reading on the Wednesday prior to the match. On the following day we trained, a full session using the facilities of the local McVities biscuit factory.

On Friday we had a light training session to loosen up on the morning before travelling to The Grand Hotel at Paddington on the morning of the Final.

We had a light lunch. I had fish before leaving for Wembley an hour before kick-off. In the period after lunch a few of us led by Len Boyd, who was a bit of comedian, went for a walk. Len decided to play a prank on Alex (Govan). We got to a public telephone box and phoned the hotel to speak to Alex. Len posed as a Sports reporter for the *Sunday People* and wanted to do an article on how he felt immediately before the FA Cup Final. Alex had no reason to doubt the authenticity of the call and was pleased when the 'reporter' confirmed that a fee was payable. The rest of us were uncontrollable with laughter. When we got back to the hotel, Alex approached us to inform us of the fact that he was getting a fee for an article in the *Sunday People*. Len, keeping a straight face, said how lucky Alex was.

Sometime after the Final Len kept asking Alex if he had got the fee yet and if not he should chase it up. This went on for some time until we were on a train and Len said to Alex, 'You see that guy sitting over there, he's the reporter from the *Sunday People*' It wasn't until Alex threatened to go over and sort him out that Len confessed."

1956 FA Cup Final Programme Cover

EAST
STANDING
ENCLOSURE

ENTER AT TURNSTILES
(See plan & conditions on back)

ENTRANCE

D

10

EMPIRE STADIUM, WEMBLEY
The Football Association
Cup Competition

FINAL TIE

SATURDAY, MAY 5th, 1956
KICK-OFF 3 p.m.

Price 3/6
(Including Tax)

Chairman & Managing Director
Wembley Stadium Limited

THIS PORTION TO BE RETAINED
This Ticket is issued on the condition that
it is not re-sold for more than its face value

1956 FA Cup Final Ticket

George Edwards Cartoon Strip

5.

TREVOR SMITH

– LEAGUE CUP WINNERS 1962–63

*Trevor Smith shakes hands with Barcelona's
skipper Juan Segarra in Spain on 13 November 1957*

FULL NAME: TREVOR SMITH.
DATE OF BIRTH: 13 April 1936.
PLACE OF BIRTH: Brierley Hill.
DATE OF DEATH: 9 August 2003.
PLACE OF DEATH: Essex from lung cancer at the age of 67.

PLAYING CAREER:

Youth Career:
Blues 1951–53

Senior Career:
Blues 1953–1964 making 365 appearances and scoring 3 goals.
Walsall 1964–66 making 12 appearances. 0 goals.

Later he was a permit player in the Lichfield Sunday League and he was manager of Mile Oak Rovers in season 1970–71. After leaving the game Smith went into the licensed trade, first with a public house. The Fox in Tamworth, then as manager of off-licences in Birmingham and later in Dagenham. He retired to Walton-on-the-Naze in Essex.

International:
1955–59 England Under-23 – 15 appearances
1955–57 England 'B' – 2 appearances
1959 Full International – 2 appearances

Smith attended Quarry Bank Secondary Modern School. In 1951 he captained the local schools' representative side, Brierley Hill, Sedgley and District, to their first Final of the English Schools FA Trophy, in which they lost to Liverpool Schools 5–3 on aggregate. A feature of the first leg, according to the Brierley Hill local newspaper, was the 'solid play of the two centre-halves, Parkes for Liverpool and Smith for the home team', while the match programme from the second leg described him thus:

> In Trevor Smith, a tall and weighty boy (nearly twelve stones) who captains the side and plays at centre-half, Brierley Hill have a sheet anchor. Few centre-forwards have been happy against him this season and, in addition to his stopper role, he finds time to distribute the ball effectively to his forwards.

When he left school he signed for Blues as an amateur, and played for the team that won the European Youth Cup (now called Blue Stars/FIFA Youth Cup) the following year. He turned professional on reaching his 17th birthday in April 1953, and made his first-team debut for Birmingham, then in the Second Division, six months later on 31 October 1953, scoring an own goal in a 4–2 win away at Derby County. Purdon, Stewart, Astall and Murphy scored in front of 18,278 spectators. He had to wait until the

1959–60 season before he scored again for the Blues: 19 September 1959 at home to Leicester City scoring in a 3–4 defeat with a crowd of 24,950. Hooper scored the other two goals, one of which was a penalty. Apart from interruptions due to injury or to National Service obligations, he was a regular choice for the first team from then on.

Smith's career at Birmingham coincided with probably the best period in the club's history. Under the management of Arthur Turner, they won promotion to the First Division in 1954–55, reached the FA Cup Final and achieved their highest ever finishing position (sixth place) the following season, and then the FA Cup semi-final in 1957, only to lose to Manchester United's Busby Babes. As Blues' captain he went on to play on the losing side in two successive Inter-Cities Fairs Cup Finals.

1958–60 Tournament.

Final First Leg: 29 March 60 v Barcelona (H) 0–0 Crowd: 40,524
Team: Schofield, Farmer, Allen, Watts, Smith, Neal, Astall, Gordon, Weston, Orritt, Hooper.
Final Second Leg: 4 May 60 v Barcelona (A) lost 4–1 Crowd: 75,000
Hooper scored
Team: Schofield, Farmer, Allen, Watts, Smith, Neal, Astall, Gordon, Weston, Murphy, Hooper.

1960–61 Tournament.

Final First Leg: 27 September 61 v A.S. Roma (H) 2–2 Crowd: 21,005
Team: Schofield, Farmer, Sissons, Hennessey, Foster, Beard, Hellawell, Bloomfield, Harris, Orritt, Auld Scorers; Hellawell and Orritt .
Final Second Leg: 11 October 61 v A.S. Roma (A) lost 0–2 Crowd: 50,000
Team: Schofield, Farmer, Sissons, Hennessey, Smith, Beard, Hellawell, Bloomfield, Harris, Singer, Orritt.

Smith represented his country at schoolboy and youth levels, and won no fewer than 15 caps at Under 23 level He was selected to represent England 'B' against their West German counterparts when still only 18. He had all the attributes necessary for a top-class centre-half. Tall and powerfully built, he was good in the air and in the tackle and read the game well, combining an uncompromising physical game with good technique. When the great Billy Wright retired from international football, the 23-year-old Smith was chosen to take his place, making his England debut against Wales at Ninian Park on 17 October 1959. A calf injury sustained early on, which hampered his movement meant he failed to do himself justice, but he kept his place for the next match, against Sweden later that month. England performed poorly overall against the Swedes, Smith and his defence failed to cope with Swedish forward Agne Simonsson and he was not chosen for his country again; Brian Clough's England career was also restricted to these same two games.

By the early 1960s, Birmingham were past their best. The Cup Final team had dispersed, league form was poor, but the new League Cup competition provided some relief. In 1963 they reached the Final against local rivals Aston Villa, who were hot favourites having won the league meeting two months earlier by four clear goals. However, under the captaincy of the inspirational Smith, Birmingham won the home leg by a comfortable 3–1 margin, and a goalless draw in the away leg gave them their first major trophy.

At the start of the 1964–65, Smith lost his place through injury, and when he recovered he moved to Walsall of the Third Division for a fee of £18,000. His final game for Blues was 2 September away at Fulham, losing 3–1 (Beard scoring) in front of 13,100 spectators. He was able to make only 13 appearances for Walsall before arthritis forced his retirement in 1966 at the age of 29. Walsall were critical of Birmingham, believing they had knowingly sold them an unfit player.

HONOURS

As a Player:

- European Youth Cup winners: 1952.
- Second Division champions: 1954–55.
- FA Cup finalists: 1956.
- Inter-Cities Fairs Cup finalists: 1958–60, 1960–61.
- Football League Cup winners: 1963.

DETAILS OF SUCCESS

27 May 1963 – Villa Park – Crowd: 37,921

DRAW 0–0

23 May 1963 – St.Andrew's – Crowd: 31,580

WON 3–1 – scorers - Bloomfield and Leek 2

Team: J. Schofield, S. Lynn, C. Green, T. Hennessey, T. Smith, M. Beard. M. Hellawell, J. Bloomfield, J. Harris, K. Leek, B Auld.

They did things differently in 1963. There was no colour television and little sunshine, so it was essential to pretend that life was good. It was the year they shot an American president, the year they deified a pop group and the year that fashion gurus devised a standard that made drainpipe trousers compulsory attire. The whole world was in transition and even football, then a means of escape for the working classes, was unsure of its role in society. Everton won the League, Manchester United the FA Cup and George Best moved from Belfast to Old Trafford. When Blues played Villa in the League Cup Final first leg at St Andrew's that May, they could not sell out the stadium. Such a scenario would be unthinkable today but in 1963, Britain was a cold place, constrained by recession and not yet ready to embrace a competition that was ignored by the top clubs. The League Cup which was won on a 3–1 aggregate, suffered from an identity crisis. Readers who shelled out three old pence for *The Birmingham Post* on Tuesday 23 May would not have been surprised to find that the report of the second leg at Villa Park was not even the most substantial story. 'League Cup draw earns Blues their first major honour' went the headline but the match report by Cyril Chapman was inexplicably smaller than the article for the Kent versus Warwickshire cricket match at Gravesend. Charlie Aitken was not complaining. The owner of the thickest head of hair in the game. Aitken was a young defender who, like many of his teammates, wondered what the hell the League Cup was all about. In those days, there was no direct entry into Europe and no prize money. The two encounters in the League Cup Final are more important now than they were then. Whenever opposing fans taunt Bluenoses with chants of 'you've never won f*** all' they miss the point about 1963. Schoey was baffled why the competition was deemed to be so irrelevant: "We found this strange as it had been such a big thing when Villa won it in 1961. We had a good team. Our playmaker was Jimmy Bloomfield who had been persuaded to come out of London to join us following a spell at Arsenal. He was responsible for improving the skill of Mike Hellawell who was a fast-raiding winger."

It is a mystery how Blues won but they did produce perhaps their most impressive display of the season to win the first leg 3–1 at St Andrew's in front of 31,580 people. Blues served up a treat of attacking football taking the lead through Leek in the 14th minute and controlling the game with such assurance that their supporters must have wondered why the team had performed so badly in the First Division. Villa equalised through Thomson but were no match for their opponents. Leek scored again in 52 minutes and Bloomfield made it 3–1 in the 66th minute. The second leg at Villa Park four nights later attracted 37,921 but was an anti-climax. Villa did not have the craft to stage a fightback and Blues eager to protect their lead, rather than add to it, spent most of the match kicking the ball out for throw-ins. The tactic worked and by the start of the 63–64 season Blues were able to distribute photos of their team sitting proudly on benches with the trophy in the foreground.

Gil Merrick remembers:

"We had struggled a bit in the league and the Final came when the season was over. I think the rivalry between us and the Villa made it a special occasion. Our defence was very good. We had Johnny Schofield in goal, Stan Lynn and Colin Green as our full-backs. Stan, from the Villa was the best buy I ever made, he was an outstanding player and a great personality. Our half-back line consisted of Terry Hennessey, Trevor Smith and Malcolm Beard, two of whom came up through the junior ranks. The forward line included Mick Hellawell, Ken Leek, Jimmy Harris, Jimmy Bloomfield and Bertie Auld. It was a memorable victory for us. It's amazing to think that the club has not been to a major final since, but that's the way football is, isn't it? We had had a bad season and the board of Directors decided that a change was needed. It was one of those things but I was very bitter about it at the time. I had always wanted to go into management after I finished my playing career and it was even more special to do that at the club that I had actually played for, for so many years. I really enjoyed it and what gave me the most satisfaction was to watch young apprentices like Terry Hennessey, Malcolm Beard, Malcolm Page and Johnny Vincent come through into the first team. We had a few players like that come through the system and I took pride in that. We won the League Cup and reached the Final of the Inter-Cities Fairs Cup in 1960 and 1961. We were the pioneers for English football in Europe."

League Cup Appearances 1963

Player	Appearances	Goals
Schofield	4	0
Lynn	7	3
Sissons	3	0
Hennessey	8	0

Smith	7	0
Beard	7	0
Hellawell	9	0
Bullock P.	1	1
Harris	6	4
Leek	8	8
Auld	9	4
Stubbs	3	1
Bloomfield	6	2
Watts	5	0
Withers	5	0
Sharples	1	0
Foster	1	0
Regan	2	0
Green	3	0
Rushton	2	0
Wolstenholme	2	1

Surname	Appearances	Goals	Seasons
SCHOFIELD	237	0	14
LYNN	148	30	5
GREEN	217	1	9
HENNESSEY	202	3	6
SMITH	430	3	12
BEARD	403/2	32	11
HELLAWELL	213	33	8
BLOOMFIELD	147	32	4
HARRIS	115	53	4
LEEK	120	61	4
AULD	145	31	5

The 1963 League Cup Winning team, where did they go?

Surname	Outcome
SCHOFIELD	WREXHAM 1966
LYNN	STOURBRIDGE 1966
GREEN	WREXHAM 1971
HENNESSEY	NOTTINGHAM FOREST 1965
SMITH	WALSALL 1964
BEARD	ASTON VILLA 1971
HELLAWELL	SUNDERLAND 1965
BLOOMFIELD	BRENTFORD 1964
HARRIS	OLDHAM 1964
LEEK	NORTHAMPTON 1964
AULD	GLASGOW CELTIC 1965

The second leg was held on 27 May 1963 and was a massive anti-climax with Blues stifling Villa in a goalless draw.

There has been much talk regarding how important the League Cup was in 1963.

Of the 22 teams in the First Division in 1962–63 season only 11 entered the competition, those which did not enter with their final positions were:

EVERTON (1), SPURS (2), BURNLEY (3), WOLVES (5), SHEFFIELD WEDNESDAY (6), ARSENAL (7), LIVERPOOL (8), NOTTINGHAM FOREST (9), WEST BROMWICH ALBION (14), IPSWICH (17), MANCHESTER UNITED (19).

The sides that did enter were:

LEICESTER CITY (4), SHEFFIELD UNITED (10), BLACKBURN ROVERS (11), WEST HAM (12), BLACKPOOL (13), ASTON VILLA (15), FULHAM (16), BOLTON WANDERERS (18), MANCHESTER CITY (21), LEYTON ORIENT (22).

Blues had finished 20th just escaping relegation Played 42 Won 10 Drew 13 Lost 19 GF 63 GA 90 Points 33.

THE ROAD TO VICTORY

FIRST ROUND	BYE
SECOND ROUND	DONCASTER ROVERS (H) WON 5–0, 26 September, Leek 2, Bloomfield, Harris, Auld. Crowd: 11,384.
THIRD ROUND	BARROW (A) DREW 1–1, 15 October, Wolstenholme. Crowd: 6,289.
THIRD ROUND REPLAY	BARROW (H) WON 5–1, 29 October, Harris 2 Stubbs, Leek, Arrowsmith (og). Crowd: 11,765.
FOURTH ROUND	NOTTS COUNTY (H) WON 3–2, 14 November, Lynn (pen), Harris, Auld. Crowd: 13,187.
FIFTH ROUND	MAN.CITY (H) WON 6–0, 11 December, Lynn 2 (1 pen), Leek, Auld, Leivers (og), Sears (og). Crowd: 18,012.
SEMI-FINAL FIRST LEG	BURY (H) WON 3–2, 27 March, Bullock, Leek, Auld. Crowd: 11,293.
SEMI-FINAL SECOND LEG	BURY (A) DREW 1–1, 8 April, Leek . Crowd: 9,177.

Not since 1956 had Blues contested a domestic Final and this was one they simply had to win, as the opposition were their neighbours and arch rivals, Aston Villa.

Villa went into the match as the bookmaker's favourites having beaten Blues two months earlier in a League match 4–0. Both sides were at full strength in front of a first-leg St.Andrew's crowd of 31,580 who were licking their lips with relish in anticipation of this Birmingham derby, which to the winner was worth much more than just 'the bragging rights'.

Blues started well with near misses from Jimmy Harris and Ken Leek, both of which were well saved by the Villa goalkeeper Sims. Blues had their best chance to date soon after when another shot from Harris was deflected onto the crossbar by Sims.

The competitiveness of both sides began to show when Bobby Thomson clattered Blues' 'keeper Schofield with an unnecessary late challenge for the ball and in another incident, Leek sent Crowe flying with another late tackle, both fouls coming in the early stages, as the teams 'sorted each other out' in what was a typically eagerly fought out derby. There was a lot at stake! The first goal came, and for celebrating home fans it was scored by Leek after 14 minutes. A ball from midfield by Harris released Bertie Auld whose left wing cross was blasted home by Leek, this time giving Sims no chance of making a stop. Jimmy Bloomfield, with the tackles still flying in became the first casualty, leaving to have a thigh injury dealt with and he returned only to hobble on the wing so that he could try to run the knock off, this he successfully did much to the relief of both the Blues' fans and Gil Merrick, the Manager. However, Villa were not beaten and got back into the game via an equaliser by Thomson. Gordon Lee started the move and after driving into Blues final third he sent in a hard, low cross which Thomson hit first time, it sped past Schofield as he was coming out to narrow the angle for the Villa man.

The second period began badly for Villa defender Sleeuwenhoek who collided with his own goalkeeper, which resulted in an injury which forced him to leave the field to receive treatment. Soon after that Blues lost their centre-half too when Trevor Smith was hurt in another rash tackle from Thomson. The first real chance to score was taken and it restored back the lead for Blues after 52 minutes. Again Harris and Auld were the architects, and Leek the goalscorer, with a low drive in the area from Auld's pinpoint pass. The match was still bad-tempered and referee Crawford began to lose his patience with the persistent niggling fouling. Crowe became the next victim, when he was elbowed in the face after a tussle with Auld. Charlie Aitken was then given a sharp tongue-lashing when he shoved Hellawell in the chest in yet another heated exchange. Fraser and Harris came close to blows as they squared up to one another and teammates had to drag them apart. Crawford also gave them a warning as they continued to infuriate the Doncaster official. Blues finally killed the game with their third goal after 66 minutes. From a Harris right wing cross, Bloomfield dashed in unmarked (apart from the wound on his thigh) by Villa's sleeping defence to push the ball past Sims and in off the upright. Blues were leading 3–1 up, in the ascendancy and they were strolling through the rest of the game, content to take their lead to Villa Park for the second leg. In the dying moments, Sims saved Villa once again saving two excellent shots on goal from Leek then Auld. The final whistle came with Blues still holding a two-goal advantage and counting the bruises from this gruelling encounter.

1963 League Cup Winners

Stan Lynn and Trevor Smith drink from the trophy and winner's tankard

League Cup Action

League Cup Action

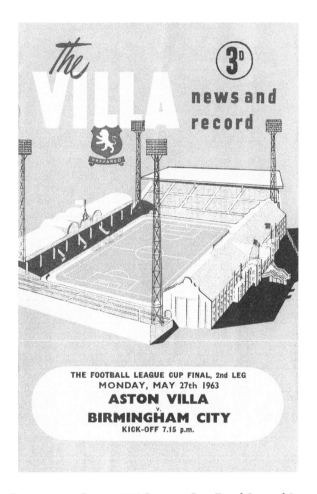

Programme Cover 1963 League Cup Final Second Leg

Jimmy Harris at home with this trophy

BLUES CAREER

SEASON	League Appearances	League Goals	FA Cup Appearances	FA Cup Goals	League Cup Appearances/ Goals	Inter-Cities Apps/Goals
1953–54	24	0	1	0	0	0
1954–55	24	0	4	0	0	0
1955–56	30	0	6	0	0	0
1956–57	37	0	7	0	0	1/0
1957–58	37	0	1	0	0	3/0
1958–59	27	0	6	0	0	2/0
1959–60	41	1	1	0	0	4/0
1960–61	31	0	4	0	2/0	5/0
1961–62	39	0	2	0	2/0	2/0
1962–63	37	0	2	0	7/0	0
1963–64	34	2	1	0	1/0	0
1964–65	4	0	0	0	0	0

6.

STAN HARLAND

– PROMOTION TO DIVISION ONE – 1971–72 & THIRD PLACE IN FA CUP 1973

1971-72 Team Group – Stan Harland on far right

FULL NAME: Stan Harland.

DATE OF BIRTH: 19 June 1940.

PLACE OF BIRTH: Liverpool.

DATE OF DEATH: 30 August 2001.

PLACE OF DEATH: Tintinhull Somerset from a heart attack at the age of 61.

PLAYING CAREER:

Youth Career:

New Brighton

Senior Career:

1959–61 Everton 0 Appearances 0 goals. 1961–1964 Bradford City 120 appearances 20 goals. 1964–1966 Carlisle United 77 appearances 7 goals. 1966–71 Swindon Town 237 appearances 6 goals. 1971–75 Blues 38 appearances 0 goals. 1975–78 Yeovil Town as player-manager.

Harland's move to the Blues came about directly because of Swindon Town's disappointing 1970–71 season. In response to the situation they recruited Dave Mackay from Derby County, which resulted in Stan losing not only his position as a first team regular but also the captaincy. Manager Fred Ford initially gave him the role of auxiliary defender but Harland was dropped completely from the team when Mackay took over the coaching at the club as player-manager. Stan was sold to Blues for £15,000. His league debut was a 0–0 draw away at Middlesbrough on 4 December 1971 with an attendance of 15,671. His final league game was 30 December 1972 at home to Ipswich Town which Blues lost 1–2 (Hatton scoring) in front of a crowd of 32,705. He never scored for the Blues in any competition apart from the Penalty Shoot-out in the FA Cup Third-Place match.

Stan only made 38 league appearances for Birmingham but he captained us to promotion to the First Division in 1972, the FA Cup semi-final of the same year and third-place in the FA Cup competition on 1973. His career was ended through injury although he moved to become player-manager of Yeovil Town and later worked with Frank Burrows at Portsmouth in a coaching capacity.

Harland was married to an ice-dancing champion and had two daughters; he also often played in the Professional Footballers' Golf Championship. After leaving football he worked in the Supermarket business and continued working up until his death.

SEASON BY SEASON

Season	League Appearances/Goals	FA Cup Appearances/Goals	League Cup Appearances/Goals
1971–72	19 (0)	5 (0)	0 (0)
1972–73	18 + 1 (0)	1 (0)	3 (0)

HONOURS

As a Player:

- Carlisle United – Third Division Champions 1964–65.
- Swindon Town;

  Second Division promotion winner 1969.

  League Cup winner 1969.

  Anglo-Italian League Cup winner 1969.

  Anglo- Italian Cup winner 1970.

- Birmingham City – Second Division Promotion winner 1972.

PROMOTION 1971–72

2 May 1972 versus ORIENT (Away) Won 1–0

Attendance: 33,383

Scorer: R. Latchford.

Team: Cooper, Carroll, Pendrey, G. Smith, Hynd, Whitehead, Campbell, Francis, Latchford, Hatton, Taylor.

PLAYER	League Appearances/Goals	FA Cup Appearances/Goals	League Cup Appearances/Goals
Kelly	19 (0)	0 (0)	0 (0)
Martin	14+ 1 (0)	0 (0)	1 (0)
Page	38 +1 (0)	5 (1)	1 (0)
Smith G	22+3 (0)	1 +1 (0)	1 (0)
Hynd	42 (1)	5 (1)	1 (0)

Pendrey	40 (1)	5 (0)	1 (0)
Campbell	42 (4)	5 (0)	1 (0)
Bowker	6 (2)	0 (0)	0 (0)
Latchford R	42 (23)	5 (4)	1 (0)
Summerill	7+2 (1)	0 (0)	1 (0)
Taylor	27 + 3 (1)	4 + 1 (0)	1 (0)
Robinson	10 + 2 (0)	0 (0)	0 (0)
Phillips	6 + 1 (0)	0 (0)	0 (0)
Latchford D	11 (0)	2 (0)	1 (0)
Francis	39 (12)	5 (2)	1 (0)
Burns	7 + 1 (0)	0 (0)	0 (0)
Carroll	27 (0)	5 (0)	0 (0)
Hatton	26 (15)	5 (2)	0 (0)
Harland	19 (0)	5 (0)	0 (0)
Cooper	12 (0)	3 (0)	0 (0)
O'Grady	2+1 (0)	0 (0)	0 (0)
Whitehead	3 (0)	0 (0)	0 (0)

The equation was simple, one game left, one point required to gain promotion to Division One after seven years in the Second Division. The Blues travelling army of 18,000 were up for this one and in a confident mood. They swelled the Brisbane Road crowd to 33,383 for the evening kick-off. Many were locals who were full time supporters of the club next in line to benefit from any Blues slip up on the night, Millwall; and they were clearly intent on causing havoc should things start to go right for Blues. Orient, the other side in this huge game, had nothing but professional pride to play for and the result no matter what, would not affect their position in the table. Blues got the game under way and within minutes it was clear how much they were under pressure, their play dominated by the fear of a single error. It was no surprise then that the opening exchanges were almost entirely made in midfield, Blues were content to sit back and earn their draw by rigid defending even from deep in the Orient half. One of the few chances that did come the Blues way was snatched at by Latchford and the ball sailed over the bar. At the other end Pendrey bravely blocked a goal bound strike from Lazarus, and striker Mickey Bullock almost broke Blues hearts but he was stopped by a fine save from Cooper. Blues best chance came just before the half-time break when Goddard acrobatically tipped over a shot from Hatton.

Blues started the second period with much more confidence; obviously Freddie Goodwin's talk had done the trick. They showed no sign of fear and were prepared to chase the game now, as if they had been told only a win, not a draw, was required. Straight away it was noticeable that Francis, who had hardly been involved in the first half, was now seeking possession and when he received the ball for the first time after the restart, he struck a beauty from outside the area, which Goddard saved brilliantly. Then minutes later he sent a spectacular volley from Taylor's cross just inches wide. Blues looked increasingly likely to score and on 58 minutes they put one foot firmly into Division One, with a goal from Bob Latchford. A corner from Taylor was headed in by the Blues centre-forward who was being pulled back by the 'keeper. The goal sparked chaos all around, Orient's players surrounded the referee complaining that Latchford's foul on Goddard, Blues fans invaded the pitch and then the Millwall fans decided to introduce themselves. Chaos prevailed for some time as police tried to shepherd fans back to their place. Play eventually resumed in full swing and it was Blues again dominating. Taylor broke through and almost made the game safe, but he was denied again by a superb diving save from Goddard. This brought about another pitch invasion; only this time it was the Millwall fans. Play was halted again and when it restarted Blues were soon attacking the Orient goal. A lob by Hatton just cleared the bar in the closing minutes; this led to loud whistling from the crowd as well as 'Keep right on to the end of the Road' which was even louder. The referee finally signalled the end of the game after almost 100 minutes play, including stoppage time, and the players charged off.

Blues fans stormed the pitch and the promotion party started, even the announcement of a bomb in the ground did not stop the celebrations, but after a time the police did and everyone was evacuated. Everyone it seems apart from the Blues team and chairman Keith Coombes who were still in the dressing room, choosing not to leave. Coombes summed up the mood of the club by saying after the game, "I didn't care even if it was a real bomb, I can go happy now I know we are back in Division One."

Orient: Goddard, Arber, Rose; Hoadley, Harris, Allen, Lazarus, Brisley, Bullock, Walley, Bowyer.
Referee: Mr M Lowe (Sheffield). Garry Pendrey captained the side on the day.

PARTY ON THE M1

If ever there was an occasion, which typified the resilience you need to be a Bluenose it was the night of 2 May 1972, the night we got promoted at the end of season 1971–72. Blues beat Orient 1–0 at Brisbane Road and 15,000 of us travelled to the capital city to ensure our boys went up. We were singing our battle hymn well before the end of the game when Bob Latchford headed home the eventual winner in the 58th minute. Before the end of the ninety minutes Millwall fans invaded the pitch and approached the Blues fans in the vain hope of getting the game abandoned (Blues needed just one point to go up, but a victory meant that Millwall finished third one point behind the Blues). Once the police had cleared them off the pitch, the final whistle blew and it was the turn of the Bluenoses to get onto the pitch to acclaim our heroes. As we were celebrating on the pitch there was an urgent loudspeaker appeal for the main stand to be cleared. No one moved even though it was during a time when the I.R.A. were active on the U.K. mainland, we wanted to salute the team. Suddenly there was a loud bang and a blinding flash in the corner of the terracing under the main stand. Fortunately no one was hurt and it was eventually found out to be a hand-made incendiary device. After dealing with a few suicidal Millwall thugs who were waiting for us outside, the Blues fans travelled North on the M1 in party mood. Scarves flew from car windows, horns honked and every car window was open with the face of a delighted Blues fan leaning out singing *'Keep Right On to the end of the Road'* as loudly as they could, beer cans littered the hard shoulder (this was before drink driving legislation) as cars pulled in to allow fans the opportunity to relieve themselves. It was a slow, slow journey home but no one complained as we were in the First Division for the first time in seven years.

FA CUP THIRD PLACE PLAY OFF
5 August 1973 v. STOKE CITY (home)

Attendance: 25841 Drew 0–0

Scorers: Campbell, Francis, Hope, Harland.

Blues Won 4–3 on penalties

PLAYER	APPEARANCES	GOALS
COOPER	26	0
CARROLL	47	0
WANT	122 + 5	2
CAMPBELL	202 + 7	14
HYND	198 + 8	5
HARLAND	44 + 1	0
HOPE	42 + 4	5
FRANCIS	327 + 2	133
LATCHFORD	190 + 4	84
HATTON	212 + 6	73
TAYLOR	189 + 14	10

7.

ARCHIE GEMMILL

– PROMOTION TO DIVISION ONE 1979–80

Archie Gemmill Team Group

FULL NAME: Archibald Gemmill.
DATE OF BIRTH: 24 March 1947.
PLACE OF BIRTH: Paisley, Renfrewshire, Scotland.

PLAYING CAREER:

Youth Career:
Drumchapel.

Senior Career:

1964–67 St Mirren 65 appearances 9 goals, 1967–70 Preston North End 99 appearances 13 goals, 1970–77 Derby County 261 appearances 17 goals, 1977–79 Nottingham Forest 58 appearances 4 goals, 1979–82 Blues 97 appearances 12 goals, 1982 Jacksonville Tea Men 32 appearances 2 goals, 1982 Wigan Athletic 11 appearances 0 goals, 1982–84 Derby County 63 appearances 8 goals. Total 686 appearances 65 goals

International:

1971–81 Scotland 43 Full Internationals 8 goals. Under-23 1 appearance.

Management Career:

1994–96, Rotherham United – joint manager with John McGovern. Their first game was against Blues in September 1994 a game, which resulted in a 1–1 draw. – 2005–2009 Scotland Under-19.

A split between Clough and Gemmill led to him signing for Birmingham City. He made his debut on 18 August 1979 in a 4–3 defeat at home to Fulham in front of a crowd of 19,330 with Evans, Dillon and Bertschin scoring for Blues. He played 97 League matches for the Blues, scoring 12 goals. His first league goal was scored on 20 October 1979 at home against Swansea, a game Blues won 2–0, Lynex scored the other goal in front of 18,624. His last game was 6 February 1982 at home in a goalless draw with Middlesbrough in front of a crowd of 10,715.

SEASON BY SEASON

SEASON	LEAGUE APPEARANCES/ GOALS	FA CUP APPEARANCES/ GOALS	LEAGUE CUP APPEARANCES/ GOALS
1979–80	37 (8)	3 (1)	3 (0)
1980–81	41 (3)	3 (0)	5 (1)
1981–82	19 (1)	1 (0)	2 (0)

HONOURS

As a Player:

- Derby County – First Division – Champions: 1971–72, 1974–75.
  FA Charity Shield – Winners: 1975.
- Nottingham Forest – First Division – Champions: 1977–78.
  Football League Cup – Winners: 1978, 1979.
  European Cup – Winners: 1979.

As a Manager:

- Rotherham United – Football League Trophy – Winners: 1996.
  3 May 1980 versus NOTTS COUNTY (home) Attendance: 33,863
  Drew 3–3.

Blues promoted to Division One in 3rd Place.

Played 42 – Won 21 – Drew 11 – Lost 10 – Goals For 58 – Goals Against 38 – Points 53.

The team on the day: Wealands, Broadhurst, Lees, Curbishley, Gallagher, Todd, Ainscow, Givens, Bertschin, Gemmill and Dillon.
Scorers: Bertschin, Curbishley and Dillon.

PLAYER	LEAGUE APPEARANCES/ GOALS	FA CUP APPEARANCES/ GOALS	LEAGUE CUP APPEARANCES/ GOALS
FREEMAN	2 (0)	1 (0)	0 (0)
CALDERWOOD	1 (0)	0(0)	0 (0)
DENNIS	40 (0)	2 (0)	3 (0)
CURBISHLEY	40+2 (3)	3 (0)	3 (0)
VAN DEN HAUWE	1 (0)	0 (0)	0 (0)
PAGE	3 (0)	0 (0)	0 (0)
AINSCOW	37 (6)	3 (0)	3 (2)

EVANS	10+3 (4)	0 (0)	2 (0)
BERTSCHIN	34+3 (12)	3 (3)	1+1 (0)
GEMMILL	37 (8)	3 (1)	3 (0)
DILLON	30+1 (6)	0 (0)	3 (0)
WEALANDS	40 (0)	2 (0)	3 (0)
GALLAGHER	41 (1)	3 (1)	3 (0)
TOWERS	22 (0)	0 (0)	3 (0)
LEES	9+1 (0)	1 (0)	1 (0)
LYNEX	20+10 (8)	0+3 (0)	2 (1)
TODD	33+1 (0)	3 (0)	1 (0)
GIVENS	7+3 (2)	0 (0)	1 (0)
JOHNSTON	15 (0)	3 (0)	0 (0)
WORTHINGTON	17+2 (4)	3 (0)	0 (0)
BROADHURST	23 (1)	3 (0)	0 (0)

MATCH REPORT:

Birmingham with one of the best home records in the Division went into this crucial game against mid-table opposition needing just a draw to ensure promotion. So, although not taking anything for granted, the crowd, which swelled to 33,863, arrived at St.Andrew's confident the Blues would sweep aside the Magpies and make sure of a promotion spot with a victory, after all you can always rely on Blues, can't you? Blues as you would expect started in dominant mood against a County side playing only for professional pride. A goal for Blues was imminent and it duly arrived, well before anyone suffered an anxiety attack within the crowd, scored by Bertschin after 18 minutes. A neat move saw Dillon beat his full-back on the right put in a clipped cross to Givens who rather than shoot from an acute angle, screwed the ball across the face of the goal for Bertschin to nod in at the far post. It was all going suspiciously to plan and when Blues added a second four minutes later, even the most pessimistic of Blues fans were convinced. The goal came directly from a Curbishley free-kick 25 yard out, after Givens had been fouled by Kilcline. Moments later the Blues further teased the crowd with the help of Avramovic who brilliantly saved a Gemmill free kick from almost the same spot as Curbishley's strike two minutes before. Then just at the point when the fans started to believe this promotion game was a doddle, a lapse in the Blues defence allowed County back in the game at 2–1. A great cross from Hunt on the right was met by the alert Mair who nipped in to poke the ball past Wealands at the near post. Just four minutes later Mair turned from goalscorer to goal provider when putting Christie clean through after Broadhurst slipped. Taking the ball on the County striker made the one-on-one with the 'keeper look easy with a crisp low shot past the oncoming Wealands. That was it the reality stick had given everyone a huge smack in the face and we all stood on the terraces trying to convince ourselves, we knew all along and they hadn't really fooled us. Within minutes Blues were back in the lead through Dillon. Bertschin's cross from the right was too long for Dillon and Givens in the centre, however, the latter after chasing the loose ball centred from the left, this fell to Bertschin who laid the ball off to Dillon to sweep a low left-foot drive into the corner of the net. The tension resumed early in the second half when Mason's fierce volley was brilliantly saved by Wealands, an early indication that County were not going to easily surrender. With just 27 minutes of the game remaining Brian Kilcline got forward for a set piece and prodded home a close range equaliser to ensure a heart-stopping finale to a game that had already left most people emotionally drained. Time after time innocuous looking forward passes by County had the crowd wincing at the potential danger. However the Blues defence of Broadhurst, Lees, Gallagher and Todd held firm right up to the long awaited final whistle. A mass, but good humoured pitch invasion ensued and the promotion party got into full swing when the players arrived in the main stand directors enclosure to thank the crowd who in turn thanked them for the season's achievements and for that unforgettable 90 minutes of football.

Notts County: Avramovic; Richards, O'Brien; Benjamin, Stubbs, Kilcline; McCulloch, Masson, Christie, Hunt, Mair.
Referee: Mr K.G. Salmon (Barnet).

Blues players celebrate Givens, Bertschin, Dillon, Ainscow

8.

BILLY WRIGHT

– PROMOTION TO DIVISION ONE 1984–85

1984-85 Team Group – Billy Wright front row fourth from left

FULL NAME: William Wright.
DATE OF BIRTH: 28 April 1958.
PLACE OF BIRTH: Liverpool.

PLAYING CAREER:

Youth Career:
1974–77 Everton.

Senior Career:
1977–83 Everton 166 appearances 10 goals, 1983–86 Birmingham City 111 appearances 8 goals, 1986 Chester City (loan) 6 appearances 1 goal, 1986–88 Carlisle United 87 appearances 3 goals, 1988 Morecambe 13 appearances 1 goal.

International:

1979–80 England Under-21 6 appearances 0 goals, 1979–80 England 'B' 2 appearances 0 goals.

Management:

1988–89 Morecambe

Billy played 370 games in the football league appearing in all four divisions.

Wright moved to Blues on a free transfer from Everton. He made his league debut on 27 August 1983 away at West Ham United losing 4–0 with a crowd of 19,729, his first league goal was a penalty against Wolverhampton Wanderers in a 1–1 draw at Molineux, attendance 15,933.

SEASON BY SEASON

SEASON	LEAGUE APPEARANCES/ GOALS	FA CUP APPEARANCES/ GOALS	LEAGUE CUP APPEARANCES/ GOALS
1983–84	40 (5)	5 (3)	8 (0)
1984–85	42 (2)	4 (1)	4 (0)
1985–86	29 (1)	0+1 (0)	3+1 (2)

Of his 14 goals for Blues only one came from open play in FA Cup 3rd Round tie on 23 January 1985 in a 1–1 draw at Carrow Road in front of 11,883

He missed only two games in all competitions in his first two seasons, was appointed captain and penalty-taker, and helped the club to promotion back to the First Division in 1985. His form began to be affected by weight problems, and Birmingham released him the following year. His final game was ironically against his hometown on 26 April 1986 at Anfield, which resulted in a 5–0 defeat with an attendance of 42,021.

After four seasons of struggle in Division One Blues had been relegated to Division Two under the management of Ron Saunders. Unlike today he kept his job, got the backing of the Board and was looking for an immediate return to the top league. As always happens to a relegated side we began to lose players; Noel Blake and Howard Gayle had moved on in the summer and were ultimately followed by Blues stalwarts, Mick Harford, Tony Coton, Pat Van den Hauwe and Mick Ferguson.

During the season we used 29 players with only Billy Wright as an ever-present. To show how things changed during the season only Robert Hopkins, Brian 'Harry' Roberts, Wayne Clarke, Gerry Daly and the skipper where in the line-up for the final game as well as the first!

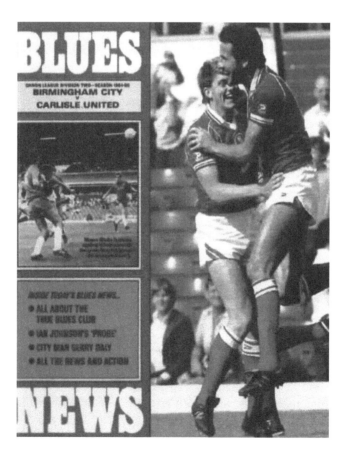

1984-85 Home Programme Cover

		HOME					AWAY					
	P	W	D	L	GF	GA	W	D	L	GF	GA	Pts	GD
Oxford	42	18	2	1	62	15	7	7	7	22	21	84	+48
BLUES	42	12	6	3	30	15	13	1	7	29	18	82	+26
Man City	42	14	4	3	42	16	7	7	7	24	24	74	+26
Portsmouth	42	11	6	4	39	25	9	8	4	30	25	74	+19
Blackburn	42	14	3	4	38	15	7	7	7	28	26	73	+25
Brighton	42	13	6	2	31	11	7	6	8	23	23	72	+20
Leeds	42	12	7	2	37	11	7	5	9	29	32	69	+23
Shrewsbury	42	12	6	3	45	22	6	5	10	21	31	65	+13
Fulham	42	13	3	5	35	26	6	5	10	33	38	65	+4
Grimsby	42	13	1	7	47	32	5	7	9	25	32	62	+8
Barnsley	42	11	7	3	27	12	3	9	9	15	30	58	0
Milton Keynes	42	9	8	4	40	29	7	2	12	31	46	58	-4
Huddersfield	42	9	5	7	28	29	6	5	10	24	35	55	-12
Oldham	42	10	4	7	27	23	5	4	12	22	44	53	-18
C Palace	42	8	7	6	25	27	4	5	12	21	38	48	-19
Carlisle	42	8	5	8	27	23	5	3	13	23	44	47	-17
Charlton	42	8	7	6	34	30	3	5	13	17	33	45	-12
Sheff Utd	42	7	6	8	31	28	3	8	10	23	38	44	-12
Middlesbro	42	6	8	7	22	26	4	2	15	19	31	40	-16
Notts Co	42	6	5	10	25	32	4	2	15	20	41	37	-28
Cardiff	42	5	3	13	24	42	4	5	12	23	37	35	-32
Wolves	42	5	4	12	18	32	3	5	13	19	47	33	-42

Final League Table 1984-85

PROMOTION 1984–85

11 May 1985 Versus LEEDS UNITED (home) Won 1–0.

Attendance: 24 847

The team on the day was: Seaman, Ranson, Roberts, Wright, Armstrong, Kuhl, Daly, Clarke, Bremner, Geddis, Hopkins.

Scorer: Kuhl.

Any attempts to celebrate on the final day were deemed hopeless when the Leeds United fans caused a riot ,which resulted in the death of a young fan when a brick wall collapsed on him. A total of 96 police officers were also injured in the incident, which resulted in the second-half starting 30 minutes later.

That day coincided with the infamous Bradford stand fire and these two incidents resulted in the setting up of the Popplewell enquiry, which ultimately brought about major changes in the way fans were treated at football matches.

The promotion was clinched two days before the Leeds United game at Cardiff City on 4 May 1985 when Robert Hopkins and Andy Kennedy both scored in the 2–1 victory in front of a crowd of 15,868.

Promoted to Division One in second place- Played 42 – won 25 – drew 7 – lost 10 – Goals For 59 – Goals Against 33 – Points 82.

PLAYER	LEAGUE APPEARANCES/ GOALS	FA CUP APPEARANCES/ GOALS	LEAGUE CUP APPEARANCES/ GOALS
COTON	7 (0)	0 (0)	0 (0)
ROBERTS	41 (0)	4 (0)	4 (0)
VAN DEN HAUWE	6 (0)	0 (0)	0 (0)
WRIGHT	42 (2)	4 (1)	4 (0)
HAGAN	21+8 (0)	1+2 (0)	4 (0)
DALY	29+1 (1)	4 (0)	2 (0)
STEVENSON	6 (0)	0 (0)	0 (0)
CLARKE	40 (17)	4 (0)	2 (0)
FERGUSON	2 (1)	0 (0)	0 (0)
GORMAN	6 (0)	0 (0)	1 (0)
HOPKINS	39 (9)	4 (0)	2 (1)
KUHL	25+2 (2)	0 (0)	4 (0)
ARMSTRONG	36 (0)	3 (0)	4 (0)
HARFORD	12 (2)	0 (0)	3 (1)
HALSALL	2+1 (0)	0 (0)	2 (0)
McDONOUGH	1 (0)	0 (0)	0 (0)
BREMNER	30 (0)	4 (0)	3 (0)
SEAMAN	33 (0)	4 (0)	0 (0)
JONES	9+1 (0)	0 (0)	1+1 (0)

REES	5+4 (2)	0 (0)	1+1 (1)
SHEARER	2+2 (0)	0 (0)	1 (1)
RANSON	28 (0)	4 (0)	0 (0)
LINFORD	1+1 (0)	0 (0)	0 (0)
MORLEY	4 (3)	0 (0)	0 (0)
PLATENAUR	11 (1)	4 (0)	0 (0)
GEDDIS	18 (12)	4 (1)	0 (0)
RUSSELL	1 (0)	0 (0)	0 (0)
PRUDHOE	1 (0)	0 (0)	4 (0)
KENNEDY	4+3 (4)	0 (0)	0 (0)
STORER	0 (0)	0 (0)	1 (0)
BROWN	0 (0)	0 (0)	0+1 (0)

9.

VINCE OVERSON

– LEYLAND DAF WINNERS 1990–91

Back row : Dougie Bell, Dean Peer, Mark Yates, Colin Gordon, Martin Thomas, Matthew Fox, Dean Williams, Trevor Matthewson, Nigel Gleghorn, Ian Rodgerson, Simon Sturridge.
Middle Row : Brian Caswell (Youth Team Coach), Ian Clarkson, Sean Francis, Andy Harris, Paul Masefield, Trevor Aylott, Eamonn Dolan, Robert Hopkins, Phil Robinson, Nigel Larkins, Peter Henderson (Physio).
Front Row : John Frain, John Deakin, John Gayle, Lou Macari (Manager), Chick Bates (Asst Manager), Vince Overson, Greg Downs, Mark Rutherford.

1990–91 Team Group – Vince Overson is on front row three from the right

FULL NAME: Vincent David Overson.
DATE OF BIRTH: 15 May 1962.
PLACE OF BIRTH: Kettering.

PLAYING CAREER:

Youth Career:
Corby Town – Long Buckby – 1978–79 Burnley.

Senior Career:

1979–86 Burnley 254 appearances 7 goals, 1986–91 Blues 202 appearances 3 goals, 1991–96 Stoke City 215 appearances 7 goals, 1996–98 Burnley 10 appearances 0 goals, 1997 Shrewsbury Town (Loan) 2 appearances 0 goals, 1998 Halifax Town 1 appearances 0 goals. Total 695 appearances 18 goals in all competitions.

Management:

2003 Padiham, 2003–04 Ramsbottom United.

Overson followed his brother Richard to Burnley after playing non-league football with Corby Town and Long Buckby. He turned professional in November 1979 and spent seven seasons at Turf Moor making 254 appearances scoring seven goals. During that time Burnley suffered relegation three times whilst they won the Third Division title in 1981–82

He joined Blues in June 1986 He made his league debut for the Blues on the opening day of 1986–87 season away at Stoke City winning 2–0 with goals from Whitton and Hemming (own goal) in front of a crowd of 11,548.

His first league goal was scored in the 4–1 win over Crystal Palace on 18 October 1986 with the other goals coming from Whitton, Bremner and Clarke, the attendance was 5,987. He captained Birmingham to success in the 1991 Football League Trophy defeat of Tranmere Rovers, which was his final game for the Blues. His final league game was on 11 May 1991 a 1–0 win away at Huddersfield Town watched by 5,195, John Gayle scored the winner. After making 213 appearances for Birmingham in five seasons he followed manager Lou Macari to Stoke City with a fee of £55,000 being decided at a tribunal.

SEASON BY SEASON

SEASON	LEAGUE APPEARANCES/ GOALS	FA CUP APPEARANCES/ GOALS	LEAGUE CUP APPEARANCES/ GOALS
1986–87	34 (1)	0 (0)	3 (0)
1987–88	37 (0)	2 (0)	1 (0)
1988–89	41 (0)	1 (0)	3 (0)
1989–90	27+3 (0)	3 (0)	3+1 (0)
1990–91	40 (2)	2 (0)	1 (0)

During his time at Blues he was managed by John Bond, Garry Pendrey, Dave Mackay and finally Lou Macari.

HONOURS

As a Player:

- Burnley
  Football League Third Division champions: 1981–82.
- Birmingham City
  Football League Trophy winner: 1991.
- Stoke City
  Football League Trophy winner: 1992.
  Football League Second Division champions: 1992–93.

DETAILS OF SUCCESS

LEYLAND DAF FINAL

26 May 1991 versus TRANMERE ROVERS at Wembley Won 3–2

Attendance: 58,756.

Scorers: Gayle 2, Sturridge.

Gayle lifts the Leyland Daf Cup after the memorable Wembley victory in 1991.

John Gayle with the trophy

The team on the day was: Thomas, Clarkson, Frain, Yates, Overson, Matthewson, Peer, Gayle, Robinson, Gleghorn, Sturridge. Substitute for Sturridge – Bailey at 62 minutes – Unused Substitute – Hopkins

PLAYER	LEAGUE APPEARANCES/ GOALS	FA CUP APPEARANCES/ GOALS	LEAGUE CUP APPEARANCES/ GOALS
THOMAS	45 (0)	1 (0)	2 (0)
ASHLEY	3 (0)	0 (0)	2 (0)
DOWNS	16+1 (0)	0 (0)	2 (0)
FRAIN	42 (3)	2 (0)	2 (0)
OVERSON	40 (2)	2 (0)	1 (0)
MATTHEWSON	46 (3)	2 (0)	2 (0)
PEER	37+3 (2)	2 (0)	2 (0)
BAILEY	25+7 (5)	2 (0)	2 (0)
HOPKINS	18+5 (3)	1 (0)	2 (0)
GLEGHORN	42 (6)	2 (0)	2 (0)
TAIT	17 (3)	1 (0)	2 (0)
STURRIDGE	33+5 (6)	2 (1)	0+2 (0)
FOX	9+2 (0)	0 (0)	1 (0)
MORAN	2+6 (1)	0 (0)	0+1 (0)
CLARKSON	34 (3)	1 (0)	0 (0)
RUTHERFORD	1+2 (0)	0 (0)	0 (0)
AYLOTT	23 (2)	0+1 (1)	0 (0)
GORDON	3+2 (0)	0+1 (0)	0 (0)
GAYLE	20+2 (6)	1 (0)	0 (0)
RODGERSON	25 (2)	0 (0)	0 (0)
DOLAN	5+5 (1)	0 (0)	0 (0)
FRANCIS	0+3 (0)	0 (0)	0 (0)
BELL	1 (0)	0 (0)	0 (0)
YATES	8+1 (1)	0 (0)	0 (0)
O'REILLY	1 (0)	0 (0)	0 (0)
ROBINSON	9 (0)	0 (0)	0 (0)
WILLIAMS	1 (0)	1 (0)	0 (0)

Never before and probably never again would Wembley see scenes like these, 48,000 Blues fans in a crowd of 58,576 converged on the twin towers in the hope of seeing their team lift their first cup there. The Blues team didn't disappoint. Led by Lou Macari and inspired by big Brummie John Gayle they dominated as much on the field as the Bluenoses did in the stands. After a bright start Blues swept ahead on 21 minutes when a long clearance was headed on by Gayle to the nippy Simon Sturridge who raced on to beat Nixon with a neatly placed shot just inside the penalty area. Blues settled on the lead and were happy to keep Tranmere at bay. The tactic worked well and Tranmere hardly troubled Martin Thomas at all. As half-time approached a pass out of defence came to Gayle who stepped over the ball throwing his marker. He smashed a rising shot, which beat Nixon from just inside the penalty area to put Blues 2–0 up on 41 minutes. Blues still had time to almost score a third, when Peer had a volley brilliantly saved by Nixon. This was the sort of game where you did not want a half-time break as, sure enough, Blues, never a team to do anything the easy way, lost their momentum, Tranmere rallied after the break and gave themselves real hope on 61 minutes when Cooper halved the deficit. Blues wobbled, and five minutes later Tranmere were level through Jim Steel. The game then ebbed end-to-end, as if the next goal was the winner. As the game entered the final few minutes it now certainly would be. With one moment of magic required, up stepped John Gayle. A free-kick to Blues near the halfway line, and Clarkson floated the ball into the Tranmere box. Overson beat Higgins in the air, looping his header to a waiting Gayle. With his back to goal he sprung an amazing scissors kick, and the ball smashed into the corner of a bemused Nixon's net in the 86th minute. The goal was indeed the winner. What a goal, and what a winner it was!!!

TRANMERE: Nixon, Higgins, Bronman, McNab (Martindale), Hughes, Vickers (Malkin,) Morrissey, Irons, Steel, Cooper, Thomas.
Referee: Mr J.E. Martin (Alton, Hants.).

LEYLAND DAF CUP FIRST ROUND
Monday 18th February 1991
Kick Off 7.45 p.m.

BIRMINGHAM CITY

V

SWANSEA CITY

Tonight's Match Sponsors are

**EVANS HALSHAW/LEYLAND DAF
ROVER CARS**

30p.

Leyland Daf First Round Programme Cover

TO BE RETAINED

**LEYLAND DAF
CUP FINAL**

Sunday 26th May 1991

Turnstiles Open at 1.00 pm
Please take your position by 2.15 pm
Kick Off at 3.00 pm

TURNSTILE M

BLOCK	ROW	SEAT
227	26	100

£7.00
6   407 070591 102159A

Leyland Daf Final ticket

Leyland Daf Final Souvenir Brochure

ROAD TO WEMBLEY

Preliminary Rounds:

06 November 1990 v Walsall (A) won 1–0 scorer: Skipper(og). Attendance 5,053.

27 November 1990 v Lincoln City (h) won 2–0 scorers: Sturridge, Clarke(og). Attendance 2,922.

First Round:

18 February 1991 v Swansea City (h) drew 0–0 won 4–2 on penalties. Attendance 3,555.

Southern Area Quarter-Final:

26 February 1991 v Mansfield Town (h) won 2–0 Scorers: Matthewson, Gayle. Attendance 5,358.

Southern Area Semi-Final:

05 March 1991 v Cambridge United (h) won 3–1 Scorers: Peer, Gleghorn and Overson. Attendance 9,429.

Southern Area Final First Leg:

26 March 1991 v Brentford (h) won 2–1 Scorers: Rodgerson, Gayle. Attendance 16,219.

Southern Area Final Second Leg:

09 April 1991 v Brentford (a) won 1–0

> **Scorer:** Sturridge
> **Attendance:** 8,745.

LEYLAND DAF APPEARANCES and GOALS

PLAYER	APPEARANCES	GOALS
THOMAS	8	0
HOPKINS	1	0
DOWNS	2	0
FRAIN	8	0
OVERSON	8	1
MATTHEWSON	8	1
PEER	8	1
STURRIDGE	8	3
BAILEY	1+3	0
AYLOTT	4+1	0
CLARKSON	7+1	0
GLEGHORN	8	1
TAIT	1	0
GAYLE	5+1	4
RODGERSON	4	1
DOLAN	2	0
HARRIS	0+1	0
YATES	3	0
ROBINSON	2+1	0

LITTLE KNOWN FACTS

- For the Final Blues had to wear their ordinary league shirts as the newly designed kit was wrongly sent to the Blues Shop and promptly sold to supporters.
- Six out of the 13-man squad were from Blues YTS or Apprentice scheme.
- John Gayle told Chairman Samesh Kumar that he would get the Wembley winner. Kumar took the bet and had to hire a top of the range Mercedes for Gayley to use for a whole weekend.

Robert Hopkins recalls:

In preparation for the Final we went to Reading University where
there were no luxuries, no TV as we slept in the Halls of Residence.
On the day before the game, Peer, Sturridge, Robinson and myself
were spoken to by Lou Macari the manager. He told us that there
were three places up for grabs in the starting line up for the Final
and who got them would be decided on the outcome of a race.
"The first three to complete four laps of the athletic track would get
a place. I told him what I thought of the idea and came last."

John Frain remembers:

Our dramatic 3–2 victory in the Final came as due reward for per-
severance at the end of some pretty lean times. I think everyone
knew about Lou's (Macari) work ethic – it was unbelievable. We
had a great run in the Cup but had a long three weeks from the
end of the season until Wembley. Lou was a mad fitness man and
he said he was going to get us fit in that time. My God, it was the
hardest training I've done in my life and we never saw a ball each
week until Thursday or Friday. He had us running all over Birmingham. But, at Wembley, we had an absolutely fabulous day, so
he got his reward.

Colin Tattum recalls:

Manager Lou Macari invited the press to travel with the team to
their pre-final hideaway. The day before the Final, in blistering heat,
Macari put them through a gruelling session that included track
work. And he ordered the media to join in, probably for light relief.
The sight of Tom Ross trying to hold off a pursuing John Gayle in
a 'hare and hounds' race around the 800m circuit was hilarious.
And in one 11 versus 11 game, I was fouled badly by Robert Hopkins and also berated by Gayle for not tackling Vince Overson hard
enough. There were a couple of images that stuck. The sight of Ian

Rodgerson at the back of the coach, almost in tears, knowing that he was unfit to play. And then there was Hopkins, one of the biggest bluenoses you will ever find, being denied the chance to come on as substitute for the club he loved at Wembley, even for the last couple of minutes. He was so upset that he almost didn't turn up for the open top bus celebration around Birmingham.

10.

IAN CLARKSON

– PROMOTION FROM DIVISION THREE TO DIVISION ONE 1991–92

Ian 'Clarky' Clarkson' in action

FULL NAME: Ian Stewart Clarkson.
DATE OF BIRTH: 4 December 1970.
PLACE OF BIRTH: Solihull.

PLAYING CAREER:

Youth Career:

1987–88 Blues.

Senior Career:

1988–1993 Blues 174 appearances 0 goals, 1993–96 Stoke City 90 appearances 0 goals, 1996–99 Northampton Town 94 appearances 1 goal, 1999–2002 Kidderminster Harriers 114 appearances 0 goals, 2002 Nuneaton Borough 12 appearances 0 goals also Stafford Rangers, 2003 Stafford Rangers also Forest Green Rovers, 2012 Alvechurch. Total 422 appearances 1 goal (All competitions).

He began his football career as a YTS trainee with Blues the club he had supported since childhood, in 1987. He made his first team debut as a 17-year-old in the League Cup Second Round at home, losing 0–2 against Aston Villa on 27 September 1988 in front of a crowd of 21,177, and his football league debut a few days later on 1 October at home to Barnsley a game we lost 3–5 with Atkins, Langley and Robinson scoring in front of paltry crowd of 4,892. He signed his first professional contract in December 1988. In 1991 he played in Birmingham's winning side in the Associate Members Cup Final at Wembley. The following season he captained the side to promotion from the Third Division while still only 21, an achievement which he considers to be the highlight of his career.

Former Birmingham manager Lou Macari brought Clarkson to First Division side Stoke City in September 1993 for a fee of £40,000.

Clarkson qualified as a coach and coach educator, and worked for Birmingham City's Football in the Community programme. During the later years of his playing career he was keen to get involved in media work; from 2002 he was employed as a football reporter and journalist by the *Birmingham Post* and *Sunday Mercury* newspapers and by the Professional Footballer's Association (PFA)'s website. In 2006 he was appointed to manage a scheme designed to involve young people in sport and physical activity, as part of a wider programme of regeneration of the deprived areas of North Solihull

DETAILS OF SUCCESS

DIVISION THREE RUNNERS UP 1991–92

Second to Brentford Played 46, won 23, drew 12, lost 11, GF 69, GA 52, Points 81.

Because of the introduction of The Premiership in 1992–93 Blues went from Division 3 to Division 1 in a season.

Final game of the season was on 8 May 1993 v Stockport County (away) lost 2–0 in front of a crowd of 7,840.

The team that day was: Dearden, Clarkson, Frain, Rennie, Hicks, Matthewson, Rodgerson, Cooper, Rowbotham, Gleghorn, Sale. Substitutes: Sturridge and Mardon.

SEASON APPEARANCES 1991–92

PLAYER	LEAGUE APPEARANCES/ GOALS	FA CUP APPEARANCES/ GOALS	LEAGUE CUP APPEARANCES/ GOALS
THOMAS	16 (0)	1 (0)	6 (0)
CLARKSON	42 (0)	1 (0)	7 (0)
MATTHEWSON	35+1 (6)	1 (0)	5 (0)
FRAIN	44 (5)	1 (0)	7 (0)
HICKS	41+1 (1)	1 0)	5+1 (1)
MARDON	31+4 (0)	1 (0)	7 (0)
RODGERSON	38+1 (9)	1 (0)	6 (2)
GAYLE	2+1 (1)	0 (0)	0 (0)
PEER	18+3 (1)	0+1 (0)	7 (3)

GLEGHORN	46 (17)	1 (0)	7 (5)
STURRIDGE	38+2 (10)	1 (0)	7 (1)
YATES	1+1 (0)	0 (0)	2 (1)
OKENIA	2+5 (1)	0 0)	1+3 (0)
DOLAN	1+1 (0)	0 (0)	2 (0)
DONOWA	20+6 (2)	1 (0)	5 (0)
AYLOTT	2 (0)	0 (0)	0+1 (0)
COOPER	27+6 (4)	4+1 (0)	0 (0)
ATKINS	5+3 (0)	0 (0)	0 (0)
JONES	0+1 (0)	0 (0)	0+1 (0)
TAIT	10+2 (0)	0 (0)	2 (0)
DRINKELL	5 (2)	0 (0)	0 (0)
CARTER	2 (0)	0 (0)	0 (0)
PASKIN	8+2 (3)	0 (0)	0+1 (0)
CHEESEWRIGHT	1 (0)	0 (0)	0 (0)
HOGAN	0+1 (0)	0 (0)	0 (0)
MILLER	15 (0)	0 (0)	0 (0)
ROWBOTHAM	21+1 (4)	0 (0)	0 (0)
BECKFORD	2+2 (1)	0 (0)	0 (0)
FRANCIS	0+3 (0)	0 (0)	0 (0)
RENNIE	17 (2)	0 (0)	0 0)
O'NEILL	2+2 (0)	0 (0)	0 (0)
DEARDEN	12 (0)	0 (0)	0 (0)
SALE	2+4 (0)	0 (0)	0 (0)
FOY	0 (0)	0 (0)	0+1 (0)

Team Group with Ian Clarkson on the back row second from right next to Trevor Matthewson

SEASON BY SEASON

Season	League	FA Cup	League Cup	Leyland DAF	Autoglass Trophy	Anglo-Italian Cup
1988–89	9 +1		2			
1989–90	15 + 5	3	1	2	0	0
1990–91	34 + 3	1	0	7+1	0	0
1991–92	42	1	7	0	2	0
1992–93	25 + 3	0	2	0	0	5
1993–4	0	0	0	0	0	1
Total	125 + 12	5	12	9 + 1	2	6

Blues Total 174 appearances 0 goals.

HONOURS

As a Player:

- Birmingham City – Football League Trophy winners: 1991, Football League Third Division runner-up: 1991–92.
- Northampton Town – Football League Third Division play-off winner: 1997.
- Kidderminster Harriers – Conference National champions: 1999 – 2000.

On 1 August 2014 it was announced by Caroline Jones and Zena Hawley:

Former Birmingham City FC captain and Derbyshire PE teacher to play football in five countries in 48 hours

A Derbyshire PE teacher who was formerly captain of Birmingham City is taking part in a world record attempt five-match football challenge – playing in five countries in just 48 hours from today to Sunday.

Ian Clarkson, who teaches at Foremarke Hall, Repton and also played at Stoke City, is part of an all-star Charity X1.

It also includes another former Blues player Dele Adebola and former Manchester United star Lee Sharpe, as well as television stars Eastenders Jamie Lomas and Hollyoaks Nick Pickard.

Mr Clarkson said the event is in aid of Children in Need and Special Olympics Ireland.

He said: "I have ordered an extra lung and a new body so I should be fine.

"It's a worthwhile cause as Children In Need is a great charity to support and the chance to be part of a potential world record is always exciting.

"The opening match of the 48-hour challenge will take place on Friday at Meadow Park Stadium, home of Threave Rovers FC, in Castle Douglas in Scotland at 5pm, on Saturday, the team plays Crusaders FC, Belfast at 10am and Paramount FC, Dublin, 5pm, and on Sunday, against Penycae FC, Wrexham, 10am and finishing at Nantwich Town FC in Cheshire at 2.30pm."

DETAILS OF SUCCESS

THIRD DIVISION –RUNNERS UP

Blues 1 Shrewsbury 0

Date: 25 April 1992.
Venue: St Andrew's.
Attendance: 19,868.
Blues: Dearden, Clarkson, Frain, Rennie, Hicks, Matthewson, Rodgerson, Cooper, Rowbotham, Gleghorn, Sturridge.
Substitute: Mardon for Rowbotham.

At 4.47 pm the announcement came over the Public Address system that Stoke City had lost at home and as a result Blues were promoted. Blues had waited six years for promotion and it was a 34th minute goal from Nigel Gleghorn that had finally got us out of the doldrums of the Third Division.

Blues had not beaten the Gay Meadow outfit for 12 years but Blues despatched their bogey side in a more convincing manner than the score-line suggests.

The quality of the football was severely impacted by a gusty wind that blew straight down the ground from the Railway End. Shrewsbury should have taken the lead after 20 minutes when ex-Blues favourite Robert Hopkins deceived Kevin Dearden with a lob which just dipped over the bar.

The vital goal was down to the resilience of Ian Rodgerson and Simon Sturridge. The latter shook off a challenge from Steve Mackenzie to get a return pass to Rodgerson. The former Cardiff player then delivered a deep cross towards the far post, which Gleghorn powered in with his head.

Blues pulverised the Shrews' goal only to find keeper Ken Hughes in tremendous form saving efforts from Rennie, Rodgerson and Rowbotham.

Shrewsbury Town: Hughes, Clark, Lynch, MacKenzie, Spink, Blake, Taylor, Summerfield, Bremner, Hopkins, Lyne.
Substitutes: Henry for Clark and O'Toole for Hopkins.

CLARKY RECALLS:

July 1991

After ten days on pre-season tour of Ireland, Bill Coldwell let us off the leash and a monumental drinking session followed with various renditions of *'Music Man'* this all wound up at about 5 a.m. with the prospect of a match against Kilkenny City in twelve hours time not at all appealing! New manager Terry Cooper was introduced to the players before that game and he announced he was there to observe! Ian Rodgerson developed a 'hamstring' – we scrapped a 1–0 win and TC's post-match comment was "There's plenty to work on!"

August 1991

I was appointed captain after the second game of the season

September 1991

With John Gayle ruled out for most of the season the goals had to come from elsewhere – enter Ian Rodgerson and Nigel Gleghorn who netted 35 goals between them in the season – problem solved!

October 1991

Another unbeaten month resulted in a few beers being sunk in the city centre on Saturday nights. The social scene in those days was an integral part of football and the manager knew exactly the right time to let us play hard off the pitch.

November 1991

We lose 3–1 to one of our main rivals – Huddersfield Town.

December 1991

Only one win – cracks are appearing.

January 1992

Terry Cooper was excellent throughout the difficult times as he always ensured that training was fun and upbeat without ever switching off from the job in hand. He had some old-fashioned ways such as the option of having a nip of whisky before kick-off that he brought with him from the successful Leeds United team of the seventies.

February 1992

A pitch invasion at St Andrew's against Stoke City meant the players had to wait for an hour in the dressing room for the trouble to subside. We were then called back out on to the pitch to play the remaining 35 seconds in front of a deserted stadium!

March 1992

We attempted to play 'five at the back' for a couple of away games but the players were so unhappy that we went to see TC on the coach on the way home and we agreed to revert to 4–4–2.

April 1992

Robert Hopkins was playing for Shrewsbury Town in the match that clinched promotion – I am sure he was wearing his Blues chain under his kit!

May 1992

A 2–0 defeat at Stockport on the last day of the season meant that Brentford pipped us for the title and that is still a disappointment to this day. However the post-season jaunt to Tenerife was memorable as we had a lot to celebrate!!!!

I had the pleasure to interview Clarky for the now defunct *'BLUES MAGAZINE'*.

Middle Name Stewart?

My Dad has a number of Scottish relatives so it was inevitable that I got a Scottish name – I guess if I was playing now I would qualify for Scotland's International squad!

Born in December? What star sign are you and are you superstitious?

Sagittarius – not really superstitious but I had three things that I felt helped my performance:

- As a youngster I liked to prepare my own chicken and pasta on a Friday night.
- I liked to run out onto the pitch in a Sweat Top whilst the rest of the lads were in their shirts.
- I always preferred long sleeved shirts as they felt like proper shirts.

How did you get spotted by BLUES?

I was playing for North Star in the Central Warwickshire league when I was invited to BLUES by their scout Norman Bodell. After being signed under the Youth Training Scheme I did not kick a football for two weeks. I got paid £28.50 a week plus a Bus Pass with a £4 win bonus and a £2 draw bonus for Youth and Reserve games. In those days we could play two games in five hours, a reserve game in the afternoon and a Midweek Floodlit game in the evening.

Being born in Solihull does that make you a BLUENOSE?

Yes my first introduction was as a 10-year-old during season 1976–77, I had the same initial experience that every BLUENOSE gets – Loss, Loss, Loss, Loss! My childhood heroes were most definitely COLIN TODD and FRANK WORTHINGTON.

Why do you think the atmosphere has been lost at St Andrew's in recent times?

I think seating has made a difference but there are other social factors, supporters reflect the way people are these days – IMPATIENT and very much ME orientated – it makes a difference to how fans see the game.

Who were the characters during your time at the BLUES?

There were a number of funny guys – STEVE WHITTON, PAUL FITZPATRICK (remember him? Seven appearances between January–March 1993) and DARREN ROWBOTHAM. DAVID RENNIE was the complete opposite – very serious.

Did you make your debut against the Villa?

Yes I did it was Second Round League Cup first leg on 27 September 1988 at St Andrew's, we lost 0–2 in front of 21,177.

The team that day was: Tony Godden, Ray Ranson, Harry Roberts, Ian Atkins, Vince Overson, Ian Clarkson, Ronnie Morris, Kevin Langley, Mark Yates, Colin Robinson, Steve Wigley. Sub: Des Bremner. We lost the second leg 5–0!

You captained the BLUES – how did that happen?

Trevor Matthewson was skipper at the time and he got injured in the first match of the season against Bury at home on August 17 1991. Terry Cooper threw me the armband and that was that, when Trevor came back at the end of September, the lads had a vote and I kept the captaincy. I guess I was chosen because I am 'gobby', but I do get on with people and if someone isn't pulling their weight then I will tell them!

How many managers did you serve under?

Four – Garry Pendrey, Dave Mackay, Lou Macari and Terry Cooper. Oh and for about 3 games Bill Coldwell in his caretaking role).

I got on with them all but Lou introduced me to fitness, he was a fitness nut – one day he got us to run down to the Aston Villa Leisure Centre on the pretext that there would be transport to get us back – no transport was there so we had to run all the way back to St Andrew's. He would organise five a side games with no boundaries so the game would just go on and on, I liked him he had no favourites!

Who are your favourite six best BLUES players?

Wayne Clarke, Tony Coton, Dave Langan, Kevin Dillon and, of course Todd and Worthington.

What's bad about the current game?

Diving and all-seater stadiums.

What was the best and worst thing about playing for BLUES?

The best thing was playing for the club I supported and the worst thing was the TRITON strip of 1992–93.

How did you career develop after leaving BLUES?

They signed Scott Hiley from Terry Cooper's previous cub Exeter City for £100,000 in March 1993 and TC wanted me to go to Exeter but I said no. So I was on a weekly deal and missed a pre-season tour to Italy, I trained with Peterborough for a while then on 1 September 1993 we played at Stoke in an Anglo-Italian preliminary round losing 2–0, Lou Macari was managing them and I moved to Stoke City for a fee of £50,000. My first three games at Stoke were against Middlesbrough, Nottingham Forest and Manchester United we won all three games, in the United game I was marking Lee Sharpe, who was released by Blues as a 16-year-old.

When Joe Jordan and Jez Moxey came to the Potteries I was signed by Ian Atkins to join Northampton Town. I stayed with the Cobblers for four years before suffering an injury that forced me to retire from the game. I trained with Nuneaton Borough and Kidderminster and got a contract with the Harriers after they had repaid my insurance payout of £15,000, Jan Molby was the Manager and we went on to win the Conference thanks to an incredible run when we only lost one game in 28!

Ian who possesses a Level One FA Tutor qualification still finds football exciting and will take any opportunity to play a game and he regularly takes part in charity games for the Former Players Association team – The Birmingham City All-Stars XI who have raised in excess of £750,000 for local charities since its inception in 1991.

What follows appears on the website www.bcfclegends.co.uk.

The formation of the Birmingham City Official Former Player's Association is the culmination of a dream that Kevan Broadhurst and myself (Tom Ross) have had for many years. It all started with the formation of the Blues All Stars charity fundraising team of Ex-Players in 1991.

That first team included Kevan Broadhurst, Joe Gallagher, Micky Evans, Tom Ross, Terry Cooper, Ron Green, Trevor Morgan, Garry Pendrey, Robert Hopkins, Tony Evans, Tony Taylor and Steve Lynex to name but a few. Over the years, the Blues All Stars have raised around three quarters of a million pounds for many deserving charities around the Birmingham area.

During those years, we have had many supporters turn out for the team such as Steve Bruce, David Gold, Barry Fry and Noel Blake. The current team includes Geoff Horsfield, Martin O'Connor, Graham Hyde, Ian Clarkson, Paul Devlin, Phil Hawker, Dave Buust, Ron Green, Ian Atkins, Robert Hopkins, Guy Russell, and Micky Clarke.

About a year ago, Kevan and I discussed the logistics of forming

a proper Former Players Association. The club bought into the idea
and with the great help of committee member Jessica Birch and the
club's Head of Corporate Sales Adrian Wright we got it off the ground
and the association now boasts over 100 members all ex-players from
every era from the 1940s through to the 2000s.

It is our aim to find as many ex-players as possible. The major
reason for the association is to build a bridge between the club, the
supporters and its history. It also allows all ex-players to keep in con-
tact with each other. By virtue of pitch and hospitality appearances,
the ex-players can keep in touch with the club's fans.

We believe that every single ex-player who has worn the Royal
blue shirt should be recognised and made welcome at St Andrew's

Back to the interview….

What qualifications have you got?

8 O levels – RSA Level 1 Typing – Distinction.

BII Pub Management Course – Passed.

RSA Level 1 CLAIT – Passed.

FA Coaching Certificate.

Emergency Aid Course.

FA Coaching Licence (UEFA 'B' Award).

SAQ Preliminary Award.

FA Coach Educator Level 1.

What about your journalist career?

I retired from professional football due to injury in October 1999 and
I started work as a sports journalist at the *Heartlands Evening News* in
November 1999.

This daily newspaper was based in Nuneaton and it gave me a good
grounding in meeting deadlines and the workings of a daily newspaper. I worked on all aspects of sport, primarily football, for six months

through to June 2000. I left the newspaper because I had the chance to return to full time professional football with Kidderminster Harriers. I joined the *Birmingham Post* in September 2005 and benefited from working on a daily newspaper covering primarily Birmingham City and West Bromwich Albion. However, I often found myself covering Aston Villa, Coventry and Walsall as well as continuing a regular flow of boxing copy.

I originally wrote a column for the *Sunday Mercury* from July 1999 – May 2000 before working on a freelance basis from 2002.

I joined the paper on a contracted basis in June 2003 and built up valuable contacts at all our local clubs and within the fields of cricket and boxing during my two-year stint at the newspaper. I covered Birmingham City on a freelance basis from January – May 2003 for both the *Express and Star* and *Sporting Star*. This involved daily copy; match reports as well a Birmingham City feature page every Saturday. On numerous occasions I have written match reports for the *Daily and Sunday Express*.

I have written for the PFA website www.givemefootball.com since May 2001. My contract is similar to that of a daily paper in that I have to meet deadlines and am required to produce a certain amount of articles each week. I have been able to build up an invaluable network of contacts through my time working with the PFA.

I have appeared on Carlton Television's ITV's *'Kicking it around'* programme as well as making appearances on *Midlands Today* for the BBC. For Radio WM I spent two years presenting a fifteen-minute slot on the *Chris Ashley Breakfast Show* every Saturday morning talking about the six local football teams to that area. This gave me an insight into broadcast journalism and I did a lot of the same at Talk Sport, BBC Radio Five Live and Capitol Gold.

11.

LIAM DAISH

– DIVISION TWO CHAMPIONS & AUTOWINDSCREENS SHIELD WINNERS 1994–95

Liam Daish

FULL NAME: Liam Sean Daish.
DATE OF BIRTH: 23 September 1968.
PLACE OF BIRTH: Portsmouth.

PLAYING CAREER:

Youth Career:

1984–86 Portsmouth.

Senior Career:

1986–88 Portsmouth 1 appearance 0 goals, 1988–94 Cambridge United 138 appearances 0 goals, 1988 Barnet (Loan) 12 appearances 0 goals, 1994–96 Blues 72 appearances 1 goal, 1996–99 Coventry City 31 appearances 0 goals, 1999–2003 Havant and Waterlooville 120 appearances 10 goals. Total 374 appearances 12 goals.

International:

1992–96 Republic of Ireland 5 appearances 0 goals.
1994 Republic of Ireland 'B' 1 appearances 0 goals.

Management:

2000–04 Havant and Waterlooville (joint), 2004–05 Welling United (caretaker), 2005–2013 Ebbsfleet United.

2014–Current Nuneaton Borough.

Despite being born in England, Daish played internationally for the Republic of Ireland due to his Irish ancestry. He only made one appearance for Portsmouth's first team before he was released in 1988. He went in search of first-team football, which he found at Cambridge United. While at Cambridge, Daish helped the club to successive promotions from the Fourth to the Second Division. He also made his international debut for the Republic of Ireland, on 19 February 1992 at home to Wales while Cambridge were pushing for a third successive promotion. However, they fell in the playoffs and were relegated a year later. The quality of his performances for Cambridge United inspired Barry Fry to sign him for Blues for a fee of £50,000 in January 1994. He made his league debut v Notts County on 11

January 1995 in a 1–2 defeat away In front of 7,212, Cooper scoring the Blues goal. His first goal for the Blues came on 10 December 1994 away to Chester City in a 4–0 victory with Lowe, Claridge and McGavin scoring the other goals. The attendance that day was 3,946. In the ensuing celebrations, some Blues fan threw a toy trumpet onto the pitch, which Daish proceeded to play. Although he wasn't sent off, the referee booked him, taking his season's points tally to 41 and resulting in a three-match ban. Fry was not amused: "I know the referee has directives to adhere to, but to get banned through being booked for that seems a bit harsh."

Daish spent just over two years at St Andrew's, making nearly 100 appearances in all competitions. He captained the side to the Division Two championship in 1994–95 and to victory in the Football League Trophy final at Wembley. Fry, who managed him throughout his spell at Birmingham, once said of Daish that if a squadron of F-111s attacked the Birmingham penalty area he would attempt to head them away.

In February 1996, Daish joined Coventry City for a fee of £1.5 million

DETAILS OF SUCCESS
AUTO WINDSCREENS WINNERS 23 April 1995. At Wembley versus Carlisle United, 1–0 after extra-time/sudden death.

The team on the day was: Bennett, Poole, Cooper, Ward, Barnett, Daish, Hunt, Claridge, Francis, Otto, Shearer.
Scorer: Tait. Crowd: 76,663.
Subs: Tait for Shearer on 62 minutes, Donowa for Francis on 76 minutes.

Auto Windscreens Shield Final Programme Cover

BLUES BECAME THE FIRST WEMBLEY WINNERS THROUGH THE 'GOLDEN GOAL' DECIDER.

AUTO WINDSCREENS APPEARANCES and GOALS

PLAYER	APPEARANCES	GOALS
PRICE	1	0
SCOTT	2	0
FRAIN	1	0
WARD	7	1
BARNETT	8	0
DAISH	7	0
HUNT	3	3
CLARIDGE	7	4
McGAVIN	1+3	1
BULL	2	1
POOLE	7	1
DOMINGUEZ	2+2	1
WALLACE	0+1	0
BENNETT	7	0
DONOWA	5+1	1
DESOUZA	1	0
DOHERTY	0+2	0
SHEARER	4	3
WHYTE	3+1	0
LOWE	2+1	0
COOPER	4+1	0
TAIT	2+3	3
OTTO	5	1
FRANCIS	3	1
SAVILLE	1	0
ESTEVES	1	0
ROBINSON	1	0
WILLIAMS	1	1

For the second time in six years the Blue Army converged on Wembley's Twin Towers to roar on their team to another trophy win. An estimated 48,000 were behind the team out of the 73,633 crowd and although never a spectacular game the day was a memorable one. With Jose Dominguez away on international duty with Portugal, Barry Fry made three changes to the side that beat Orient in the second leg at Brisbane Road in the semi-final. Gary Cooper came in at left-back for Chris Whyte, Jonathon Hunt replaced Rui Estevez and Kevin Francis made the starting line up in place of Steve Robinson. On the bench was Paul Tait despite his sudden death winner over Swansea which had set up the Orient tie, and Brummie John Frain was missing from the squad altogether. Blues soon showed why they were installed as firm favourites as they dominated the early stages, Otto in particular exploiting the huge Wembley pitch, but after Francis picked up an early knock, the crosses he had been winning easily were now dealt with comfortably by a Carlisle back four which included man-of-the-match, Derek Mountfield. At the other end Carlisle did little to trouble the Blues defence and Ian Bennett was left to soak up the atmosphere for the majority of the first half. At the break the game remained goalless. The second half too, was a cagey affair, which only opened up after Fry made further substitutions with 13 minutes of normal time remaining. Tait had already been tactically introduced into the game just after the hour mark for Shearer, but the second change saw Donowa replace the struggling Francis. Within minutes he had two glorious chances to win the game but both were in the air and failed to trouble the 'keeper. As the prospect of the 'sudden death' goal loomed Blues almost snatched the game late on. Gary Poole had surged forward and as people waited for the cross he let fly from outside the area with a fiercely hit angled drive, which went just wide of the upright. Extra time got under way with Blues stepping up the pace, and the turning point came 10 minutes into the first period, when Mountfield, who had been a pillar of strength in the centre of Carlisle's defence, had to leave the field following a cut to his forehead, replaced by Jamie Robinson. Just three minutes later a floated cross by Otto fell into the territory Mountfield had controlled commandingly all afternoon but without his presence Tait rose to flick a header which cleared the outstretched arm of Caig and dropped into the corner of the net.

CARLISLE: Caig, Edmondson, Gallimore, Walling, Mountfield (Robinson 100), Conway, Thomas, Currie, Reeve, Hayward, Prokos (Thorpe 90).
Referee: Mr P Foakes (Clacton-on-Sea).

ROAD TO WEMBLEY
First Round
27 September 1994 v Peterborough United (away) won 5–3.
Scorers: Bull, Dominguez, Hunt (3). Crowd 2,044.

Second Round
18 October 1994 v Walsall (home) won 3–0.
Scorers: Shearer (2), Donowa. Crowd 10,089.

Third Round
29 November 1994 v Gillingham (home) won 3–0.
Scorers: McGavin, Poole, Tait. Crowd: 17,028.

Fourth Round
10 January 1995 v Hereford United (home) won 3–1.
Scorers: Claridge, Ward (pen), Otto. Crowd 22,351.

Southern Area Semi-Final
31 January 1995 v Swansea City (h) won 3–2 after extra-time/sudden death.
Scorers: Claridge, Francis, Tait .Crowd: 20,326.

Southern Area Final – First Leg
28 February 1995 v Leyton Orient (h) won 1–0.
Scorer: Shearer. Crowd 24,002.

Southern Area Final – Second Leg

14 March 1995 v Leyton Orient (a) won 3–2 (4–2 on aggregate).

Scorers: Claridge (2),Williams. Crowd 10,830.

Celebrating at Wembley

Auto Windscreens Shield Final ticket

Paul Tait with the trophy

Taity celebrates his golden goal

HONOURS

As a Player:
- Cambridge United: Fourth Division (level 4) promotion 1990 – Third Division (level 3) champions 1991.
- Birmingham City: Second Division (level 3) champions 1995 – Football League Trophy winners 1995.

As a Manager:
- Havant and Waterlooville: FA Trophy semi-final 2003.
- Ebbsfleet United: FA Trophy winners 2008 – Conference South Playoff Winners 2011.

SEASON BY SEASON

SEASON	LEAGUE APPEARANCES/ GOALS	FACUP APPEARANCES/ GOALS	LEAGUE CUP APPEARANCES/ GOALS
1993–94	19 (0)	0 (0)	0 (0)
1994–95	37 (3)	5 (0)	3 (1)
1995–96	16+1 (0)	2 (0)	7 (2)

DID YOU KNOW THAT?

Portuguese midfielder RUI ESTEVES made his Blues debut in the away leg of the Southern Area Final but walked off the pitch complaining that the challenges were too tough and vigorous! HE DID NOT PLAY FOR BLUES AGAIN!

Steve Claridge remembers:

Karren (Brady) could also be really tight when it came to money, as my contract negotiations with her always revealed. That season we reached the Final, against Carlisle United, of the Auto Wind-screens Shield after seven tough games, during which I scored four goals. We were going down to Wembley for the Friday and Satur-day nights before the game on Sunday, but Karren announced that the club would only pay for one night at our hotel, The Swallow at Waltham Abbey. Luckily Barry (Fry) found a wealthy friend who sponsored our second night, saving us £40 each. We were also only allowed to buy – buy not receive – ten tickets for our friends and relatives. The club said that because tickets were so scarce, with an amazing 55,000 allocation out of 76,000 revealing the depth of our support, players should pay. That added to the dissatisfaction that we were on a bonus of only £1,000, with all that extra revenue com-ing in. On top of that we each had to pay £8 for our club tie. Things like that knocked you back, undermined your morale. When you are doing badly, you expect nothing; you just get your head down and get on with things. But when you are doing well you expect to be treated well with things like perks. And we did do well, winning the trophy with a goal by Paul Tait – a true Blue, having grown up supporting the club – in sudden death extra-time (as he had also done in an earlier match against Swansea). But even that could not pass without controversy, this being Birmingham City. We only knew about it the next day when we read the papers, but Paul had lifted the trophy wearing a T-shirt saying 'Shit on the Villa'. We did not take any notice but everybody overreacted and there were a lot of problems at the club for a few days. On one side of the City he was the dog's bollocks, on the other he was like Salman Rushdie. He had to keep his head down for a while, which was a bit difficult for Taity as he is a very social animal. Actually he was beginning to settle down a bit and stay in a few nights by then, although this may have had something to do with the fact that he was barred from quite a few places…

Tales from the Boot Camps

Barry Fry with the two trophies from our double season

CHAMPIONS – DIVISION TWO – SEASON 1994–95

Played 46, won 24, drew 14, lost7, GF 84, GA 37, Points 89.

6 May 1995 v Huddersfield (Away) won 2–1.

> **Attendance:** 18,775.
> **Scorers:** Huddersfield: Bullock 87. Blues: Claridge 73, Tait 85.

THE OPENING OF THE MCALPINE STADIUM

Blues won the championship with 89 points a seasonal record points total to date.

> **The team on that day was:** Bennett, Poole, Frain, Ward, Whyte, Daish, Hunt, Claridge, Hendon, Williams, Cooper. Substitutes: Donowa for Hunt and Tait for Williams.
> **HUDDERSFIELD TOWN:** Francis, Trevitt, Cowan, Bullock, Scully, Sinnott, Collins (Moulden 74), Duxbury, Booth, Jepson, Dunn (Billy).
> **Referee:** Mr J. Winter (Middlesbrough).

Blues arrived at their last game of the season needing a point to ensure promotion and with it the Second Division Championship. Blues started with an unfamiliar cautious approach and clearly looked shaky. However after Bennett had saved brilliantly from Jepson in the opening 10 minutes, they settled well. Hunt had Blues best chance of the half on 13 minutes. A corner evaded everyone in the middle and ran to Hunt on the far post, he stubbed his shot from an acute angle and the ball rolled agonisingly wide. Claridge was unlucky when a glorious lob looked a goal all the way as it cleared the head of 'keeper Francis, but the ball dropped onto the crossbar. Blues had to settle for an evenly balanced 0–0 draw at the interval which meant one firm hand at least was on the trophy.

Huddersfield playing only for pride started the brighter in the second half, and a header from Booth went narrowly wide just five minutes after the restart. An evenly fought battle lasted for almost 22 minutes, then

Blues grabbed the lead to mass jubilation amongst the 4,000 travelling fans behind the goal. The scorer was Claridge. From a great run and pass by full-back Cooper, the striker collected and spun around to smack a low drive past Francis from within the penalty area. Blues were now in pole position and they grew more confident. With just eight minutes remaining Tait who had come on as a substitute scored the decisive goal to make it 2–0. It was the result of a fine strike from Cooper which Francis couldn't hold, when the ball dropped from his grip Tait prodded it over the line from barely a yard out. Huddersfield scored a late 88th minute goal when Bullock nodded in a Jepson cross. The final whistle went and the party began for the Blues fans who refused to move until the team had come out to receive their due congratulations.

The 1994–95 campaign forever holds a special place in the hearts of Bluenoses – the season when Birmingham City went a long way to winning back the self-respect that had taken a battering over the past decade. A solid start in the league, holding Liverpool to a draw in the FA Cup at home, before cruelly going down on penalties in the replay at Anfield, boosted confidence, and by late April the Second Division Championship and an appearance at Wembley, against Carlisle United in the Autoglass Windscreens Shield had hovered into view.

For Liam Daish , as skipper, the next few weeks proved to be the best of his career.

"The first day of the season, Barry said that we were going to win the league, score 100 goals and go to Wembley, so from then on he treated every game with the utmost Importance, We lost the first game but had a decent run from then on and started to believe that if we went a goal down it wasn't a problem because we'd come back. The way Baz wanted us to play, as long as you scored more goals than the opposition it didn't matter. His passion for the game spilled over into the players, and the fans appreciated that because the crowds we were getting – up to 24,000 – were unbelievable. We had a big turnover of players but, to be fair, we had a pretty solid spine, with Benno in goal, Dave Barnett and myself at the back,

Mark Ward in midfield and Steve Claridge up front. I think Steve had thirteen strike partners that season – maybe Barry should have looked at him instead of the others!

There were some real good lads at the club – and some real good nights out! – and we enjoyed our success. Baz was one of those managers who let you do anything you wanted as long as you were doing it on the pitch on Saturday. You soon knew about it if you weren't but you could get away with murder. Wardie was very influential, as was Steve Claridge. Mark brought a bit of quality, he was a great passer and he had the right character as well. He wasn't the biggest but he had a heart as big as a barn door and he'd fight the world, while Steve would run his socks off all day up front. But most of the players in that side struck up a good relationship with the supporters; guys like Paul Tait, Peter Shearer and Kevin Francis all had an understanding of what the club was about and wanted to do well. You could feel it, everything snowballed, and everyone wanted to be part of it. It started at the top with the Board, and filtered down, and as we started winning games we gained a touch of arrogance. I'd been to Wembley with Cambridge, but it was a different kettle of fish going there with Blues. The place was full up and passionate and it was a great day. There was a little bit of pressure on us because we were on a hiding to nothing, we were the favourites, so to come away from Wembley with a bit of success was brilliant. It was probably the highlight of my career to go up and get the trophy with all those supporters there. You saviour those memories and it set us up for a great end to the season.

But the big game was against Brentford at St Andrew's three days later, because they were flying at the time. They were on a good run and had some good players, and they'd fancied their chances after watching us at Wembley. But we just went out there, got about them, and ended up comfortable winners. Big Kev had done his cruciate ligament at Wembley but he was determined to play against Brentford. He basically played with a cruciate ligament in his knee, but he scored and that summed up the spirit in the side. Everyone wanted to be out there and anyone not in the team was gutted, I got the second goal to make it 2–0 – I nearly did two laps after it! – and that was that. A couple of weeks later, the champagne corks were popping after goals from Claridge and Tait secured the victory at Huddersfield that clinched the title – and Blues were back in the first division.

Blues won the championship with 89 points a seasonal record points total to date, leaving them four points ahead of runners up Brentford.

Steve Claridge remembers:

Yet again I was involved in a last match that had so much riding on it, this time against Huddersfield Town, who were a top six team. It was a tense day and I did not help our cause early on when I missed a simple chance, my shot hitting a defender on the line. But I made amends by turning home a close-range shot to set us on our way and we eventually came through 2–1. It was my 20th league goal of the season – 25 in all competitions – making me the first Blues player since Trevor Francis, twenty years earlier, to reach that figure in a season, and won me the supporter's award for Player of the Year. I was particularly pleased because I played the end of the season with two broken ribs. About six minutes from the end of a game with Plymouth Argyle I was kicked under my chest and could not breathe. The bench were giving me stick but I stayed on and scored, although I knew something was not right. Every game after that I was in a lot of pain whenever I was elbowed or pushed, but I have always liked to play if I possibly could so I struggled on with a cricket thigh pad strapped around my rib cage. It had been a great season. We were averaging crowds of 20,000 in the Second Division, with very few away fans, the stand was finished and the ground was looking magnificent. I really felt that I was at what would very soon be a Premiership club, that finally I had a chance of getting in with the big boys. I really felt I could make an impression in the First Division

Tales from the Boot Camps

12.

MARTIN O'CONNOR

– WORTHINGTON CUP FINALISTS 2000–01

FULL NAME: Martin O'Connor.
DATE OF BIRTH: 10 December 1967.
PLACE OF BIRTH: Walsall.

PLAYING CAREER:

Youth Career:
1991–92 Bromsgrove Rovers.

Senior Career:
1992–94 Crystal Palace 2 appearances 0 goals, 1993 Walsall (Loan) 10 appearances 1 goal, 1994–96 Walsall 94 appearances 21 goals, 1996 Peterborough 18 appearances 3 goals, 1996–2002 Blues 186 appearances 16

goals, 2002–2003 Walsall 48 appearances 2 goals, 2003–05 Shrewsbury Town 56 appearances 2 goals, 2005–06 Kidderminster Harriers 12 appearances 0 goals. Total 426 appearances 45 goals.

International:

2000 Cayman Islands 2 appearances 0 goals.

Management:

2009–2011 Walsall (assistant).

O'Connor started his career at Bromsgrove Rovers in the early 1990s before moving to Crystal Palace. He then spent the first of three spells at Walsall, joining on loan in March 1993 before signing permanently the following year. His most prominent role at the Saddlers was winning promotion to Division Two in 1995. He then joined Peterborough United, followed by Birmingham City, whom O'Connor represented in the 2001 Football League Cup Final against Liverpool, which Birmingham lost in a penalty shootout.

He made his league debut for Blues on 30 November 1996 against Norwich City at Carrow Road in a match which Blues won 0–1. The scorer was O'Connor in front of a crowd of 12,764. His final game in Royal Blue was on 19 January 2002 at St Andrew's against Wimbledon. Blues lost 0–2 in front of a crowd of 17,766.

O'Connor re-joined Walsall in 2002, but his contract was not renewed at the end of the 2002–03 season. He then signed for Shrewsbury Town in July 2003 before ending his playing career with Kidderminster.

O'Connor was called up to the Cayman Islands national football team in 2000, but FIFA soon ruled that he could not play for them. The Cayman Islands had been attempting to exploit their status as a British Overseas Territory by picking British passport holders who would not ordinarily be eligible to play for them.

HONOURS

As a Player:
- Walsall: Football League Third Division runner-up 1994–95
- Birmingham City – Worthington League Cup runner-up 2000–01.

DETAILS OF SUCCESS

WORTHINGTON LEAGUE CUP FINAL – RUNNERS-UP

25 February 2001 v. LIVERPOOL Millennium Stadium Cardiff Drew 1–1 after extra time

Scorer: Purse (pen).

Lost 5-4 on penalties.

The team that day was: Bennett, Eaden, Grainger, Sonner, Purse, Johnson (M), McCarthy, Adebola, Horsfield, O'Connor, Lazaridis. Substitutes: Johnson (A) for Adebola , Hughes for Sonner, Marcelo for Horsfield.

LEAGUE CUP APPEARANCES & GOALS

PLAYER	APPEARANCES	GOALS
BENNETT	10	0
EADEN	10	1
PURSE	8+1	1
M. JOHNSON	8	2
GRAINGER	10	1
McCARTHY	1	0
SONNER	9	1
O'CONNOR	9	0
LAZARIDIS	5+2	0
HORSFIELD	5+1	4

ADEBOLA	6+2	5
HUGHES	6+3	1
HOLDSWORTH	4	0
NDLOVU	5+1	1
MARCELO	2+3	1
WILLIAMS	0+1	0
A.JOHNSON	1+6	3
GILL	7	0
BURROWS	0+2	0
HYDE	0+1	0
ROBINSON	0+2	0
BURCHILL	3+1	1
JENKINS	1	0

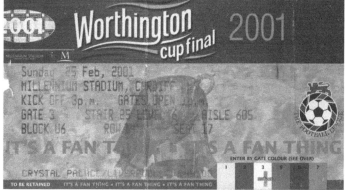

Worthington Cup Final ticket

What a magnificent start to the new temporary home of English Cup Finals. With Wembley closed for refurbishment Cardiff's Millennium Stadium hosted the Worthington Cup Final of 2001. Premiership Liverpool were hot favourites and quickly took control. It took them just 29 minutes before Heskey flicked on Westerveld's deep goal kick, for Fowler to volley home from 25 yards. At 1–0 it seemed the Nationwide team would fold, however it only inspired Blues to fight back and in the end they came so very close to a major upset. Darren Purse was giving an impressive solid defensive display, after being beaten by Heskey for the opening goal he rarely put a foot wrong, this gave Blues the opportunity to attack more. In the second half the first real chance fell to substitute Andrew Johnson who might have made more of his snap shot from a fired in cross by Eaden. With normal time almost up Blues threw everything forward looking for an equaliser and eventually a neat move ended with a loose ball in the Reds' area, O'Connor chased it and as he was about to control the ball Hamann's outstretched leg brought him down, referee Elleray immediately awarding a penalty. After a long nervous pause whilst O'Connor received treatment for the knock, Purse, with 35,000 Blues fans congregated behind the goal he was facing, strode up striking his penalty to Westeveld's left firmly into the corner, the keeper had no chance. During extra time the pressure from Blues was relentless, a superb 35-yard chip from Hughes almost caught out the Reds' 'keeper, a solitary hand just pushing the ball wide of the post. Then came the moment Blues will never forget, on a breakaway, Hughes played the ball to Eaden and he knocked it onto the on-rushing Andrew Johnson, as he was about to collect the ball he was clearly tripped by his marker, but amazingly Elleray who seemed to have a perfect view waved play on. In the last minute of extra time a quick Liverpool free kick found Hamann who hit a fierce shot which came back off the Blues post to safety. So at 1–1 the match was to be decided on a penalty shoot out, Liverpool's fortune held and they took the cup, their first of a superb treble winning season.

LIVERPOOL: Westerveld, Babbel, Henchoz, Hypia, Carragher, Gerrard (McAllister 78), Hamann, Biscan (Ziege 96), Smicer (Barmby 83), Heskey, Fowler.

Referee: Mr D Elleray (Harrow).

PENALTY SHOOT OUT

NUMBER	PLAYER	TEAM	SCORE	
1	McAllister	Liverpool	1–0	
2	Grainger	Blues	1–0	Missed
3	Barmby	Liverpool	2–0	
4	Purse	Blues	2–1	
5	Ziege	Liverpool	3–1	
6	Marcelo	Blues	3–2	
7	Hamann	Liverpool	3–2	Missed
8	Lazaridis	Blues	3–3	
9	Fowler	Liverpool	4–3	
10	Hughes	Blues	4–4	
11	Carragher	Liverpool	5–4	
12	A. Johnson	Blues	5–4	Missed

The despair of Andy Johnson whilst Liverpool celebrate in the background

ROAD TO CARDIFF

Round 1 First Leg

22 August 2000 v Southend United (away) won 5–0.

> **Scorers:** Eaden, Johnson (M), Hughes, Marcelo, Adebola. Crowd 3,694.

Round 1 Second Leg

5 September 2000 v Southend United (home) drew 0–0. Crowd 9,507.

Round 2 First Leg

19 September 2000 v Wycombe Wanderers (away) won 4–3

> **Scorers:** Horsfield (2), Johnson A (2). Crowd 2,537.

Round 2 Second Leg

26 September 2000 v Wycombe Wanderers (home) won 1–0

> **Scorer:** Ndlovu. Crowd 8,960.

Round 3

31 October 2000 v Tottenham Hotspur (away) won 3–1

> **Scorers:** Adebola (2), Burchill. Crowd 27,096.

Round 4

29 November 2000 v Newcastle United (home) won 2–1.

Scorers: Adebola, Johnson (M). Crowd 18,520.

Round 5

12 December 2000 v Sheffield Wednesday (home) won 2–0

Scorers: Sonner, Adebola. Crowd 22,911.

Semi-Final First Leg

9 January 2001 v Ipswich Town (away) lost 0–1. Crowd 21,684.

Semi-Final Second Leg

31 January 2001 v Ipswich Town (home) won 4–1 after extra-time 2–1 after 90 minutes.

Scorers: Grainger, Horsfield (2), Johnson (A). Crowd 28,624.

Probably the most dramatic match at St Andrew's ended late into the night as Blues, of the Football League, defeated Ipswich Town, of the Premiership, to secure a place in the Final of the League Cup. It needed extra time, it needed a remarkable display of fortitude, but Blues defeated Ipswich 4–1 on the night (4–2) on aggregate to secure a place with Liverpool at the Millennium Stadium in Cardiff.

Two goals from Geoff Horsfield led the way on a wonderful night for Trevor Francis's team. Goals either side of the break by Martin Grainger and Horsfield reversed Ipswich's 1–0 lead from the first leg. Blues' advantage lasted less than a minute though as James Scowcroft scored, but Horsfield and Andrew Johnson then struck in extra time to assure an historic night for Blues.

If the 90 minutes at St Andrew's was stressful for the Bluenoses, the extra 30-minute period is one that will live long in the memory. Seven minutes into extra time, TF sent on Johnson and the shape of the match changed. It was Horsfield, though, who struck the blow. Danny Sonner's astute pass caught the defence square and Horsfield took the ball in his stride before stroking it precisely across Richard Wright into the far corner of the goal. Johnson added the final blow, when with three minutes remaining, Wright made a horrible hash of a kick, allowing the substitute to roll the ball into the unguarded net.

After match celebrations after Semi-Final victory over Ipswich

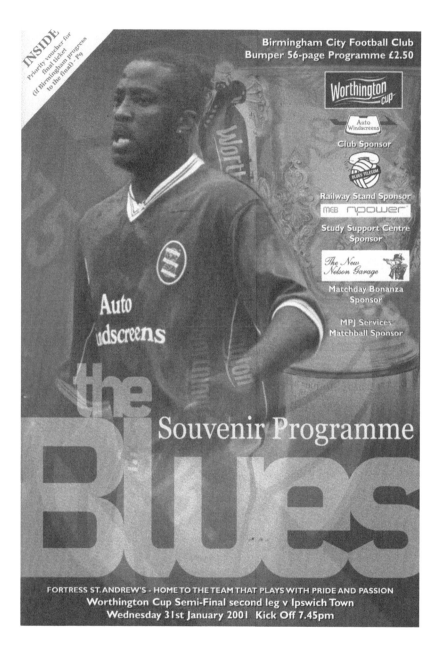

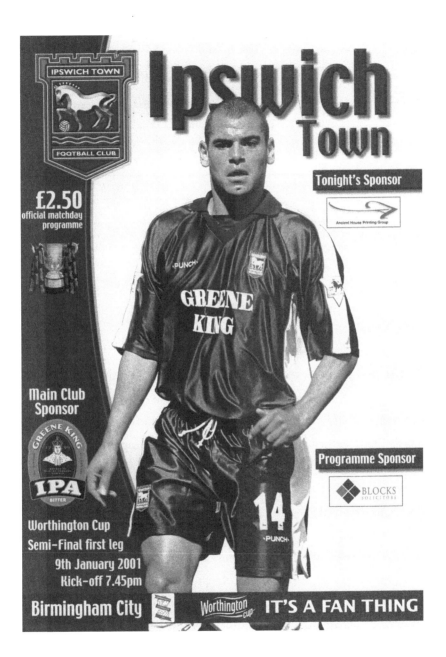

SEASON BY SEASON

SEASON	LEAGUE APPEARANCES/ GOALS	FA CUP APPEARANCES/ GOALS	LEAGUE CUP APPEARANCES/ GOALS
1996–97	24 (4)	0 (0)	0 (0)
1997–98	32+1 (1)	3 (0)	3 (0)
1998–99	37+2 (4)	1 (0)	4 (0)
1999–2000	40+1 (2)	1 (0)	6 (3)
2000–01	30+2 (5)	1 (0)	9 (0)
2001–02	24 (0)	1 (0)	0+1 (0)

I had the pleasure to interview Martin for the now defunct *BLUES MAGAZINE.*

How did things start for you?

'I started my professional career late in life after being rejected by the Development Centres of Aston Villa and West Bromwich Albion at the age of 14. Although I have worked for the Wolves' Academy and the Blues' College, I feel that the current scouting system lets a lot of kids down. It is virtually impossible to predict a boy's development and progress from the age of 7 through to 15.'

'After my rejection at 14, I lost interest in football for two years before joining the Afro-Caribbean Centre team that was run by one of my mate's Dad. I recall my first game was at Swinfen Hall Prison – getting into the place was a problem – they had to unlock a door get the team in then lock the door behind us before they unlocked the next door and so on and that's an Open prison!'

'In my second season our goalkeeper passed his driving test but he was dropped for the next game. What did he do? He parked his car in between the goal posts and demanded to be picked – our manager refused – the car stayed put and the match was abandoned. You couldn't make it up.'

'I had by now qualified as a freight train driver at Bescot having completed my training in the shunting yard and as a guard, I'd been a train driver for six months when I began playing for Bloxwich Town who were managed by Nicky Higgs – after half a season Higgs informed me that Bobby Hope (ex-Blues and WBA) had watched me and wanted me to go for a pre-season trial at Bromsgrove Rovers. I was offered a two-year contract and I recall Bobby Hope and later Chris Nicholl, at Walsall, were the two managers who helped make me a better player. Bobby taught me a lesson – I wanted to go to a party on a Friday night, so I told him on the Thursday that I would not be available for the following Saturday's match. Bobby said OK but you will have to tell your teammates that you no longer wish to play with them. I told them a huge row broke out – outcome? I didn't go to the party and played on the Saturday.'

'I was about 25 when Bromsgrove informed me that Cambridge, Bournemouth, Oxford, Wimbledon and Premiership side, Crystal Palace were interested in signing me. After a trial at Cambridge for John Beck, I signed for Palace in June 1992 for £15,000 and moved to London, the PFA organised the move on my behalf that included free hotel accommodation, which I didn't enjoy. It was all a bit too much for me living in London and moving to the Premiership. When I arrived for pre-season I was so unfit compared to the other lads that they sent me to Lilleshall to improve my fitness levels, I originally went for one week and stayed for four! There was huge competition for midfield places at Palace: Gareth Southgate, John Solanko, Geoff Thomas, Alan Pardew and Simon Osborn but I was in the Premiership albeit as Captain of the reserve team. Kenny Hibbitt was Walsall's manager at the time and he travelled to watch me at Southampton and he took me on loan in 1992–93, I helped The Saddlers get into the play-offs and scored my first league goal against Darlington. Then it was back to Palace who had been relegated to join the first team squad on a pre-season trip to Portugal, I had made it to the first team squad but just never broke through. I travelled to and from the Midlands with Stan Collymore who eventually went to Southend and I had the choice to go to either Chesterfield or Walsall – it was no contest – I moved in February 1994 for £40,000 of which half was paid for by the supporters!'

Martin was an instant success at Walsall becoming Captain and making 80 appearances, scoring 19 goals. He was also picked for the Division 3 Representative side for consecutive seasons (94–95 and 95–96). At the end of the season Martin was out of contract and Derby had had a £350,000 offer refused. 'Walsall only offered me a one year contract obviously hoping to cash in on me early the next season. I was disappointed and refused the deal.'

How did your move to Blues come about?

Barry Fry answers that in his book *Big Fry* – 'I talked to a couple of players who were out of contract about coming to join Peterborough and the position with them was that their fees would be fixed by a tribunal. I did manage to get hold of O'Connor for £350,000 which was a club record.'

Martin spent four months at Peterborough scoring three goals in 18 games, during this time Graeme Souness, the Southampton Man-ager, offered £1m for Martin's services but the deal was for £500k plus players and Barry refused. 'Barry was always saying he would get a million pounds for me, then we were drawn against Cheltenham in the FA Cup. On the Saturday we drew and therefore had a replay on the following Tuesday at Cheltenham, it was important to the club to win the game as they needed the cash. Unfortunately during the weekend my daughter had an asthma attack and was hospitalised. Barry was more than happy to let me miss the replay but I just had to be there, so I played and we won and on my way back to the hospital, Barry rang to say Trevor Francis wanted to speak to me. It all happened so quick, I met Trevor on the Wednesday had a medical and signed on the Thursday and met up with the lads on the Friday night prior to an away game at Norwich. I roomed with Dave Barnett who told me how great the Blues were and I responded by scoring the winner the next day.'

Barry Fry takes up the story: 'Then I sold Martin O'Connor to Birmingham for £528,000 up front and everybody said what a great deal it was. Oh Yeah? It was a shit deal. I would have got a million for him if I had not been put under pressure. Trevor Francis had be me by the short and curlies.'

What were your initial thoughts of the Blues?
'Everything was so much bigger and professional than I had been used to – the training for instance, At Peterborough it was predominantly all 5-a-sides whilst at Blues it was fitness, technique, drills etc. My Mom used to say it was noisy at St Andrew's unlike the other clubs I had been at. Dave Barnett told me that I would be a success with the Bluenoses because they loved players that gave their all.'

What was your most memorable game for Blues?
'No question that was the League Cup Final at the Millennium Stadium, Cardiff. I am never nervous before a game but that day I had butterflies in my stomach and felt nauseous. I knew it was probably my last chance to win a major trophy and as Captain I would be the one to lift the trophy in front of 50,000 Blues fans. This was the year my Dad died and I am part of a large close family with six brothers and sisters and five half brothers and sisters, needless to say they were all there! (Martin recalls it was a happy household but with 12 children it was a race for the toilet!)

What do you remember of the game?
'At the beginning it was witnessing Trevor having to tell Gilly (Jerry Gill), Bugsy (David Burrows) and David Holdsworth that they were missing out. As Captain I had to try and reduce their disappointment but there was nothing I could say.'

'At the end of the game I felt totally gutted knowing that Elleray had copped out (or should that be Kopped?) in not giving us a second penalty. Robbie Fowler was great after the game going round shaking all the boys' hands and inviting us into their dressing room for a drink. My Mom's got my medal!'

What was your proudest moment?
'Being given the captaincy by Trevor, who for me was 100%, it was prior to an away game at Barnsley. I was captain in a side that included senior pros like Bruce, Ablett, Furlong and Newell – what an honour. I just lead by example something that I would do with or without the armband.'

What was your happiest moment?
'Winning the League Cup Semi-Final second leg at St Andrew's 4–1 against Ipswich. I just knew we would get there it was destined to be our night. It was fantastic to be chaired off the field by the Bluenoses who were trying to get hold of my shirt, shorts everything! Prior to the Final TF dropped me for a game against Sheffield United as a booking would have meant me missing the Final. I didn't like the decision and said so, but that's me I just want to play football.'

How many times did you play for the Cayman Islands?
'Twice. I qualified because my Dad was born in Jamaica and I had an English passport. The first game was a warm-up match against Jamaica prior to a World Cup qualifying game against Cuba. We had a 60-year-old Brazilian coach who trained us on the beach. Normally 200 or so people turn out to see the Cayman Islands play and they normally get beaten 10–1, on this occasion 6,000 fans were there to see us lose 1–0. We lost the Cuba game by the same margin. TF was great about letting me have the time off! I didn't get a cap you got a medal for each game. My Mom's got them!'

How did you career end at Blues?

'Once Steve Bruce was appointed Manager I was his first departure, I think it was Bryan Hughes who replaced me. I played 24 games in that promotion season. Colin Lee was manager at Walsall and I was signed on a free in January 2002 and immediately made Captain and remained at Walsall until the end of 2002–03.'

What did you do then?

'I was disillusioned with the game and turned down a number of opportunities before joining Jimmy Quinn at Shrewsbury, which enabled me to get my Coaching qualifications (I have my A Licence) During my time at Gay Meadow we got them back into the Football League before I joined Stuart Watkiss as player-coach at Kidderminster Harriers. After Stuart was sacked I spent three months as caretaker manager. After spells with Wolves and Blues youth schemes, then I joined Halesowen Town as player-coach when they were third from bottom and we got very close to the play-offs. I was with to ex-Blues favourites at Halesowen: Graham Hyde and Paul Devlin.'

13.

JEFF KENNA

– CHAMPIONSHIP PLAY-OFF WINNERS 2001-02

FULL NAME: Jeffrey Jude Kenna.
DATE OF BIRTH: 27 August 1970.
PLACE OF BIRTH: Dublin Ireland.

PLAYING CAREER:

Youth Career:

1987–1989 Southampton.

Senior Career:

1989–1995 Southampton 114 appearances 4 goals, 1995–2002 Blackburn Rovers 157 appearances 1 goal, 2001 Tranmere Rovers (Loan) 11 appearances 0 goals, 2001 Wigan Athletic (Loan) 6 appearances 1 goal, 2001–02 Blues (Loan) 6 appearances, 2002–2004 Blues 69 appearances 3 goals, 2004–06 Derby County 65 appearances 0 goals, 2006–08 Kidderminster Harriers 57 appearances 1 goal, 2008 Galway United 6 appearances 0 goals, 2009 St Patrick's Athletic 0 appearances 0 goals.

International:

1988–92 Republic of Ireland U 21 8 appearances 0 goals, 1994 'B' 1 appearance 0 goals, 1995–99 Full 27 appearances 0 goals.

Management:

2008–09 Galway United, 2009 St Patrick's Athletic, 2011 he joined the coaching staff of the IMG Academy in Bradenton, Florida.

Kenna was born in Dublin, but began his club career in England, at Southampton in 1988. He made his debut on 4 May 1991 in a 6–2 league defeat by Derby County at the Baseball Ground. He became a first team regular in the 1992–93 and remained a fixture in the first team until 15 March 1995, when he moved to Blackburn Rovers for a fee of £1.5 million, playing a part in the run-in to the club's Premier League title that year.

He had played 114 league matches for the Saints, scoring four goals.

He was a regular in the Blackburn team until the 1999–2000 season, after Blackburn had been relegated to Division One. He made his final six appearances for Rovers in the 2000–01 season. During that campaign he had loan spells with Tranmere Rovers and Wigan Athletic, before finally exiting Ewood Park after nearly seven years to join Blues on a free transfer on 24 December 2001.

He made his league debut for Blues on 26 December 2001 against Sheffield Wednesday at Hillsborough. It was a game Blues won 1–0 with Geoff Horsfield scoring the winner in front of a crowd of 24,335. After nearly twelve months he scored his first goal for Blues on 30 November 2002 against Tottenham Hotspur in the 1–1 draw in front of a St Andrew's crowd of 29,505. His final game in the Royal Blue was on 6 March 2004 against Bolton Wanderers at home when he came on as a substitute in the 2–0 win in which Forssell and Hughes scored in front of a crowd of 28,003.

Kenna scored three goals for Birmingham City after their promotion to the Premier League as Division One playoff winners at the end of the 2001–02 season – their first top division campaign in nearly 20 years.

He joined Derby County on a free transfer in March 2004, and was appointed club captain 2005, but was released at the end of the season in May 2006.

Kenna is the brother of heavyweight boxer Colin Kenna and second cousin of football manager Pat Scully. His father Liam is a former Irish snooker international. Since his days at Birmingham City Kenna's family had been settled in the West Midlands and he commuted to Ireland for training activities.

HONOURS

As a Player:
- Southampton – Full Members Cup finalist: 1992.
- Blackburn Rovers – FA Premier League: 1994–95.

DETAILS OF SUCCESS
CHAMPIONSHIP PLAY-OFF WINNERS 2001–02
12 May 2002 v. NORWICH CITY –drew after extra time (0–0 at 90 minutes).

Scorers: Norwich: Roberts 91, Blues: Horsfield 102, won 4-2 on Penalties.

At Millennium Stadium Cardiff.

Attendance: 71, 597.
The team that day was: Vaessen, Kenna, Vickers, Johnson M, Grainger, Mooney, Tebily, Hughes, Devlin, Horsfield, John.
SUBS: CARTER for Vickers (71), LAZARIDIS for Mooney (69,) A. JOHNSON for Horsfield (113). SUBS unused: BENNETT and D. JOHNSON.

PENALTY SHOOT OUT

NUMBER	PLAYER	TEAM	SCORE	
1	Roberts	Norwich	1–0	
2	John	Blues	1–1	
3	Mulryne	Norwich	1–1	Missed
4	Devlin	Blues	2–1	
5	Sutch	Norwich	2–1	Missed
6	Lazaridis	Blues	3–1	
7	Easton	Norwich	3–2	
8	Carter	Blues	4–2	

Carter's penalty has gone in

It took 16 years, four failed attempts in the play-off semi-finals, 120 minutes and eight penalty kicks, but Blues were finally back in top flight football. When Darren Carter smashed in the winning spot kick the noise in the Millennium Stadium reached record levels. Blues fans were left wallowing in the glory of the club's biggest win for years, a memorable day that will be celebrated for years to come. Blues started the game clear favourites, having beaten Norwich twice in the regular season 4–0 at St Andrew's and 0–1 at Carrow Road. Blues were also the team with the best current form, unbeaten in their last 12 games. Norwich scraped into the play-off places on the last day of the season, on goal difference over Burnley, but showed in the two-legged semi-final against Wolves that they were not to be taken lightly.

Blues got off to a great start and on 15 minutes John was given a glorious chance after a ball from Hughes sent him clean though on goal. However, with just the 'keeper to beat he made a hash of trying to bend the ball round Green with the outside of his boot, and it drifted well wide of the target. Still Blues went forward and were denied another chance of a goal via the penalty spot when Horsfield was apparently tripped by MacKay but, referee Barber ignored the incident. Norwich, who had yet to trouble the Blues goal suddenly became a threat and finished the half looking the better side, but still could not force a save of any note from Vaesen in the Blues goal. Not so at the other end, and right on the stroke of half-time Green produced a magnificent reflex save to stop a volley from Horsfield, who had been put clear just four yards out from Mooney's headed knock down.

Chances soon dried up in the second half as both sides sensed the pressure mounting. The best chances however both fell to Blues and Tebily. Two minutes into the half his header was cleared off the line by Drury, and four minutes from the end his snap shot from eight yards just cleared the crossbar. At the other end a timely interception from Kenna stopped the ball running to Norwich substitute Roberts, who would have had a simple chance. Roberts soon got his opportunity to hit the target and Norwich took the lead 43 seconds into extra-time. Grainger badly misjudged a pass to Notman on the right and from his beautifully flighted cross Roberts rose unmarked in the area to steer his header into the bottom corner of the net. Blues battled back and Norwich frantically defended for 12 minutes before they finally succumbed to a deserved equaliser from Horsfield's header after a great knock down from John. Blues continued to stream forward looking for a winner and with three minutes of extra-time remaining Michael Johnson almost snatched a dramatic headed goal, but the ball struck the bottom of the post.

So the game now hinged on the outcome of a penalty shoot out, Blues were given the early boost of winning the toss. They would take their penalties in front of their own 33,000 fans, but they also wanted to avoid the goal where they lost the shoot out against Liverpool in the Worthington Cup Final.

NORWICH: Green, Kenton, Drury, Mackay, Fleming, Rivers (Notman 90), Holt, Mulryne, Nielsen (Roberts 83), McVeigh (Sutch 102), Easton.
Referee: Mr G. Barber (Tring).

Blues celebrate promotion

OFFICIAL MATCHDAY PROGRAMME £4

Nationwide
FOOTBALL LEAGUE

DIVISION ONE PLAY-OFF FINAL
SUNDAY 12TH MAY 2002
KICK OFF 3.30PM

Birmingham City

V

Norwich City

Nationwide

Finished 5th Division One behind Manchester City (Champions), West Bromwich Albion (Runners Up), Wolverhampton Wanderers and Millwall.

Played 46, won 21, drew 13, lost 12, Goals For, 70 Goals Against 49, Points 76.

APPEARANCES

PLAYER	LEAGUE APPEARANCES/ GOALS	FA CUP APPEARANCES/ GOALS	LEAGUE CUP APPEARANCES/ GOALS
VAESEN	25+1	0 (0)	2 (0)
GILL	14 (0)	1 (0)	0 (0)
GRAINGER	42+1 (4)	0 (0)	3 (0)
SONNER	10+5 (1)	0 (0)	3 (0)
PURSE	37+1 (3)	1 (0)	1 (0)
JOHNSON M.	31+2 (1)	0 (0)	3 (1)
EADEN	24+5 (1)	0 (0)	3 (0)
MOONEY	32+14 (13)	1 (0)	1 (2)
HORSFIELD	36+7 (12)	1 (0)	3 (0)
O'CONNOR	24 (0)	1 (0)	0+1 (0)
LAZARIDIS	22+13 (0)	0 (0)	1+1 (0)
HUGHES B.	30+4 (8)	0+1 (0)	2 (1)
HOLDSWORTH	3+1 (0)	0 (0)	1 (0)
FURLONG	2+9 (1)	0 (0)	0+2 (0)
WOODHOUSE	18+10 (0)	1 (0)	2+1 (0)
MARCELO	17+4 (12)	0+1 (0)	0+3 (0)
KELLY	6(0)	0 (0)	0 (0)
JOHNSON A.	9+16 (3)	1 (0)	2 (1)
BURROWS	9+3 (0)	1 (0)	1+1 (0)
BRAGSTAD	3 (0)	0 (0)	0 (0)
LUNTALA	9+6 (0)	0 (0)	1 (0)
HUTCHINSON	0+3 (0)	0 (0)	0+1 (0)

FERRARI	0+4 (0)	0 (0)	0 (0)
FLEMING	6 (0)	0 (0)	0 (0)
VICKERS	15+1 (1)	1 (0)	0 (0)
BENNETT	18 (0)	1 (0)	0 (0)
HYDE	1+4 (0)	0 (0)	0 (0)
KENNA	24 (0)	0 (0)	0 (0)
McCARTHY	3+1 (0)	0 (0)	0 (0)
BAK	2+2 (0)	1 (0)	0 (0)
CARTER	13+2 (1)	0 (0)	0 (0)
DEVLIN	13+2 (1)	0 (0)	0 (0)
JOHN	18 (8)	0 (0)	0 (0)
JOHNSON D.	6+3 (1)	0 (0)	0 (0)
WILLIAMS	4 (0)	0 (0)	0 (0)
TEBILY	10 (0)	0 (0)	0 (0)
HUGHES M.	3 (0)	0 (0)	0 (0)
POOLE	0 (0)	0 (0)	1 (0)

PLAY OFF SEMI-FINALS

First Leg 28 April 2002 v Millwall (home) drew 1–1

   Scorer: Hughes B. Crowd 28,282.

Second Leg 2 May 2002 v Millwall (away) won 1–0

   Scorer: John. Crowd 16,391.

SEASON BY SEASON

SEASON	LEAGUE APPEARANCES/ GOALS	FA CUP APPEARANCES/ GOALS	LEAGUE CUP APPEARANCES/ GOALS
2001–02	24 (0)	0 (0)	0 (0)
2002–03	36+1 (1)	1 (0)	1 (0)
2003–04	14+3 (2)	4 (0)	0 (0)

Paul Devlin remembers:

What was your most memorable game at Blues?

'That has to be the Division One Play-Off Final at Cardiff against Norwich that we won on penalties. Taking my penalty was the worst experience of my life. In fairness those of us who were the nominated penalty takers had practised but it does not prepare you for the emotional aspects. In my mind all I could think of was 'don't let me be the one to miss.' I had a further problem because I was suffering from cramp and therefore could not take the long run up I usually took, as I said earlier I just blasted it. When it went in there was no joy it was just pure relief. The next 3–4 days were something of a blur as we shared a few Shandies to celebrate!!'

14.

DAMIEN JOHNSON

– PROMOTION TO PREMER LEAGUE 2006–07

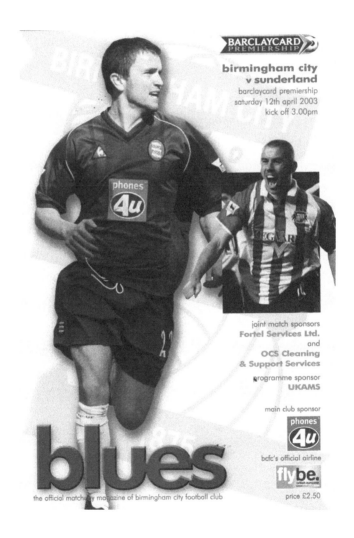

FULL NAME: Damien Michael Johnson.

DATE OF BIRTH: 18 November 1978.

PLACE OF BIRTH: Lisburn Northern Ireland.

PLAYING CAREER:

Youth Career:

Portadown F.C.

Senior Career:

1997-2002 Blackburn Rovers 59 appearances 3 goals, 1998 Nottingham Forest (loan) 6 appearances 0 goals; 2002-10 Blues 193 appearances 4 goals; 2010–12 Plymouth Argyle 20 appearances 0 goals; 2010–11 Huddersfield Town (loan) 16 appearances 0 goals; 2011–12 Huddersfield Town 16 appearances 0 goals; 2012–13 Fleetwood Town 22 appearances 0 goals.

International:

1998–99 Northern Ireland Under-21 11 appearances 0 goals, 1999–2010 Northern Ireland Full International 56 appearances 0 goals.

He began his career with Portadown FC in his native Northern Ireland from whom he signed as a trainee for Blackburn Rovers and spent five years with the club, as well as spending time on loan with Nottingham Forest. He moved to Blues in 2002, where he spent the next eight seasons and became the club's captain. Johnson was transferred to Plymouth Argyle in 2010 and spent the 2010–11 and 2011–12 season on loan with Huddersfield Town. He represented Northern Ireland over an eleven-year period, earning 56 caps.

His first English team was Blackburn Rovers, for whom Johnson signed as a trainee, from Portadown F.C. in 1997, making his debut in the League Cup on 30 September 1997, a 1–0 defeat to Preston North End, in which he picked up a yellow card.

Loaned to Nottingham Forest on 28 January 1998, Johnson played in five games, and, despite accruing a yellow card in his last appearance in February he performed well for the team.

On 8 March 2002, Johnson moved to Blues for £50,000 and in

September 2004, he signed a new three-year contract. His Blues debut was on 12 March 2002 against Bradford City away, which Blues won 3–1 with goals from Purse, Horsfield and John in front of a crowd 13,105. He scored his first goal for Blues on 31 August 2002 at St Andrew's against Leeds United which Blues won 2–1 with Devlin scoring the other goal in front of a crowd of 27,164

Johnson was named the Birmingham City captain for the 2006–07 season, but in one of his first games as captain, he angered fans when he first threw his captain's armband and then his shirt on the floor when he was substituted late on.

On 28 October 2006, Johnson's jaw was broken in two places after he was elbowed in the face by West Bromwich Albion defender Paul Robinson during a tackle. Despite the broken jaw, Johnson played on until the final whistle.

In 2007, he signed a three-year deal keeping him at Birmingham City until 2010.

At the opening of the 2007–08 season he injured his hamstring in a pre-season friendly. Further injuries followed, and Johnson only regained fitness in December. He made his final appearance in Royal Blue as a substitute in the Christmas fixture against Chelsea on 26 December 2009 in a goalless draw in front of a crowd of 28,958. Described by Blues boss Steve Bruce as his best signing, he was Player of The Year in 2005–06 and was again a key man in leading the Blues to promotion back to the Premiership in 2007.

Johnson signed for Championship club Plymouth Argyle, on 1 February 2010, on a free transfer, signing a two-and-a-half year contract. Upon Johnson's departure, Birmingham manager Alex McLeish said: 'He is always a terrier of a player and played a significant part in us returning to the Premier League. I wish him all the best.'

Johnson earned his first Northern Ireland call up on 29 May 1999, when he came on as a substitute in the 1–0 away win against the Republic of Ireland. Further appearances as substitute followed against Finland,

Luxembourg, Malta and Hungary, before he made his first full appearance versus Yugoslavia at Windsor Park Belfast, in August 2000.

After a period when his international appearances were restricted by serious injury, Johnson made his 49th appearance for Northern Ireland in the 3–0 World Cup Qualifying victory in San Marino on 11 February 2009, when he was the BBC's 'Man of the Match'.

On 29 July 2010, Johnson announced his retirement from international football.

HONOURS

As a Player:

- Huddersfield Town: Football League One play-off winner 2011–12.
- Birmingham City: Promotion to the Premiership 2006–07.

SEASON BY SEASON

SEASON	LEAGUE APPEARANCES/ GOALS	FA CUP APPEARANCES/ GOALS	LEAGUE CUP APPEARANCES/ GOALS
2001–02	6+3 (1)	0 (0)	0 (0)
2002–03	28+2 (1)	1 (0)	0+1 (0)
2003–04	35 (1)	4 (0)	1 (0)
2004–05	36(0)	2 (0)	0+1 (0)
2005–06	31 (0)	4 (0)	3 (0)
2006–07	24+2 (1)	3 (0)	0 (0)
2007–08	17 (0)	0 (0)	1 (0)
2008–09	8+1 (0)	0+1 (0)	0 (0)
2009–10	0+1 (0)	1+1 (0)	0 (0)

DETAILS OF SUCCESS

PROMOTION TO PREMIER LEAGUE 2006–07.

Second in the table after Sunderland

P 46, HW 15, HD 5, HL3, HGF 37, HGA 18, AW11, AD 3, AL9, AGF 30, AGA 24, PTS 86, GD +25.

Appearances and Goals

Player	League Apps	League Gls	FA Cup Apps	FA Cup Gls	League Cup Apps	League Cup Gls
N. Bendtner	38(4)	11	1 (1)	0	0 (4)	2
D. Campbell	15 (17)	9	3 (0)	2	2 (2)	1
S. Clemence	31 (3)	4	0 (0)	0	1 (0)	0
A. Cole	5 (0)	1	0 (0)	0	0 (0)	0
N. Danns	11 (18)	3	0 (3)	0	3 (0)	0
C. Doyle	19 (0)	0	0 (0)	0	3 (0)	0
D. Dunn	9 (2)	1	0 (0)	0	0 (1)	0
M. Forssell	3 (5)	1	0 (0)	0	2 (0)	0
J. Gray	2(5)	0	0 (0)	0	3 (0)	0
R. Jaidi	38 (0)	6	1 (0)	0	3 (0)	0
C. Jerome	20 (17)	7	2 (0)	0	4 (0)	2
D. Johnson	24 (1)	1	3 (0)	0	0 (0)	0
S. Kelly	35 (1)	0	1 (0)	0	3 (1)	0
N. Kilkenny	0 (8)	0	0 (3)	0	2 (1)	0
S. Larsson	27 (16)	4	3 (0)	3	4 (0)	2
A. Legzdins	0 (0)	0	0 (0)	0	0 (0)	0
Maik Taylor	27 (0)	0	3 (0)	0	1 (0)	0
Martin Taylor	29 (2)	0	2 (1)	1	4 (0)	0
G.McSheffery	40 (0)	13	3 (0)	1	1 (1)	2
F. Muamba	30 (4)	0	3 (0)	0	3 (1)	0

B. N'Gotty	25 (0)	1	2 (0)	1	0 (0)	0
M. Nafti	18 (14)	0	0 (1)	0	1 (0)	0
M. Painter	1 (0)	0	0 (0)	0	1 (0)	0
M. Sadler	36 (0)	0	3 (0)	0	2 (0)	0
O. Tebily	5 (1)	0	0 (0)	0	1 (0)	0
M. Upson	8 (1)	2	3 (0)	0	0 (0)	0
R. Vine	10 (7)	1	0 (0)	0	0 (0)	0

Birmingham City 2 Sheffield Wednesday 0

Date: 28 April 07

Venue: St Andrew's

Attendance: 29,317

Blues: Doyle, N'Gotty, Jaidi, Taylor, Kelly, Larsson, Muamba, Clemence, McSheffrey (Nafti),Cole (Vine), Bendtner (Jerome).

Wednesday: Adamson, Simek (Clarke), Bullen, Wood, Spurr, Tudgay, Lunt, Whelan, Brunt (Johnson) MacLean, Burton.

And so it was that St Andrew's welcomed play-off hopefuls Sheffield Wednesday for the penultimate game of the season. To say the game was full of nerves was an understatement and at half-time it was goalless.

On 57 minutes things turned against Blues when midfielder Fabrice Muamba was sent off. Down to 10 men, the Bluenoses responded and drove their team forward and it was no surprise when Jerome scored the opening goal. The match was won by arguably the goal of the season when Larsson ran from the halfway line to fire a shot past 'keeper Chris Adamson in front of the Tilton End.

The fans went mad, as did the players as they formed a human mound on top of Larsson soon to be joined by the management and staff!

Stephen Clemence recalls:

'As soon as Fabrice got sent off, the fans really, really got going and gave us a lift. They were magnificent. We scored quite early after the sending off and then that gave us something to hang onto, but I think when the second goal went in, it was like the roof was going to come off the stadium. It was electric. The fans were absolutely unbelievable'.

It was then onto Sunday when Palace played Derby, things were as tense in Birmingham as they were in London, and when Palace won 2–0, with a goal from ex-Blues forward Clinton Morrison that was enough to send Blues back to the Premiership.

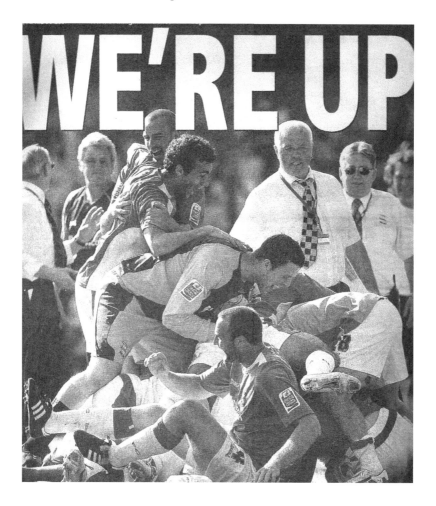

15.

LEE CARSLEY

– PROMOTION TO PREMIER LEAGUE 2008–09

FULL NAME: Lee Kevin Carsley .
DATE OF BIRTH: 28 February 1974.
PLACE OF BIRTH: Birmingham.

PLAYING CAREER:

Senior Career:
199299 Derby County 138 appearances 5 goals, 1999–2000 Blackburn Rovers 47 appearances 11 goals, 200002 Coventry City 47 appearances 4 goals, 2002–2008 Everton 166 appearances 11 goals, 2008–2010 Blues 48 appearances 2 goals, 2010–11 Coventry City 25 appearances 0 goals. Total 471 appearances 33 goals.

International:
1997–2008 Republic of Ireland 40 appearances 0 goals.

Management:
2011 Coventry City (assistant), 2012 Coventry City (caretaker), 2013 Sheffield United (assistant – technical).

Carsley began his career at Derby County where he played more than 150 games in all competitions He was sold to Blackburn Rovers in March 1999 for £4.5 million and was their top scorer in 1999–2000, his only full season with the club. In December 2000 he moved on to Coventry City for a fee of around £3.0 million but spent only 14 months with the club before moving on again, this time to Everton for £1.9 million. Carsley enjoyed mixed fortunes during his first two seasons at Everton, but the 2004–05 season saw him become an increasingly important player within the team. He was a regular starter in the 4–1–4–1 formation, sitting just in front of the defence and just behind the midfield.

In December 2004, Carsley scored the winner in the 200th Merseyside derby between Everton and Liverpool. The win took Everton temporarily to second place in the Premier League. He continued to perform well and Everton ended up finishing fourth, thus gaining entry to the third qualifying stage of the Champions League

His contract with Everton was due to expire at the end of 2007–08; he chose not to accept the offered extension, and signed for home-town club Blues in May 2008. With club captain Damien Johnson expected to be out of action for several months following a back operation, Carsley started the 2008–09 season as captain. At the end of the season, Birmingham were promoted back to the Premier League, and Carsley won the Players' and Junior Blues' Player of the Season awards.

His League Debut for Blues was in the opening game of the 2008–09 season on 9 August 2008 at home to Sheffield United. Blues won 1–0 with Kevin Phillips scoring in front of a crowd of 24,019. His first goal was the winner in a 1–0 victory over Plymouth Argyle (away) on 9 December 2008 with an attendance of 10,446.

In November 2009, he was at the centre of controversy in Birmingham's Premiership match against Liverpool at Anfield. Following his tackle on David N'Gog, a penalty was awarded which Steven Gerrard converted to bring the scores level. Carsley believed that N'Gog had dived to win the penalty and described it as 'an embarrassing case of cheating'. After a season disrupted by injury, he confirmed in April 2010 that he would leave the club at the end of the season.

His final game for Blues was on 9 November 2009 as a substitute against Liverpool at Anfield in a 2–2 draw in front of 42,560

Carsley returned to former club Coventry City in July 2010, signing a one-year contract. He was appointed club captain by manager Aidy

Boothroyd After he was released at the end of his contract, he retired from professional football.

Carsley qualifies for the Republic of Ireland National team through his grandmother, who is from Dunmanway County Cork.

Carsley was involved in the qualification for both the 1998 and 2002 World Cups. He was part of the Ireland squad that reached the last 16 of the 2002 World Cup, making one appearance in the finals, in their 3–0 win over Saudi Arabia in the group stages.

Carsley and wife Louisa live in Solihull and have three children. He is patron of the local Down's Syndrome support group, with which the Carsley's became actively involved because their second son has the condition.

DETAILS OF SUCCESS

Second in the table after Wolverhampton Wanderers.

P 46, HW 14, HD 5, HL 4, HGF 30, HGA 17, AW 9, AD 9, AL 5, AGF 24, AGA 20, PTS 83, GD +28.

Appearances and Goals

Player	League Apps	League Gls	FA Cup Apps	FA Cup Gls	League Cup Apps	League Cup Gls
G. Agustien	18 (5)	0	1 (0)	0	1 (0)	0
S. Aydilek	0 (0)	0	0 (0)	0	0 (0)	0
M. Bent	16 (17)	3	1 (0)	0	1 (0)	0
H. Bouazza	9 (7)	1	0 (0)	0	0 (0)	0
l. Bowyer	17 (0)	1	0 (0)	0	0 (0)	0
S. Carr	13 (0)	0	0 (0)	0	0 (0)	0
L. Carsley	41 (0)	2	1 (0)	0	2 (0)	0
C. Costly	3 (5)	0	0 (0)	0	0 (0)	0
U. De la Cruz	0 (1)	0	0 (0)	0	0 (0)	0
C. Doyle	1 (1)	0	0 (0)	0	2 (0)	0
K. Fahey	15 (4)	4	0 (0)	0	0 (0)	0
N. Hunt	9 (2)	0	0 (0)	0	0 (0)	0
R. Jaidi	30 (0)	0	1 (0)	0	0 (0)	0

C. Jerome	25 (18)	9	1 (0)	0	0 (1)	1
D. Johnson	8 (1)	0	0 (1)	0	0 (0)	0
S. Kelly	2 (3)	0	0 (1)	0	1 (0)	0
A. Krysiak	0 (0)	0	0 (0)	0	0 (0)	0
S. Larsson	35 (3)	1	0 (0)	0	1 (0)	0
D. Lyness	0 (0)	0	0 (0)	0	0 (0)	0
Maik Taylor	45 (0)	0	1 (0)	0	0 (0)	0
Martin Taylor	23 (1)	1	0 (0)	0	1 (0)	0
J. McFadden	22 (8)	4	0 (0)	0	0 (0)	0
M. McPike	0 (0)	0	0 (0)	0	0 (0)	0
G.McSheffery	3 (3)	0	0 (0)	0	2 (0)	0
D. Murphy	28 (2)	0	0 (0)	0	2 (0)	0
J. Mutch	0 (0)	0	0 (0)	0	0 (1)	0
M. Nafti	6 (5)	0	0 (0)	0	1 (0)	1
G. O'Connor	10 (6)	6	0 (0)	0	2 (0)	1
Q. Owusu-Abeyie	12 (7)	2	0 (0)	0	1 (1)	1
S. Parnaby	19 (2)	0	1 (0)	0	2 (0)	0
K. Phillips	24 (12)	14	0 (0)	0	1 (1)	0
N. Quashie	8 (2)	0	1 (0)	0	0 (0)	0
F. Queudrue	23 (2)	3	1 (0)	0	0 (1)	0
L. Ridgewell	36 (0)	1	1 (0)	0	2 (0)	0
A. Sammons	0 (0)	0	0 (0)	0	0 (0)	0
R. Shroot	0 (0)	0	1 (0)	0	0 (0)	0
S. Sinclair	8 (6)	0	0 (0)	0	0 (0)	0
D. Traore	2 (1)	0	0 (0)	0	0 (0)	0
J. Wilson	0 (1)	0	0 (0)	0	0 (0)	0

In the Official Birmingham City Annual 2010 there was an article entitled 'LEADING FROM THE FRONT';

Blues fan Lee Carsley had to bide his time before playing for his hometown club but proved it was worth the wait by leading the team to promotion in his first season at St Andrew's. Carsley was a Premier League regular for six years at Everton following earlier top-flight spells at Coventry City, Blackburn Rovers and Derby County.

His aim was to play his way back up there when he joined Blues before the start of the 2008–09 season and he duly delivered with some outstanding performances which earned him the Player of the Year award from his team-mates.

'That's what I wanted, to play in the Premier League with Birmingham,' said the Blues' captain. Carsley admitted that it wasn't an easy ride but praised the players and manager Alex McLeish for sticking together and staying focussed on their goal.

A sending-off against Wolverhampton Wanderers kept Carsley out for three big games during the final run-in but the tough-tackling midfielder was back for the deciding game at Reading when his experience helped Blues over the line.

And now the former Republic of Ireland international is determined to play his part in keeping Birmingham in the big league and avoid the one-season stay they endured last time round. 'We want to be a stable club and show the fans that,' added Carsley, who is just the kind of man Blues need to achieve that goal.

SEASON BY SEASON

SEASON	LEAGUE APPEARANCES/ GOALS	FA CUP APPEARANCES/ GOALS	LEAGUE CUP APPEARANCES/ GOALS
2008–09	41 (2)	1 (0)	1 (0)
2009–10	3+4 (0)	1 (0)	1 (0)

It was the day that Manchester United won the Premier League for the third successive season, this is the second time they have achieved a successive treble of titles – a new record for the Red Devils. On Sunday 3 May 2009, Birmingham City set a unique record – they are the first club to be relegated, promoted, relegated and promoted to and from the Premier League in successive seasons. Birmingham City therefore retain the description of being a yo-yo club which they have maintained throughout their history as evidenced throughout this book.

DETAILS OF SUCCESS
PROMOTION TO PREMIER LEAGUE 2008-09

After failing to secure the runners up spot, and thereby gaining automatic promotion against Preston North End at St Andrew's on 25 April, Blues needed a win the following week, the last game of the season, to ensure promotion to the Premier League.

READING 1 – BLUES 2

Date: 04 May 2009.

Venue: Madejski Stadium.

Attendance: 24,011.

Referee: H.Webb (South Yorks).

Blues: Taylor (Maik), Carr, Traore, Jaidi, Taylor (Martin), McFadden (Larsson, 66), Johnson, Carsley, Fahey, Phillips (Bouazza 72), Jerome (O'Connor 80).

Reading: Hahnemann, Rosenior, Harding (Doyle 57), Bikey, Duberry, Tabb, Karacan (Matejovsky 54), Long, Kitson, Hunt, Kebe

Bookings: Jaidi, Phillips, Traore

After the team being booed off against Preston North End, the 2,000 travelling Bluenoses hailed one of the best performances of the season as Blues brushed aside a surprisingly uninspired Reading side to secure top level football next season.

If ever a Blues side had put in a performance that was defined by the club anthem this was it. Brummie, Lee Carsley was restored to midfield in place of the erratic Lee Bowyer and regained the captain's armband. He gave a captain's performance covering every inch of the pitch and was only robbed of the 'man of the match' accolade which was awarded to Keith Fahey, who edged the judge's vote by scoring the all-important first goal. Martin Taylor came in for the injured Franck Queudrue and together with Radhi Jaidi made up for their lack of natural ability with a rugged determination never to lose a tackle and both were in with a shout for the 'man of the match' award. Other candidates included Steven Carr, James McFadden and Damien Johnson; it was that sort of game.

The first goal came on 19 minutes from a corner after a teasing run from McFadden. After a clearance at the near post the ball fell to Phillips just outside the penalty area, his flick found Fahey who sent in a shot which Marcus Hahnemann got his hands on to but was unable to prevent the ball entering the net. With Blues leading at half-time, Reading came out for the final 45 minutes with their intentions clear switching to a 3-4-3 formation. Although under pressure it was Blues who extended their lead through Kevin Phillips in the 60 minute when Fahey returned the compliment by slipping him a delightful through ball. Phillips used all his experienced and skill by rolling the ball beyond the 'keeper to score just inside the far post. It's 0–2 and we are back in the Premier League with only 30 minutes to go!

As Bluenoses know we never do things easy and within 60 seconds, Reading had pulled a goal back through their substitute Marek Matjovsky before the Blues fans had had time to celebrate Phillips' goal.

Whilst all Bluenoses were thinking 'here we go again' Hameur Bouazza came on for Phillips and Blues reverted to a five-man midfield. It was a nervous period and it seemed as if Garry O'Connor had sealed things with five minutes to go when immediately after replacing Cameron Jerome he got on the end of a Johnson pass and thumped a shot against a post. Reading took heart from this piece of good luck and from then on they were camped in the Blues' penalty area.

With the fans singing 'Keep Right On', the players responded by heading, tackling, harassing, chasing, blocking and giving their all as the clock ticked down until the celebrations could begin.

All Bluenoses would agree that in terms of performances it had been a poor season but as David Gold said after the game 'In the Summer I said "Alex, get us promoted pal". I didn't say how.' But Colin Tattum in the *Evening Mail* echoed the feelings of the fans with his comment, 'Little could the chairman have known that McLeish would take him as his word and stretch levels of incredulity, agony and ecstasy to the limit.'

The Season's results were:

August 9 – Blues 1 Sheffield United 0 (Phillips).

August 16 – Southampton 1 Blues 2 (Phillips, O'Connor).

August 23 – Blues 2 Barnsley 0 (Phillips, O'Connor).

August 30 – Norwich 1 Blues 1 (Larsson).

September 13 – Blues 1 Doncaster 0 (Jerome).

September 16 – Bristol City 1 Blues 2 (Jerome, Larsson).

September 20 – Blues 0 Blackpool 1.

September 27 – Cardiff 1 Blues 2 (McFadden, Quincy).

September 30 – Derby 1 Blues 1 (Quincy).

October 4 – Blues 1 QPR 0 (Phillips).

October 18 – Burnley 1 Blues 1 (Jerome).

October 21 – Blues 1 Crystal Palace 0 (O'Connor).

October 25 – Blues 3 Sheffield Wednesday 1 (Phillips, O'Connor (2)).

October 28 – QPR 1 Blues 0.

November 3 – Blues 0 Coventry 1.

November 8 – Nottingham Forest 1 Blues 1 (McFadden).

November 15 – Blues 3 Charlton 2 (McFadden, Phillips, Queudrue).

November 21 – Swansea 2 Blues 3 (Bent, Phillips (2)).

November 25 – Blues 2 Ipswich 1 (Ridgewell, Phillips).

November 29 – Wolves 1 Blues 1 (Jerome).

December 6 – Blues 3 Watford 2 (Phillips, Bent, Jerome).

December 9 – Plymouth 0 Blues 1 (Carsley).

December 13 – Preston 1 Blues 0.

December 20 – Blues 1 Reading 3 (Phillips).

December 26 – Ipswich 0 Blues 1 (McFadden).

December 28 – Blues 0 Swansea 0.

January 17 – Blues 1 Cardiff 1 (Bowyer).

January 24 – Blackpool 2 Blues 0.

January 27 – Blues 1 Derby 0 (Carsley).

January 31 – Sheffield Wednesday 1 Blues 1 (Phillips).

February 7 – Blues 1 Burnley 1 (Phillips).

February 14 – Blues 2 Nottingham Forest 0 (Bent, Fahey).

February 21 – Coventry 1 Blues 0.

February 24 – Crystal Palace 0 Blues 0.

March 1 – Sheffield United 2 Blues 1 (Morgan OG).

March 4 – Blues 1 Bristol City 0 (Queudrue).

March 7 – Blues 1 Southampton 0 (Fahey).

March 10 – Barnsley 1 Blues 1 (Taylor Martin).

March 14 – Doncaster 0 Blues 2 (Jerome, Bouazza).

March 21 – Blues 1 Norwich 1 (Jerome).

April 6 – Blues 2 Wolves 0 (Jerome, O'Connor).

April 11 – Charlton 0 Blues 0.

April 13 – Blues 1 Plymouth Argyle 1 (Queudrue).

April 18 – Watford 0 Blues 1 (Jerome).

April 25 – Blues 1 Preston 2 (Fahey).

May 3 – Reading 1 Blues 2 (Fahey, Phillips).

Alex McLeish achieved promotion at the first time of asking and apart from wanting it achieved with better performances on the pitch, Bluenoses have to say 'he got the job done.'

After failing to keep Blues in the Premier League in his first exposure for English football he was required to perform that almost impossible trick – of reducing the wage bill but retaining sufficient quality to get promoted at the first time of asking.

Mikael Forssell, Fabrice Muamba, Olivier Kapo, Daniel De Ridder and Rafeal Schmitz departed but he was able to persuade the Board to keep the jewels in the crown; McFadden and Larsson.

With McFadden and Larsson acting in midfield the 'spine' of the team was completed by Maik Taylor, Radhi Jaidi, Liam Ridgewell in defence and Cameron Jerome and Garry O'Connor in attack.

Major strengthening was required and apart from Marcus Bent (a forward with the strike rate of a full-back) who could argue with the contributions of Lee Carsley and Kevin Phillips. So on paper the squad looked the best in the league – it was time to test it on grass!

The ability to score goals and kill off opponents is evidenced by the number of 1–0 victories – 10 during the season and the total goals total of 54, which was beaten by three by relegated Norwich.

Blues got off to a great start achieving their best ever start to a league campaign in their history on their way to the top by the end of October 08.

Teams were raising their game against the Blues, which was testified by defeats at home by Blackpool and Reading and a draw with Swansea. Although these results ultimately proved to be just blips they aroused questions as to whether McLeish was the man for the job.

'Big Eck' reacted and got rid of Quincy Owusu-Abeyie and Nigel Quashie and brought in loan signings; Scott Sinclair, Hameur Bouazza and the questionable Lee Bowyer to bring more energy and skill into midfield. The unknown Irishman Keith Fahey was also signed from the Dublin side, St Patrick's Athletic of the Eircom League, and whilst Bluenoses thought 'Who are ya?' his impact was immediate as he brought pace and width to the midfield and whilst performances improved the score rate did not go up.

Controversially Stephen Kelly was allowed to go on a £500,000 loan deal to Stoke City leaving Blues without a recognised right-back, surprisingly Stephen Carr (ex-Newcastle United) was brought out of retirement to fill the gap and his non-stop performances have made him extremely popular with the fans. The defence has proved to be the best in the league keeping 17 clean sheets.

In April Blues showed the necessary grit and determination required for promotion and the spirit of the squad in being able to react positively to a number of incidents that could have easily derailed a lesser side;

- At St Andrew's on 6 April Lee Carsley received a red card against League leaders and eventual champions Wolverhampton Wanderers, but the ten men of Birmingham took all three points – Damien Johnson, after missing the early part of the season through injury, returned to perform doggedly in midfield.
- Against Plymouth on 13 April Maik Taylor received a straight red card and Liam Ridgewell broke his leg – Colin Doyle performed such that the defence was not compromised by Taylor's absence and Franck Querudue deputised for Ridgewell in the next game against Watford on 18 April and scored the winning goal.
- At Vicarage Road on 18 April David Murphy broke his kneecap and Traore came in and retained his place for the final two games.
- On 25 April against Preston Lee Bowyer received a straight red and back came Carsley and Johnson fitted in, whilst Queudrue was injured and Martin Taylor came in for the Reading game and performed heroics.

In the final month of the promotion run-in, Blues had suffered three red cards, two broken legs and one major injury and still managed to achieve automatic promotion.

The question is 'Can Blues retain their Premier status in 2009–2010?' it will be a big ask but at least Bluenoses have another season of 'mixing it with the big boys.'

SEASON STATISTICS
League Appearances

Position	Name	Starts	Substitute	Goals
1	Maik Taylor	45	0	0
2	L. Carsley	41	0	2
3	L. Ridgewell	36	0	1
4	S. Larsson	35	3	2

5	R. Jaidi	30	0	0
6	D. Murphy	29	1	0
7	C. Jerome	27	17	9
8	K. Phillips	24	12	14
9	F. Queudrue	23	2	3
10	Martin Taylor	23	1	1
11	J. McFadden	22	8	4
12	S. Parnaby	19	2	0
13	M. Bent	16	17	3
14	L. Bowyer	16	0	1
15	K. Fahey	15	5	4
16	G. Agustien	13	5	0
17	S. Carr	13	0	0
18	Quincy	12	7	2
19	G. O'Connor	10	6	6
20	H. Bouazza	9	7	1
21	S. Sinclair	9	5	0
22	N. Hunt	9	2	0
23	D. Johnson	9	0	0
24	N. Quashie	8	2	0
25	M. Nafti	6	5	0
26	C. Costly	3	6	0
27	G. McSheffery	3	3	0
28	D. Traore	2	1	0
29	S. Kelly	1	4	0
30	C. Doyle	1	1	0
31	U. De La Cruz	0	1	0
32	J. Wilson	0	1	0
	Own Goal			1

16.

STEPHEN CARR

– CARLING CUP WINNERS 2010–11

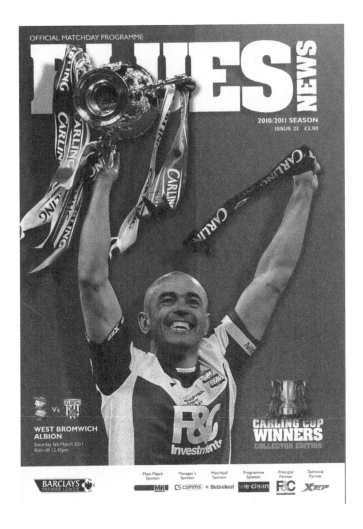

FULL NAME: Stephen Carr.
DATE OF BIRTH: 29 August 1976.
PLACE OF BIRTH: Dublin, Ireland.

PLAYING CAREER:

Youth Career:

Stella Maris – 1991–93, Tottenham Hotspur.

Senior Career:

1993–2004 Tottenham Hotspur 226 appearances 7 goals, 2004–08 Newcastle United 78 appearances 1, goals, 2009–13 Blues 106 appearances 0 goals. Total 410 appearances 8 goals.

International:

1999–2007 Republic of Ireland 44 appearances 0 goals.

As a fifteen-year-old, he went on trial from Stella Maris Football Club where he played his schoolboy football to Tottenham Hotspur and was signed up by then manager Ossie Ardiles. He made his debut for the club on 29 September 1993 away to Ipswich Town in the 1993–94 Premier League season. However he had to wait until the 1996–97 to establish himself as a regular first-team player, when he made 28 appearances that campaign.

He picked up a League Cup medal with Spurs in 1999 after contributing to a 1–0 win over Leicester City in the final. The 1999–2000 season was arguably his best ever as far as his performances are concerned, as well as scoring a 'thunderous piledriver' against champions Manchester United.

His reputation continued to grow throughout the 2000–01 season, and other clubs were beginning to show interest in signing him. However, in the summer of 2001, he began to have problems with his knee and required an operation, which he underwent in September of that year. He did not make any appearances in the 2001–02 season and also missed the 2002 World Cup Finals. It was not until October 2002 that Carr was back, fully fit. As he returned to form, interest from other Premiership clubs started to resurface. Carr was linked with Manchester United, and a move to Newcastle United was on the cards.

Carr signed for Newcastle United in August 2004 when then manager Bobby Robson signed him for a fee of £2 million on a four-year contract. Soon after he signed Robson was sacked from his managerial post by chairman Freddy Shepherd. He was replaced by Graeme Souness, who, like Robson, saw Carr as a first-team player. Carr's debut for the club came in a 2–2 draw against Middlesbrough on 14 August. He played in 26 league games in the 2004–05, scoring once. His first goal for the club came from a 'fierce shot from well outside the area' against Southampton. He helped Newcastle reach the quarter-finals of the UEFA Cup and the semi-final of the FA Cup. Newcastle finished 14th, which put pressure on Souness.

In the 2005–06 season, he only managed to make 19 league appearances for the club as the persistent knee injury ruled him out for two months. The team finished 7th in the league under the new management of Glenn Roeder, after Souness was sacked in January.

Carr was one of the many injury victims during Newcastle's 2006–07 and was out with a fractured foot for a few months. He returned for the 2–2 draw against West Ham United on 20 January 2007, filling in at an unfamiliar left-back position after impressive displays from Nolberto Solano at right-back during Carr's absence, putting question marks over his future at the club. He fell further down the pecking order during the 2007–08 season with the signings of Habib Beye and Geremi. Beye's impressive form and Carr's inability to maintain fitness resulted in Kevin Keegan deciding against renewing Carr's contract and he was released at the end of the season.

Carr was linked with moves to Aston Villa, Everton, West Ham United, Wigan Athletic, Hertha Berlin, Racing Genk and Bohemians. He was also on trial with League One side Leicester City where he would have linked up with Nigel Pearson whom he played under at Newcastle. Having failed to find a suitable club, Carr announced his retirement from all forms of football on 1 December 2008.

In February 2009 he began training with Blues with a view to coming out of retirement, and signed a one-month contract with the club on 23 February. He made his debut the following day, playing the whole of the goalless draw away to Crystal Palace. He quickly became a fans' favourite with his surging runs up the right flank. After impressing during the initial month, Carr signed an extension until the end of the season. Following Birmingham's promotion to the Premier League, Carr signed a new two-year contract with the club. Made acting captain, in the absence through injury and squad rotation of Lee Carsley, he was a member of the Birmingham team that went 15 games unbeaten in all competitions, including a club record 12 unbeaten in the top flight, during the 2009–10 Premier League season. Towards the end of the season Carr received a one-match suspension for improper conduct after making an 'offensive gesture' towards Aston Villa supporters at the end of the local derby lost by Birmingham via a late, controversial penalty.

He captained the team to victory in the 2011 Football League Cup Final as Birmingham defeated favourites Arsenal 2–1 Carr played every game of the 2010–11 Premier League season, at the end of which Birmingham were relegated to the Championship, and the club took up the option of retaining his services for another year.

Carr made his 100th appearance for Birmingham in the Europa League play-off round first leg against Portuguese club Nacional, the first time the club had participated in major European competition for nearly 50 years. He missed much of the second half of the 2011–12 season with knee cartilage damage, and his contract expired in June, but after the appointment of former Newcastle teammate Lee Clark as Birmingham's manager, he signed a one-year deal with the club. Investigation of an injury sustained in a pre-season friendly in August revealed knee damage requiring surgery predicted to keep him out for six months.

Carr was unable to play again, and at the end of the 2012–13 season he announced his retirement from football. Although Clark had hoped to persuade him to stay at Birmingham as a coach, Carr confirmed that he and his family intended to move to Spain where he had business interests.

Carr has represented his country at schoolboy, youth, under-18, under-21 and full international levels.

Carr initially retired from the international scene after the team failed to qualify for the 2006 World Cup, having played 39 times for his country. However he was convinced to continue playing international football by new Ireland manager Steve Staunton. Due to injuries and the sacking of Irish manager Staunton, Carr retired from international football on 14 November 2007.

In the Official Birmingham City Annual 2010 in an article entitled 'CARR IN THE FAST LANE WITH BLUES' the following is reported:

'Blues defender Stephen Carr thought he would have been watching the Premier League on *Match of the Day*. But following a dramatic comeback, the former Republic of Ireland international is now helping Alex McLeish's side try and gain a foothold in the top-flight of English football. Carr is no stranger to the territory after racking up more than 300 Premier League matches for Tottenham Hotspur and Newcastle United. And that experience will be invaluable to the Blues following his surprise arrival at St Andrew's in February. Carr came out of retirement to help McLeish's men to promotion and his performances at right-back were so impressive that he was rewarded with a new two-year contract in the summer. And the Dublin-born defender is delighted to be back in business. "I thought I would be okay, but I really missed playing," Carr admitted. "You think you can walk away from it, but after 17 years and when you are only 33 you realise that there is a lot still there to be done. This was an unbelievable opportunity which I thought would never come around.'

'Alex McLeish said at the time, "His hunger has been superb ever since he arrived. He is a fully motivated player with the kind of quality that counts in the Premier League. He is always positive and says the right things. He has got a winner's attitude".'

Tottenham Hotspur: 226 league appearances (7 goals), 17 FA Cup appearances (0 goals), 23 League Cup appearances (1 goal), 6 European appearances (0 goals). TOTAL 272 appearances (8 goals).

Newcastle United: 78 league appearances (1 goal), 8 FA Cup appearances (0 goals), 1 League Cup appearance (0 goals), 20 European appearances (0 goals). TOTAL 107 appearances (1 goal).

SEASON BY SEASON

SEASON	LEAGUE APPEARANCES/ GOALS	FA CUP APPEARANCES/ GOALS	LEAGUE CUP APPEARANCES/ GOALS	EUROPEAN APPEARANCES/ GOALS
2008–09	13 (0)	0 (0)	0 (0)	0 (0)
2009–10	35 (0)	4 (0)	1 (0)	0 (0)
2010–11	38 (0)	1 (0)	5 (0)	0 (0)
2011–12	20 (0)	1 (0)	0 (0)	3 (0)
2012–13	0 (0)	0 (0)	0 (0)	0 (0)

Birmingham City: 106 League appearances (0 goals), 6 FA Cup appearances (0 goals), 6 League Cup appearances (0 goals), 3 European appearances (0 goals). TOTAL 121 appearances (0 goals).

Career Total: l 410 League appearances (8 goals), 31 FA Cup appearances (0 goals), 30 League Cup appearances (1 goal), 29 European appearances (0 goals). TOTAL 500 appearances (9 goals).

HONOURS

As a Player:
- Tottenham Hotspur Football League Cup 1999.
- Newcastle United UEFA Intertoto Cup 2006.
- Birmingham City Football League Cup 2011.

Individual honours;

Premier League PFA Team of the Year 2001–02 and 2002–03.

Tottenham Hotspur Members Club Player of the Year: 1999 and 2000.

What makes Carr such a great captain?

It takes a special captain to inspire his team to victory with the odds stacked against them. To do that in a League Cup Final, having bounced back from retirement and injury, is something else. When Stephen Carr came to Blues he was out of shape and out of practice, but determination helped him go from trialist to conquering club skipper.

What was his defining moment as skipper?

For me it was Carr roaring the crowd to, 'Come On' after the final whistle of the 2011 Carling Cup Final victory over Arsenal. He'd earlier etched his name into City folklore by taunting a whole stand of Aston Villa fans with a choice hand gesture – even if it did cost him a one-match ban.

Carr retired from professional football citing persistent knee problems as the main reason for his decision. In season 2013–14 all the Blues' fans saw of him was him warming up for the first match of the season! He originally announced his retirement in 2008 when he released by Newcastle United, but he went on to captain Blues to League Cup success – an amazing story He told the Blues' website that his knee was getting to the stage where he could no longer continue playing. 'I am going on 37 and now is the time to bow out,' he said. 'I felt OK in pre-season but unfortunately my knee just crumbled away. It was unfortunate for me and the club. We knew there was a chance something could happen, but we didn't think it would be that early. It just wasn't meant to be in the end. The fans have been brilliant with me since I came in and I have had a great relationship with them. I will never forget that day lifting the cup. It was a big, big thing for me.' The defender has undergone three operations on his knee problem in 18 months and leaves a Birmingham side that narrowly missed out on the Championship play-off places this season.

'CARR – THE DRIVING FORCE'

During season 2008–09 Birmingham City were in The Championship and not enjoying their 'yo-yo' club description even though their record since the start of the Millennium meant it was well deserved:

So 'yo-yo' they were but the title of 'nearly men' would certainly have applied in the early part of the twenty-first century.

1999–00 we finished fifth behind Champions, Charlton Athletic to lose to Barnsley in the Play-Offs.

2000–01 we finished fifth behind Champions, Fulham to lose to Preston North End in the Play-Offs.

2001–02 we finished fifth behind Champions, Manchester City to beat Norwich City on penalties at the Millennium Stadium.

In 2002–03 we finished thirteenth in the Premier League gaining 48 points in 38 games and finishing two places above Aston Villa.

In 2003–04 we finished tenth in the Premier League gaining 50 points in 38 games.

In 2004–05 we finished twelfth in the Premier League gaining 45 points in 38 games.

In 2005–06 we finished eighteenth in the Premier League gaining 34 points from 38 games and were relegated along with West Bromwich Albion and Sunderland.

In 2006–07 we finished second in the Championship gaining 86 points from 46 games and were promoted as runners-up to Champions, Sunderland.

In 2007–08 we finished eighteenth in the Premier League gaining 35 points from 38 games and were relegated along with Derby County who only secured eleven points throughout the season.

In 2008–09 we finished second in the Championship gaining 83 points from 46 games and were promoted as runners-up to Champions, Wolverhampton Wanderers.

In 2009–10 we finished ninth in the Premier League, the Blues' highest finish in the top division since we finished sixth in 1955–56 season, gaining 50 points from 38 games.

In 2010–2011 our Premier League status is secure with 42 points gained in 38 games left Blues in fourteenth place. But there were distractions:

27 February 2011 we beat Arsenal at Wembley to win the Carling Cup (League Cup), which was our first major trophy since 1963!

16 April 2011 we lost to Manchester United in the semi-final of the FA Cup that was played at Wembley, although we missed out on a second Wembley Final by 3–1, the Bluenoses took over the North London venue in terms of volume of support for the second time in a season!

So what was the catalyst to bring about such a change in the fortunes of the sleeping giant of the second city in the land?

It was diminutive Irishman with an unquenchable thirst for the game and a resolute attitude to never accepting defeat.

That man was Stephen Carr.

DETAILS OF SUCCESS
CARLING LEAGUE CUP FINAL

27 February 2011

This is the day Bluenoses have been waiting for; the last time we were at Wembley was in 1994 and the last time we won a major trophy was 1963.

But this is 2011, it's the new Wembley, the League Cup is a passage to European competition and the Blues are a Premier League side.

But would the result be any different? Could we beat the Arsenal who are competing in four competitions; The Premier League, The Champions League, The FA Cup and The League Cup? The bookies think not as the Gunners are odds on favourites and a 2–1 win for the Blues is 22 to 1.

My journey began on Thursday 24 when I finally held in my hands my ticket for the Carling Cup Final at Wembley. Entrance K Section 501 Row 4 Seat 8. On the halfway line, next to the Arsenal fans and a bargain at £86. The morning of the match arrived and I wore not only my home shirt (with long sleeves), but my scarf from the Millennium Stadium Worthington Cup Final in 2001. As I joined the queue for Platform One at Solihull station for the 11.22 train, I saw Malcolm Page and Alan Campbell in amongst the excited Bluenoses as the rain came down. Upon arrival it was into the Ibis Hotel for shelter and a drink but it struck me that many of the Brummies outside in the rain were unlikely to see the end of the game in anything other than a drunken stupor. Well it is sponsored by a major lager brand!

As I made my way towards the stadium from the hotel the burning of an Arsenal scarf had brought the unwelcome attention of the police. After fish 'n chips Wembley style (how do they manage to take out the natural taste of the fish and the chips?) I settled down to watch the pre-match activities. A passionate video about Birmingham generated a huge response from the west end of the stadium that was well populated an hour before the kick off in direct contrast to the east seats where there were very few occupants. Still I guess they only had a six-mile walk from the Emirates stadium!

The team was announced and McLeish's game plan was revealed: a five man midfield with Zigic upfront alone. Blues played like every Bluenose hoped they would – with energy, commitment and a dogged belief that today could be their day to be awarded the title of 'Modern Day Heroes'.

The game was 'kicked off' when Bowyer was fouled in the penalty area only to be ruled off-side, which was later proved to be an erroneous decision. Larsson's corner was met by Johnson and Zigic out jumped the Arsenal defenders to deflect the ball into the net – Blues were winning 1–0! It was inevitable that the Gunners would equalise and sure enough Van Persie scored. The fact that Arsenal had also hit the woodwork in the first 45 minutes did not bode well for the second period. Although Arsenal increased the pressure in the second half Ben Foster proved his 'England Number One' claim with a succession of saves and stops and it was Fahey who hit the woodwork. Then with a few minutes left the unbelievable happened, a mix up between Laurent Koscielny and Wojciech Szczensy resulted in the ball dropping at the feet of Martins and Blues were 2–1 up.

When the final whistle went I felt stunned! There is no other way to describe it.

For all my time as a Bluenose I have been programmed for 'defeat and disappointment'; when we took the lead the equaliser was expected – as full-time approached I was saying to myself. 'Well at least we've not been humiliated' – 'It will be like 2001 a meaningless extra-time period and defeat in the penalty shoot-out', so when the winner went in, I was stunned! After all those years of disappointment the Blues had won some-thing – The League Cup and no one could deny that they deserved it!!

Team: Foster, Carr, Johnson, Jiranek, Ridgewell, Larsson, Ferguson, Gardner (Beausejour 50), Bowyer, Fahey (Martins 83), Zigic (Jerome 90 +2).

Substitutes not used: Taylor, Murphy, Phillips, Parnaby.

Bookings: Larsson (Dissent 41), Jerome (Time wasting 90 + 4), Ferguson (Time wasting 90 + 5).

Goalscorers: Zigic 28 minutes, Martins 89 minutes.

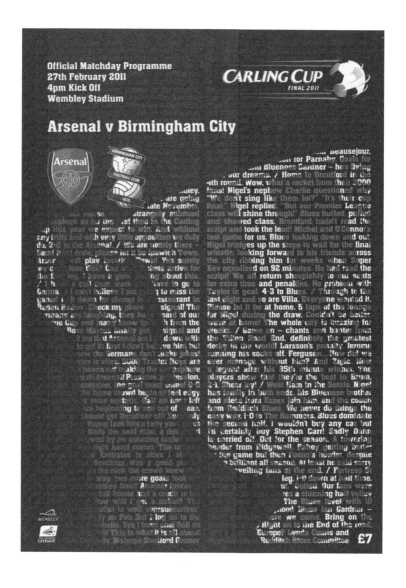

Carling Cup Winners 2010-2011)

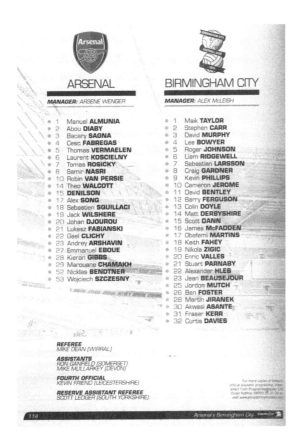

2010–2011 Carling Cup Final Line-Ups

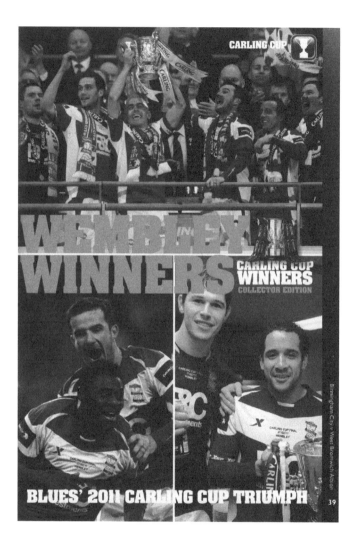

THE ROAD TO WEMBLEY

Round 2, Thursday 26 August 2010 versus ROCHDALE (H) won 3–2. Crowd: 6,431.

Team: Taylor (Maik), Fahey, Murphy, Dann, Johnson, Valles (Redmond 76), Michel, Bowyer, McFadden (Larsson 46), Derbyshire (Zigic 65), O'Connor.

Goalscorers: McFadden (28 penalty), Murphy (48), Derbyshire (53).

Round 3, Tuesday 21 September 2010 versus MK DONS (H) won 3–1. Crowd: 9,450.

Team: Taylor, Parnaby, Murphy, Johnson, Jiranek, Helb (Phillips 66), Michel (Gardner 23), Fahey, Beausejour (Valles 58), Zigic, Derbyshire.
Goalscorers: Hleb (22), Zigic (26), Gardner (28).

Round 4, Tuesday 26 October 2010 versus BRENTFORD (H) drew 1–1. Crowd: 15,166.

Won 4–3 on penalties after extra-time.

Team: Taylor, Ridgewell, Carr, Dann, Parnaby, Bowyer, Gardner, Michel (Ferguson 91), Derbyshire (Zigic 77), Phillips, O'Connor (Redmond 64).
Goalscorer: Phillips (90 + 2).

Round 5, Wednesday 1ᵗ December 2010 versus ASTON VILLA (H) won 2–1. Crowd: 27,679.

Team: Foster, Ridgewell, Carr, Dann, Johnson, Bowyer (Gardner 65), Fahey, Larsson (Murphy 88), Ferguson, Jerome, Zigic (Derbyshire 89).
Goalscorers: Larsson (12 penalty), Zigic (84).

Semi-Final First Leg, Tuesday 11 January 2011 versus WEST HAM UNITED (A) lost 1–2. Crowd: 29,034.

Team: Foster, Ridgewell, Carr, Johnson, Dann (Murphy 46), Larsson (Zigic 87), Ferguson, Gardner, Fahey, Hleb (Beausejour 83), Jerome.
Goalscorer: Ridgewell (56).

Semi-Final Second Leg, Wednesday 26 January 2011 versus WEST HAM UNITED (H) won 3–1 after extra-time. Crowd: 27,519.

Team: Foster, Carr, Ridgewell, Jiranek, Johnson, Larsson (Beausejour 101), Gardner (Murphy 101), Ferguson, Jerome, Derbyshire (Zigic Half Time), Bowyer.

Goalscorers: Bowyer (59), Johnson (79), Gardner (94).

BLUES WON 4–3 ON AGGREGATE!!!

WHO DID WHAT?

Player	Starts	Substitutes	Goals
Taylor	3	0	0
Fahey	5	0	0
Murphy	2	3	1
Dann	4	0	0
Johnson	6	0	1
Valles	1	1	0
Redmond	0	2	0
Michel	3	0	0
Bowyer	5	0	1
McFadden	1	0	1
Larsson	4	1	1
Derbyshire	4	1	1
Zigic	3	4	3
O'Connor	2	0	0
Parnaby	2	0	0
Jiranek	3	0	0
Helb	2	0	1
Phillips	1	1	1
Gardner	4	2	2

Beausejour	1	3	0
Ridgewell	5	0	1
Carr	5	0	0
Ferguson	4	1	0
Foster	4	0	0
Jerome	3	1	0
Martins	0	1	1

MATCH REPORT

From *The Guardian.*

If Birmingham City held one advantage over Arsenal it lay in the art of endurance. A side striving not to fall out of the Premier League reached a peak in their history by defeating opponents who took far too long to discover impetus in this Carling Cup Final. After 89 minutes, the substitute Obafemi Martins thrived on hapless defending to notch the winner. Alex McLeish's side had brought the club their first trophy since taking this prize in 1963.

Arsenal's defects warrant prolonged examination, but the real priority is to salute Birmingham. They are inferior in almost every respect to Arsène Wenger's team, as the 3–0 loss to them at St Andrew's in January emphasised, yet their powers of endurance were remarkable and not only for the saves that Ben Foster produced when Arsenal seemed bound for the winner.

There was a boldness to Birmingham, who understood that a Cup Final is not to be wasted by cowering in the hope that luck comes your way. Nikola Zigic may have been the man who most caused disquiet to the opposition. The Serb had scored only seven goals before this occasion, but he exposed the unsatisfactory defending of Arsenal and, in particular, of the centre-half Laurent Koscielny.

The Frenchman made a ruinous nuisance of himself with a minute remaining. Koscielny moved as if to kick a long ball from Foster and distracted his goalkeeper Wojciech Szczesny. He then let possession spill to the Nigerian Martins, who came to Birmingham last month on loan from the Russian club Rubin Kazan. No matter how brief his stay in the Midlands turns out to be, he has a permanent place in the memory of every Birmingham supporter. Arsenal, for their part, were co-conspirators in this result. After six years without a trophy, it is impossible to believe they were complacent. It is more likely that we were witnessing nervousness as they rolled the ball around to very limited effect in the first half. There were intimations even then of vulnerability in the ranks.

Zigic regularly highlighted that. He not only scored the opener, but should have added to it. After 28 minutes, Sebastian Larsson put a corner towards the fringes of the penalty area and Roger Johnson got the better of Koscielny to nod the ball into the goalmouth, where the Serb diverted the ball into the net with his head. Arsenal's apprehension was marked well before that. Although they were behind then, the situation might have been far worse. Szczensy would have been sent off in the second minute for bringing down Lee Bowyer, following a pass from Zigic, had it not been for the mistake by the assistant referee Ron Garfield in raising the flag for offside. McLeish's side showed a desire to seize the opportunity, while Arsenal lost track of where they were and why.

This may have been the least of the four prizes that Wenger's side were pursuing, but there will be further misery if they continue to be so brittle. Arsenal might as well have been out to illustrate every defect that is suspected in them. So it was that tension prevented them from showing fluency. Birmingham were close to recording their second goal much earlier in the second half, when a Keith Fahey shot came back off the crossbar.

It was to be expected that McLeish's men would raise their game. There was nothing to fear when almost everyone had taken it for granted that they would fall to inevitable defeat. The side's great feat was to believe in themselves for so long. There was nothing that resembled an Arsenal onslaught until well into the second half. When Arsenal at last achieved impetus, there was a string of saves from Foster, particularly when Samir

Nasri and then the substitute Nicklas Bendtner forced him into action. At that stage in the second half, Arsenal might well have achieved total command.

Instead they drifted away from a target that seemed well within reach. That should be at least as disquieting to Wenger as the fact that a prize has eluded him. The side's focus and standard of play were both prone to being blurred. It would have been better for Wenger if Cesc Fábregas and Theo Walcott had not been absent through injury, and many could have anticipated there would also be a craving for the presence of the defender Thomas Vermaelen, who has been absent for almost all of this season. Birmingham behaved from the outset as if every player had been convinced by McLeish that there was glory to be had if they attacked the Arsenal central defence with confidence.

There might have been a second goal for Zigic, who displayed zest and mobility that had been well disguised on other occasions. Birmingham could have extended the lead 11 minutes from the interval. Jack Wilshere's challenge on Craig Gardner merely knocked the ball to the Serb, but he did not connect properly and Szczesny blocked without difficulty.

Arsenal may attempt to trick themselves into thinking that nothing of real worth has escaped. There are greater honours to be sought, but this was an outcome to plant new doubts in men who were starting to develop faith in themselves. The immediate priority is to inch back to normality by beating Leyton Orient on Wednesday. The requirement for a replay in that FA Cup came with an 89th minute leveller for the League One team.

We should appreciate then that this continues to be an Arsenal team in the shadow of their prolonged fallibility. The weeks to come do, of course, include the return with Barcelona in the Champions League. There is much that could go wrong and Arsenal have heightened the apprehension by falling to admirable Birmingham.

17.

PLAYER – CAPTAIN – MANAGER

Although never achieving success for the club as captains, Arthur Turner, Garry Pendrey and Steve Bruce have a unique place in the history of Birmingham City Football Club having served the Blues as player, captain and manager. (Note: Kevan Broadhurst had one game in 1993 as joint caretaker manager which was lost).

How well did they perform as manager:

ARTHUR TURNER;

November 1954 to February 1958.
Played 166 games, won 74, drew 35 and lost 57 resulting in a win percentage of 44.6%.

With Pat Beasley:
February 1958 to September 1958.
Played 17 games, won 6, drew 5, and lost 6, resulting in a win percentage of 35.3%.

GARRY PENDREY;

May 1987 to April 1989.
Played 98 games, won 20, drew 27 and lost 57, resulting in a win percentage of 20.4%.

STEVE BRUCE;

December 2001 to November 2007.

Played 270 games, won 100, drew 70 and lost 100, resulting in a win percentage of 37%.

ARTHUR OWEN TURNER

DATE OF BIRTH: 1 April 1909.

PLACE OF BIRTH: Chesterton Staffordshire.

DATE OF DEATH: 12 January 1994.

PLACE OF DEATH: Sheffield at the age of 84.

PLAYING CAREER:

Youth Career:

Downing Tileries, Woolstanton PSA, 1929–1930 West Bromwich Albion.

Senior Career:

1930–39 Stoke City 290 appearances 17 goals. 1939–48 Blues 39 appearances 0 goals. 1948 Southport 28 appearances 0 goals. TOTAL 357 appearances 17 goals.

He made his league debut on 4 February 1939 at home v Charlton Athletic in a 3–4 defeat with Fred Harris hitting a hat-trick in front of 29,727.

In 1939–40 26 appearances in the Midland Regional League and League Cup.

1940–41 3 appearances in League (South) First and Second Championships and League (South) Cup.

1941-42 No Competitions.

1942–43 32 appearances and 1 goal in League (North) First and Second Championships and League (North) Cup.

1943–44 32 appearances in League (North) First and Second Championships and League (North) and Midland Cup.

1944–45 39 appearances and 1 goal in League (North) First and Second Championships and League (North) and Midland Cup.

1945–46 40 appearances and 2 goals in Football League (South) and FA Cup;

Management:

1948 Southport (player-manager).

1948–51 Crewe Alexandra.

1951–53 Stoke City (assistant manager).

1954–58 Birmingham City.

1959–69 Headington United/Oxford United.

He won the Second Division championship in 1954-55 led them the following season to the 1956 FA Cup Final and their highest ever top flight finish, and became the first man to manage an English club side in European competition when he took the club to the semi-final of the Inter-Cities Fairs Cup in 1958. Turner went on to manage the transformation of Southern League club club Headington United into Oxford United of the Second Division of the Football League.

Following a spell as an amateur with West Bromwich Albion, he signed professional forms for local club Stoke City in 1930. He was a strong defensive half-back, good in the air and on the ground, reliable and influential. He won a Second Division championship medal with Stoke in the 1932-33 season; the club history described him as one of "the real bedrocks" of the promotion side. He was appointed captain of Stoke, in a side that included Stanley Matthews, and in all competitions played over 300 games for the club. In 1939 he was sold to Blues for a fee of £6,000.

His contribution in his first few months at Birmingham was not enough to prevent their relegation from the First Division, and the suspension of league football later that year for the duration of the Second World War seriously disrupted his career. He was 30 when war was declared. During the war Turner played nearly 200 games for Birmingham, captaining them to the championship of the wartime Football League South and to the semi-final of the first post-war FA Cup

In 1948 Turner joined Southport of the Third Division North as player-manager, he played his last game in October 1948 at the age of 39. He was appointed manager of Crewe Alexandra in October 1948 and stayed there for three years, returning to Stoke City as assistant manager in December 1951 under first Bob McGrory and then Frank Taylor.

In November 1954 Turner replaced Bob Brocklebank as manager of former club Blues. When he joined, the club lay 12th in the Second Division, with one away win to their name; in the rest of the season they lost only once more away from home. They scored 92 league goals, their best goal return since the 19th century, with all five first choice forwards reaching double figures, inflicted a club record 9–1 defeat on Liverpool and confirmed themselves as champions with a 5–1 win away at Doncaster Rovers.

Birmingham City's official history rated 1955–56 as the club's best season to date. Turner led the team he inherited to their highest league finish, sixth place in the First Division, only four points off runners-up spot. They reached the 1956 FA Cup Final, losing to Manchester City 3–1. The following year he led them to the FA Cup semi-final, only to lose to Manchester United. Also in 1956, Turner became the first manager to take an English club side into European competition when Birmingham City represented the city of Birmingham in the inaugural Inter-Cities Fairs Cup. They reached the semi-final, going out to eventual winners Barcelona in a replay on a neutral ground after the original tie had finished 4–4 on aggregate.

His record in the transfer market was sound. He brought in England under-23 international Dick Neal to replace Len Boyd, bought wingers Harry Hooper and future England player Mike Hellawell, and gave their first professional contracts to youngsters Malcolm Beard and Colin Withers.

In January 1958, Pat Beasley joined the club; Beasley had believed he was coming as Turner's assistant, but chairman Harry Morris announced to the press that he was to be appointed joint manager. Turner, who found out about this arrangement not from the club but from the press, threatened to resign; he was persuaded to stay 'for the time being', but finally left in September 1958.

Oxford United's club website pinpoints the appointment of Turner as manager of the then Southern League side Headington United as a turning point in the club's history. He joined on New Year's Day 1959. Not long afterwards, First Division club Leeds United approached him to take over as their manager; though favourite to take the job, the Headington directors matched Leeds' salary offer, and Turner chose to stay.

There was no automatic promotion into the Football League in those days; clubs had to be elected, and the likelihood of election depended largely on how the chairmen of other league clubs perceived them. That year, Turner persuaded the directors to change the name of the club to Oxford United, to increase public awareness of the club and to broaden its appeal. Turner's management brought two Southern League titles in two years, and when Accrington Stanley went bankrupt in 1962, Oxford United took their place in the Fourth Division of the Football League.

Two years later Turner's team eliminated Blackburn Rovers, who at the time lay second in the First Division, in the fifth round of the FA Cup. They thus became the first Fourth Division side to reach the sixth round. In 1964–65, he led them to promotion from the Fourth Division, and three years later to the championship of the Third. By this time the young players who had been the mainstay of Oxford's rise through the divisions were ageing or retired. Turner had no money to strengthen the side for its Second Division campaign, and struggled with what he had. In April 1969, he became General Manager of the club, leaving the running of the team to Ron Saunders, and in February 1972 he was dismissed when the club admitted they were unable to afford to keep him in post.

Turner remained active in football into the 1980s. He was employed as a scout for Rotherham United and Sheffield Wednesday.

Stoke City: 312 appearances 17 goals.
Southport: 28 appearances 0 goals.
Birmingham City: 56 appearances 0 goals.
TOTAL: 393 appearances 17 goals.

SEASON BY SEASON

SEASON	LEAGUE APPEARANCES/GOALS	FA CUP APPEARANCES/GOALS
1938–39	12 (0)	0 (0)
1945–46	0 (0)	12 (0)
1946–47	27 (0)	4 (0)

HONOURS

As a Player:

- Stoke City – Second Division Champions 1933.
- Birmingham City – Football League South Champions 1946.

As a Manager:

- Birmingham City – Second Division Champions 1955, FA Cup Runners Up 1956.
- Headington United/Oxford United – Southern League Runners Up 1960, Southern League. Champions 1961 – Fourth Division promotion 1965, Third Division Champions 1968.

GARRY JAMES SIDNEY PENDREY

DATE OF BIRTH: 9 February 1949.
PLACE OF BIRTH: Birmingham.

PLAYING CAREER:

Youth Career:

1965–66 Birmingham City.

Senior Career:

1966–1979 Blues 306 appearances 4 goals.

1979–81 West Bromwich Albion 18 appearances 0 goals.

1981 Torquay United 12 appearances 0 goals.

1981–82 Bristol Rovers 1 appearance 0 goals.

1982–83 Walsall 8 appearances 1 goal.

Management:

1987–89 Blues.

In 2012, Pendrey was one of seven former players elected to Birmingham City's Hall of Fame – his claim to fame being the Blues' youngest ever captain.

He signed for Blues in 1965 as an apprentice, before agreeing professional terms in October 1966. He played for the club until 1979, making 360 appearances in all competitions and scoring five goals.

After retiring from playing in 1983, Pendrey became a coach at Walsall. Working alongside manager Alan Buckley he helped coach the team to the League Cup semi-final in 1984. In 1986, Pendrey was replaced when Walsall was sold to a new owner, Terry Ramsden. He spent a few months on the coaching staff at Wolverhampton Wanderers before returning to Birmingham as manager in June 1987. With a dwindling squad and no money to spend on replacements, Pendrey was fighting a losing battle. In April 1989, with relegation to the Third Division for the first time in the club's history confirmed, the new owners sacked him and appointed Dave Mackay as manager. Pendrey refused the offer of a coaching role, and rejoined Wolves instead.

When Gordon Strachan become manager of Coventry City in November 1996, Pendrey was appointed his assistant. When Strachan departed in 2001, Pendrey left the club also, only for them to reunite as manager and assistant at Southampton on 22 October 2002.

On 1 June 2005, Pendrey joined Glasgow Celtic as Strachan's assistant manager.

After the resignation of Gordon Strachan on 25 May 2009, Pendrey left Celtic from his role as assistant manager. He was replaced by the new Celtic assistant manager Mark Venus who joined from West Bromwich Albion after the appointment of Tony Mowbray as Celtic's new manager

On 26 October 2009, Strachan was appointed the new Middlesbrough manager in succession to Gareth Southgate after he was sacked. Garry joined Strachan as Middlesbrough assistant manager.

STEPHEN ROGER BRUCE

DATE OF BIRTH: 31 December 1960.

PLACE OF BIRTH: Corbridge, Northumberland.

PLAYING CAREER:

Youth Career:

1977–79 Gillingham.

Senior Career:

1979–84, Gillingham 205 appearances 29 goals.

1984–87, Norwich City 141 appearances 14 goals.

1987–96 Manchester United 309 appearances 36 goals.

1996–98 Birmingham City 72 appearances 2 goals.

1998–99 Sheffield United 10 appearances 0 goals. Total 737 appearances 81 goals.

International:

1979–80 England Youth 8 appearances 0 goals.

1987 England B 1 appearances 0 goals.

Management:

1998–99 Sheffield United.

1999–2000 Huddersfield Town.

2001 Wigan Athletic.

2001 Crystal Palace.

2001–07 Blues.

2007–09 Wigan Athletic.

2009–11 Sunderland.

2012– To date Hull City

He was a promising schoolboy footballer but was rejected by a number of professional clubs. He was on the verge of quitting the game altogether when he was offered a trial with Gillingham. Bruce was offered an apprenticeship and went on to play more than 200 games for the club before joining Norwich City in 1984.

In 1987, he moved to Manchester United with whom he achieved great success, winning the Premier League, FA Cup, League Cup and European Cup Winners Cup. He also became the first English player of the twentieth century to captain a team to The Double. Bruce began his managerial career with Sheffield United, and spent short periods of time managing Huddersfield Town, Wigan Athletic and Crystal Palace before joining Blues in 2001. He twice led Birmingham to promotion to the Premier League during his tenure of nearly six years, but resigned in 2007 to begin a second spell as manager of Wigan. At the end of the 2008–09 he resigned to take over as manager of Sunderland, a post he held until he was dismissed in November 2011. Seven months later, he was appointed manager of Hull City.

The elder of the two sons of Joe and Sheenagh Bruce. Joe was a local, but his mother had been born in Bangor in Northern Ireland. The family lived in Daisy Hill near Wallsend and Bruce attended Benfield School

Bruce, a boyhood fan of Newcastle United, claims to have sneaked into St James' Park without paying to watch the team play, saying, 'I have always been a Newcastle lad and when I was a kid, I crawled under the turnstiles to get in to try and save a bob or whatever it was. They were my team, I went to support them as a boy and being a Geordie it's in-bred, you follow the club still the same today.' Like a number of other future professionals from the area, he played football for Wallsend Boys Club. He was also selected for the Newcastle Schools representative team, and at the age of 13 was among a group of players from the team selected to serve as ball boys at the 1974 Football League Cup Final at Wembley Stadium.

Having been turned down by a number of professional clubs, including Newcastle United, Sunderland, Derby County and Southport, Bruce was about to start work as an apprentice plumber at the Swan Hunter dockyard when he was offered a trial by Third Division club Gillingham whose manager Gerry Summers had seen him playing for Wallsend in an international youth tournament. He travelled down to Kent with another player from the Wallsend club named Peter Beardsley, but although Gillingham signed Bruce as an apprentice, they turned Beardsley away. At the time Bruce was playing as a midfielder, but he was switched to the centre of defence by the head of Gillingham's youth scheme, Bill 'Buster' Collins whom Bruce cites as the single biggest influence on his career.

Bruce spent the 1978–79 in Gillingham's reserve team and, despite playing in defence, scored 18 goals to finish the season as top scorer. In January 1979, he was selected to represent the England Youth team, and he went on to gain eight caps, participating in the 1980 European Under-18 Championship. He came close to making his debut for the club's senior team in May 1979, but Summers decided at the last minute that, as Gillingham were chasing promotion from the Third Division, Bruce was not yet ready to handle the pressure of the occasion. He eventually made his senior debut in a Football League Cup tie against Luton Town on 11 August 1979 and made an immediate impact in the team, winning the club's Player of the Year award at the end of the 1979–80 season. He went on to make more than 200 appearances for the club, and was twice voted into the Professional Footballers' Association's Third Division Team of the Year.

Confident that he was being targeted by clubs from higher divisions, Bruce resolved not to sign a new contract with Gillingham when his existing deal expired at the end of the 1983–84. In an April 1983 match against Newport County he attempted, in a moment of anger, to deliberately injure opposition player Tommy Tynan, but connected awkwardly and succeeded only in breaking his own leg, leaving him unable to play again for six months. Arthur Cox, manager of Bruce's beloved Newcastle United, expressed an interest in signing the player, but resigned from his job before any further action could be taken. Bruce eventually opted to sign for Norwich City in August 1984 for a fee variously reported as between £125,000 and £135,000.

Bruce began the 1984–85 season by scoring an own goal in the first minute of his debut for Norwich against Liverpool but went on to score the team's winning goal in the semi-final of the Football League Cup against local rivals Ipswich Town and was named man of the match in Norwich's victory in the Final. Norwich City were relegated to the Second Division and Bruce played in every match as Norwich won promotion back to the top division at the first time of asking in the 1985–86 season after which he was chosen to replace the departing Dave Watson as club captain The following season he helped the club to its highest ever league finish of fifth position.

In 1987, he was chosen to captain the England B team in a match against the full national team of Malta, but it was to be his only appearance in an England shirt, and he has subsequently been described as one of the best defenders of his era never to be selected for the full England national team. Bruce began to attract the attention of big-name clubs in late 1987, Manchester United quickly emerged as the front-runners for his signature, and Bruce publicly expressed his desire to sign for the club. The deal came close to collapsing when Norwich asked for a transfer fee of £900,000 after initially agreeing to accept £800,000, leading to Bruce refusing to play any further matches for the club, which he felt was jeopardising his dream move. On 17 December 1987, however, shortly before his 27th birthday, the deal was finally concluded and Bruce officially left Carrow Road for a fee reported between £800,000 and £825,000. Bruce made his Manchester United debut in a 2–1 win over Portsmouth on 19 December 1987, and played in 21 of United's remaining 22 league fixtures, helping the club to a top two place in the First Division for the first time since 1980. The team could only finish in mid-table the following season, however, prompting manager Alex Ferguson to bring in a number of new players, including Gary Pallister, who joined the club in August 1989 from Middlesbrough. His partnership with Bruce in the centre of defence was described in 2006 by the then United captain, Gary Neville, as the best in the club's history. Bruce and Pallister were part of the team which won the 1990 FA Cup Final against Crystal Palace in a replay.

Following the lifting of the five-year ban on English clubs from European competitions, which had been imposed after the Heysel affair, United became England's first entrants into the UEFA Cup Winners Cup Competition in the 1990–91 Bruce played regularly, and scored three goals, in the team's progress to the final against FC Barcelona, United winning 2–1. Injuries took their toll upon Bryan Robson during the 1992–93 season which lead to Bruce captaining the team in the majority of United's matches during the first season of the new Premier League he and Robson received the trophy jointly after the home victory over Blackburn Rovers on 3 May.

He joined First Division club Blues on a free transfer at the age of 35 having signed a contract valued at nearly £2 million over two years, which made him one of the highest-paid players in the country.

Bruce was among five former Premier League players signed by Birmingham manager Trevor Francis to add experience to a squad expected to challenge for promotion. He was made captain of the team, but his Birmingham career was dogged by a series of disagreements with Francis. Director David Sullivan felt the need to publicly deny rumours that Bruce was lined up to replace Francis as manager after the club's stock market flotation. The 1997–98 season saw Bruce dropped for the first time in his career, for a match against former club Gillingham, and he described himself as 'hurt and unhappy' at being left out. By November 1997 he was being left out more frequently, and his omission against Nottingham Forest provoked a public war of words, which fuelled rumours that the manager was to be dismissed and that Bruce would take over as caretaker until the end of the season. At the end of the season he accepted the post of player-manager at Sheffield United. Though the deal was delayed while Birmingham attempted to negotiate a transfer fee for his playing contract, he took up his new position on 2 July 1998. He played eleven matches for the club before retiring as a player.

SEASON BY SEASON

SEASON	LEAGUE APPEARANCES/ GOALS	FA CUP APPEARANCES/ GOALS	LEAGUE CUP APPEARANCES/ GOALS
1996–97	32 (0)	3 (1)	4
1997-98	40 (2)	3 (0)	2

Although his Crystal Palace team began the 2001–02 season strongly, topping the First Division table and looking well placed for regaining the Premier League place that the club had last held in the 1997–98 season Bruce tendered his resignation less than three months into the season in order to return to Birmingham City as manager. Although he was initially prevented from doing so by an injunction taken out by Crystal Palace, he was eventually allowed to join the Midlands-based club after a compensation package was agreed. By now he had acquired a reputation as a manager who rarely held down a job for a significant length of time.

Upon his arrival, the Blues were in a mid-table position in the First Division, but a lengthy unbeaten run saw the team qualify for the play-offs. The team went on to beat Bruce's former club Norwich City in the final after a penalty shoot-out to gain promotion to the Premier League, ending a 16-year absence from the top level of English football. The following season began well for Birmingham, who climbed as high as fourth in the table, but the team's fortunes declined and they could only finish in tenth place at the end of the season. Despite this disappointment, Bruce signed a new contract in June 2004 designed to keep him at St Andrew's for a further five years, but just two months later Freddy Shepherd, chairman of Newcastle United, was reported to have made Bruce his main target in the search for a new manager to replace Bobby Robson. The club was reportedly prepared to pay Birmingham more than £3 million in compensation, and Bruce himself was said to be keen to take over at St James' Park, but he ultimately remained at Birmingham. He stated that, 'as far as I'm concerned, I've got a job to do [at Birmingham City] and I'm determined to get on with it', but it was also reported that Newcastle would have been required to pay a much larger compensation fee or face legal action had he been persuaded to switch clubs. Three years later Birmingham director David Sullivan publicly stated that the club had 'priced Steve out of a move to Newcastle' and gave the level of compensation, which would have been involved as £7 million. Initial expectations were high for the 2004–05 season, but the club once again finished in a mid-table position, ending the season in 12th place.

In the 2005–06, Birmingham were struggling in the league, and on 21 March 2006 were beaten 7–0 at home by Liverpool in the FA Cup quarter-finals. Some supporters of the club began to call for his resignation, but Bruce insisted that he would fight on as manager. The team managed to climb out of the relegation zone for the first time in nearly six months after a win over Bolton Wanderers in early April, but were soon overtaken by Portsmouth, whose victory over Wigan Athletic on 29 April left Birmingham mathematically unable to match their points total and were therefore relegated.

Although Bruce had the largest transfer budget in the division made available to him, Birmingham made a slow start to the 2006–07 season in the Football League Championship and, after a 1–0 defeat at home to Norwich City, the team's fifth consecutive match without a win, there were calls from fans and local journalists for the manager to be sacked. Bruce publicly accepted responsibility for the team's poor run and admitted that he feared for his job, but the team responded with a 1–0 victory over Derby County and then recorded a further five consecutive league victories to be joint leaders of the league table by late November. On 29 April 2007, Birmingham secured promotion to the Premier League, with one match to play, by virtue of Derby County's 2–0 defeat at Crystal Palace. Chairman David Gold told the press, 'There have been some dark days but Steve has been outstanding. He was determined to bounce back. He has rebuilt the team and now we are all back where we want to be.'

In May 2007, Birmingham's board agreed a new contract for Bruce, but the unwillingness of the club's prospective purchaser Carson Yeung to ratify it left his future uncertain. In October 2007, Bolton Wanderers were refused permission to speak to him about their managerial vacancy. Later that month, Bruce and Yeung held a meeting, which reportedly had positive results. However, Bruce later claimed that Birmingham's then Managing Director Karren Brady had 'shafted' him on a new contract with the club, and when Wigan Athletic requested permission to speak to Bruce about their managerial vacancy, he was receptive to their approach. As required under the terms of his contract, Wigan agreed to pay Birmingham compensation for the loss of his services of around £3m, and they were then allowed to speak to him. On 19 November, Wigan announced the signing of Bruce for a second time.

On 21 November, during a press conference which was intended to formally present Bruce as the new manager of Wigan, the club's chief executive Brenda Spencer informed the media that the deal had been put on hold by 'unknown issues' between Bruce and Birmingham City, reported to centre on the advance payment of the image rights element of Bruce's contract. On 23 November 2007, however, Wigan announced that Bruce had now signed his contract and would officially rejoin the Latics

Managerial Performance

TEAM	FROM	TO	GAMES	WON	DRAW	LOST	WIN%
SHEFFIELD UNITED	02/07/98	17/05/99	55	22	15	18	40
HUDDERSFIELD TOWN	24/05/99	16/10/2000	66	25	16	25	37.9
WIGAN ATHLETIC	04/04/01	29/05/01	8	3	2	3	37.5
CRYSTAL PALACE	31/05/01	02/11/01	18	11	2	5	61.1
BLUES	12/12/01	19/11/07	270	100	70	100	37
WIGAN ATHLETIC	26/11/07	03/06/09	68	23	17	28	33.8
SUNDERLAND	03/06/09	30/11/11	98	29	28	41	29.6
HULL CITY	08/06/12	PRESENT	99	42	18	39	42.4
TOTAL			682	255	168	259	37.4

HONOURS

As a Player:

- Norwich City – League Cup winners 1985, Second Division Champions 1985–86.
- Manchester United – Premier League Champions, 1992–93, 1993–94, 1995–96, Premier League Runners-Up 1987–88, 1991–92, 1994–95, FA Cup Winners, 1990, 1994, 1996, FA Cup Runners-Up 1995, Football League Cup Winners, 1992 – Football League Cup Runners-Up 1991, 1994, Charity Shield Winner, 1990 (shared), 1993, 1994, European Cup Winners Cup winners 1991, European Super Cup winner 1991.

As a Manager:

- Birmingham City – Championship Runners-Up 2006–07, Championship winners 2002.
- Hull City – FA Cup Runners-Up 2013, Championship Runners-Up 2012–13.

Bruce has been married since February 1983 to Janet (née Smith), who is also from the Hexham area, and went to the same school as Bruce. The couple have two children, Alex (born 1984) and Amy (born 1987). Alex is also a footballer, and was signed by his father for Hull City in July 2012. He had previously played under his father's management at Birmingham City, but left the club in 2006, in part due to accusations of nepotism levelled at his father.

In addition to an autobiography, *Heading for Victory*, Bruce has published three novels, *Sweeper!*, *Defender!* and *Striker!* featuring the exploits of fictional footballer manager Steve Barnes. *Sweeper!* was described as 'surprisingly punchy and pacey, although the plot is essentially ludicrous.'

18.

CAPTAIN'S LOG

I have been fortunate to be able to talk to a number of Blues captains to find out more about their personalities by asking questions like:

Who is your sporting hero?
What would you be if you weren't a sportsman?
Which other sportsman would you like to be?
Career highlight for Blues?... And the worst moment?
Rest of Career highlight?... And the worst moment?
If your house was burning down, what one possession would you save?
What's the best advice you've ever been given?
Favourite karaoke song? – and a whole host of other favourites!
Most-listened to songs on your iPod?
Last film you saw?
Last book you read?
Favourite pre-match meal?
Can you cook? Best dish?
In a film of your life, who would you like to play you?
What's the most expensive thing you've ever bought?
Any experiences (funny or tragic) when you were Blues captain?
What are the qualities of a good captain?
Who was the best captain you played for and why?
Enjoy this insight into some of your favourites. Read on:

STEVEN CALDWELL

Defender – Date of Birth: 12 September 1980, Stirling Scotland – Prior to Blues he played for Wigan, Burnley, Sunderland, Leeds United (Loan), Bradford City (Loan), Blackpool (Loan) and Newcastle. He joined on a two-year deal in July 2011 after being released by then Premier League Wigan Athletic at the end of his 12-month contract at the DW Stadium. Scottish International winning 12 caps he made his international debut in a 1–1 draw away in Poland at the Zdzislaw Kryszkowiak stadium on 25 April 2001.

In The Official 2013 Blues Annual, Steven answers the following questions in a section entitled 'TEAM TALK'

Favourite TV Show? *The West Wing.*

Favourite Movie? *Godfellas.*

Favourite Musician? *Ocean Colour Scene.*

Favourite Food? *Chinese.*

Favourite Gadget? *Apple Mac.*

Favourite Actor? *Leonardo Di Caprio.*

Favourite Actress? *Michelle Williams.*

Favourite Place? *New York.*

What was the last thing you listened to on your iPod? *Islands in the Stream by Feist.*

If you knew today was your last day on earth how would you spend it? *With my kids and family.*

If you could be any superhero, who would you be? *Superman.*

If you were granted one wish, what would you wish for? *Health and happiness.*

If you could go back in time for one day, where and when would you go? *Back to my days in Scotland as a 14-year-old having a kick-about with my brother.*

Who is your sporting hero? *Kenny Dalglish. He played for my team, Celtic, and remains one of the best Scottish footballers of all time.*

What would you be if you weren't a sportsman? *I'd be in films. A producer or something like that.*

Which other sportsman would you like to be? *Any F1 driver. I'd have said a golfer, but there isn't much family time with golf.*

Career highlight? *Winning promotion via the play-off Final at Wembley with Burnley a couple of seasons ago. To be the captain of a team of men like that at a club that never expected to get into the Premier League was special.*

...And the worst moment? *The manner in which I left Sunderland. I just wanted to see my contract out. I was pushed out of the door. It hurt.*

If your house was burning down, what one possession would you save? *I scored the goal that sealed promotion for Sunderland a few years ago. I have that strip framed – it would be that.*

What's the best advice you've ever been given? *When I was at Newcastle, our coach Tommy Craig told us a story about the day he signed for the club as a player. At St James' Park he bumped into Jackie Milburn, who pulled him to one side and said: 'Just show them you care.'*

Favourite karaoke song? *The Gambler by Kenny Rogers.*

Three most-listened to songs on your iPod? *The Day We Caught The Train by Ocean Colour Scene, L.I.F.E.G.O.E.S.O.N. by Noah and the Whale, Gloria by Patti Smith.*

Last film you saw? *Senna – it's a tremendous film. Get on it.*

Last book you read? *I'm reading a biography of Robert Mugabe. It's quite fascinating how these tyrants can be so charming on one hand and so utterly barbaric on another.*

Favourite pre-match meal? *Porridge, chicken and poached eggs. I like to feel empty when I go out on the park but I need energy, obviously.*

Can you cook? Best dish? No. When I was at The Blues my family were in the northeast so Mrs Burke (wife of team-mate Chris) used to cook lasagne for me, otherwise I was eating out.

In a film of your life, who would you like to play you? *Ewan McGregor.*

What's the most expensive thing you've ever bought? *A Rolex watch. I like watches but every time I go to buy a second one my wife asks: 'What for?'*

CHRIS BURKE

(Captain 2013–14 in absence of Paul Robinson)

Scottish international midfielder – Date of Birth 2 December 1983 in Glasgow, Scotland. Previous Clubs; Cardiff City and Glasgow Rangers. He joined Blues in the summer of 2011 on a two-year deal under the Bosman ruling having left Cardiff at the end of the 2010–11 campaign ending a stay that started in January 2009. His 9-year stay at his boyhood club Glasgow Rangers saw him gain UEFA Champions League experience as well as a Scottish Premier League title and League Cup victory. Height: 5' 9" (175cm) Weight: 10st 10lbs (68kg) – Was a member of Gordon Strachan's first Scotland squad in January 2013, Strachan described him as, 'Chris was fantastic in the Europa League at a good level, he has maturity about his play now…' He won his first cap on 11 May 2006 as a substitute against Bulgaria in the Kirin Cup in Japan. He scored twice in a 5–1 win.

The Official Blues Annual 2014 quizzed Chris in the section entitled 'BACK CHAT':

ABOUT YOUR TEAM MATES:
Who is the best trainer? *Paul Robinson.*

Who has the worst dress sense? *Colin Doyle.*

Who is the best dancer? *Wade Elliott.*

Who spends the longest in front of the mirror? *Wade Elliott.*

Favourite Actor? *Will Ferrell.*

Favourite Actress? *Jennifer Lawrence.*

Favourite Movie? *Scarface.*

Favourite Musician or Band? *Jay-Z.*

Favourite Place? *My house.*

Favourite Pet Hates? *Stairs.*

If not a footballer? *Property developer.*

What do you do on your days off? *Drink Coffee.*

Snow or Sun? *Snow.*

Coffee or Tea? *Coffee.*

Early Bird or Night Owl? *Night owl.*

Action or Comedy? *Comedy.*

Apple or Blackberry? *Apple.*

Sausage or Bacon? *Sausage.*

Cats or Dogs? *Neither.*

Bond or Bourne? *Bourne.*

In the Official Blues Annual 2012 he answered the following questions in the section entitled 'FOOTBALLERS' LIVES'

If you could go to a major sporting event other than football – what would it be? *The Olympics.*

When was the last time you laughed until you cried? *Saturday night when i was out with my mates.*

Favourite Actor? *Will Smith (Note: What happened to Will Ferrell?).*

Who would play the part of you in a Hollywood blockbuster? *The actor who plays Dexter, I don't know his name (note: Michael C. Hall).*

Favourite Actress? *Cameron Diaz (Note: What happened to Jennifer Lawrence?).*

What is your favourite ever movie? *Toy Story 3 (Note: What happened to Scarface?).*

If you could meet anyone, living or dead, who would it be and why? *Elvis Presley so I could really see what sort of lifestyle he had.*

What would be your X Factor audition song? *Fly Me To The Moon.*

What is your favourite gadget? *iPhone.*

When was the last time you felt really proud? *When my son was born.*

He had a tremendous first season where he made 61 appearances, scored 14 goals and provided 18 assists. His efforts saw him awarded: 2011–12 Players' Player of the Season – Player of the Season award and Junior Blues' Player of the Season.

PAUL ROBINSON

The Official Blues Annual 2014 quizzed Paul in the section called "BACK CHAT":

ABOUT YOUR TEAM MATES:

Who is the best trainer? *Me, obviously.*

Who has the worst dress sense? *Shane Ferguson and Scotty Allan.*

Who is the best dancer? *Kyle Bartley.*

Who spends longest in front of the mirror? *Wade Elliott.*

Who is the joker in the dressing room? *Wade Elliott.*

Favourite Actor? *Jason Statham.*

Favourite Actress? *Sandra Bullock.*

Favourite Movie? *Gladiator.*

Favourite Musician or Band? *Justin Timberlake.*

Favourite Place? *Portugal.*

Pet Hates? *I've got a few. Losing and Mess – I am a bit OCD, so like things to be tidy.*

If you were a character in any movie, who would it be? *– I would have to be Jason Statham in Transporter.*

What do you do on your days off? *Relax and chill out with the kids.*

Snow or Sun? *Sun.*

Coffee or Tea? *Coffee.*

Early Bird or Night Owl? *Early bird.*

Action or Comedy? *Action.*

Apple or Blackberry? *Blackberry.*

Sausage or Bacon? *Bacon.*

Cats or Dogs? *Dogs.*

Bond or Bourne? *Bourne.*

In The Official Blues Annual 2014 in the BACK CHAT section questions posed above the 7 players: MATT GREEN – DARREN RANDOLPH – CHRIS BURKE – CALLUM REILLY – SCOTT ALLAN – WILL PACKWOOD nominated Paul as The Best Trainer. JONATHAN SPECTOR went for Lee Novak

MARTIN O'CONNOR

Who is your sporting hero? *Mohammed Ali.*

What would you be if you weren't a sportsman? *I would like to have been a P.E. teacher but I would probably have stayed as a train driver.*

Which other sportsman would you like to be? *Any Golfer because I love playing the game although my handicap is 28 which means I not much good.*

Career highlight for Blues?...And the worst moment? *Captaining the Blues in the 2001 Worthington Cup Final at The Millennium Stadium Cardiff. Leading the boys out was incredible because I had fourteen members of my family in the crowd. But the manner of our defeat also meant it was the worst moment in my career.*

Rest of Career highlight?...And the worst moment? *There are two: signing my first professional contract with Crystal Palace and then getting promotion with Walsall. Worst? I think that must be getting to four Play Offs and getting nothing from it – so near and yet so far!*

If your house was burning down, what one possession would you save? *My family but also a framed photograph of my Dad who sadly passed away in 2000.*

What's the best advice you've ever been given? *That was from Bobby Hope at Bromsgrove Rovers who said, 'If you don't get your act together regarding your attitude you won't make it'.*

Favourite karaoke song? *'I believe I can fly' – R. Kelly – I'm brilliant I should be on X-Factor but I only know the one song!*

Three most-listened to songs on your iPod? *Anything by Luther Vandross or Alexander O'Neal.*

Last film you saw? *Ironman 3.*

Last book you read? *'Who stole my cheese?' by Ilene Hochber B.S., B.S.A. Amazing ways to make more money from the poor suckers that you cheated in your work and in your life.*

Favourite pre-match meal? *It would have been boiled chicken and beans back in the day.*

Can you cook? Best dish? *Yes I can – My signature dish is meatballs and pasta in my own sauce – washed down with a glass of red wine!*

In a film of your life, who would you like to play you? *Idris Alba.*

What's the most expensive thing you've ever bought? *Apart my house and car, it would be a diamond ring I had made around the time of my Dad's death – to remind me of him!*

Any experiences (funny or tragic) when you were Blues captain? *Again I go back to The Millennium Stadium when Trevor Francis announced the team and Jerry Gill and David Burrows both of whom had played in all the rounds to the Final were not included. They were angry but essentially they were incredibly disappointed. As Captain I sat with them both on the coach journey from the Hotel to the ground to try and explain TF's decision and get them in a state of mind which meant they could support the lads on one of the greatest days in the club's history – in fairness to them they both did their jobs. It was also a great experience introducing the lads to Sven Goran Erickson in Cardiff.*

IAN CLARKSON

Who is your sporting hero? *Frank Worthington/Steve Redgrave.*

What would you be if you weren't a sportsman? *I am a teacher but would like to have been in a band.*

Which other sportsman would you like to be? *Ian Botham.*

Career highlight for Blues?...And the worst moment? *Winning promotion back into the Championship – a fantastic season full of great memories... particularly winning at the Albion 1–0 along the way. Also, the 1–1 home draw against Stoke was memorable but for different reasons as I don't think Roger Wiseman refereed again after that. The worst moment for me was getting battered 5–1 at Tranmere on a Friday night in the Dave Mackay era... that was a low ebb.*

Rest of Career highlight?...And the worst moment? *Winning at Wembley with Northampton was good and winning at Stamford Bridge and beating Manchester United under Lou Macari at Stoke. We had a decent team and were 90 minutes away from the Premier League. Worst moment was breaking my leg at Northampton and having a Lincoln player leaning over me telling me I was putting it on whilst I was on the deck. That more or less finished off my career as I came back at Kidderminster but wasn't quite the same.*

If your house was burning down, what one possession would you save? *My family.*

What's the best advice you've ever been given? *Work hard, play hard, enjoy life.*

Favourite karaoke song? *'Too much too young' – The Specials.*

Three most-listened to songs on your iPod? *The Jam – To Be Someone, The Beat – Big Shot, The Clash – Janie Jones.*

Last film you saw? *Lucy – a Luc Besson film.*

Last book you read? *Chavs – the demonisation of the working classes by Owen Jones.*

Favourite pre-match meal? *It would have been chicken and beans back in the day.*

Can you cook? Best dish? *Yes I can – A chicken/pasta/cheese sauce hybrid the kids love!*

In a film of your life, who would you like to play you? *Joe Strummer, Paul Weller or Ray Davies.*

What's the most expensive thing you've ever bought? *A house!*

Any experiences (funny or tragic) when you were Blues captain? *I can remember us beating Swindon 4–1 at home and then with half an hour left Glenn Hoddle and Micky Hazard turned on the style and we lost 6–4 I came off at 4–4 and was sitting with Terry Cooper on the bench and a bloke came past in a wheelchair and said, 'I could do better than Andy Gosney in goal' and Terry said, 'You're not f****** wrong!'*

I can remember beating Albion and was feeling pretty sure of myself when a bloke came up to me and said, 'Don't I know you? I was thinking he was just about wax lyrical over our win but he said, 'Got it, you're a barman at The Rainbow! (A pub in Digbeth!).' My mates were laughing and as always it's a good way of keeping your feet on the ground.

I can remember before a home game Les Sealey being very loud and chirpy and giving John Gayle some stick as he had been sent off in the last game and asking him to pull his weight etc, etc. The thing was, if you knew Gayley well, there was a time and a place to take the mickey and you could tell this wasn't one of them but Les was always full of it...I was sitting next to Les and a size 12 boot missed my head by about an inch and flew straight onto his head. I've never seen someone shut up so quickly! He legged it out of the dressing room in his suit and didn't reappear until about 2.59 safe in the knowledge that Gayley was outside ready to kick off...

What are the qualities of a good captain? *Vocal, lead by example and stand up to people in charge – fight for the cause...*

Who was the best captain you played for and why? *Vince Overson was a decent captain at both Blues and Stoke as was Ray Warburton at Northampton. They weren't 'yes' men but they had your back in the game.*

What makes Paul Robinson a successful captain for The Blues? *All the reasons above. I have only met him once socially at a Birmingham City Supporters Club function and he seemed like a top bloke who cares about the club and more importantly the supporters. I think he has made the best of his ability and I really admire players like that. I would love to have played in the same back four as him.*

DAMIEN JOHNSON

In February 2005 – BLUES MAGAZINE – '6 1/2 MINUTES WITH JONTY'

Which sporting event would you most like to attend? *All Ireland Gaelic football Final.*

Football stadium you would love to play in? *Nou Camp.*

Favourite Sports Programme? *Match of the Day.*

Best Player played against? *Raul.*

First pair of football boots? *They were a pair called Arrow from Adidas when I was eight. I remember that they had these luminous yellow markings on them. I had them for three years. I think they must have looked good.*

First team played for? *Lisburn Youth. It was the local team where I grew up. It started from under-10s and went upwards. Quite a few decent players have* *come through their system. In my age group was David Healy, who played for Preston North End. I am still mates with him to this day.*

First Team supported as a boy? *Glasgow Celtic. Growing up in Northern Ireland, you either followed Celtic or Rangers. My family supported Celtic and I followed suit.*

First Footballing hero? *I didn't really have one hero as such, but I suppose if I had to pick a player it would be Paul McStay. I remember my brother had all these posters of him on his bedroom wall so my interest in him just followed from there. He was a tidy midfield player for Celtic.*

First match seen live? *Our boys club went over to see Manchester United v Coventry City. I was about 10 years old. I can't recall too much about the actual game other than Cyrille Regis was playing for Coventry! What did stick in my mind was Old Trafford, we were all in awe of the place. And that was before it was as good as it is today.*

First Famous Player met? *That would have to be Kenny Dalglish. I went over to Blackburn Rovers when I was 14 for a week's trial. He came over and introduced himself to me and all the other lads there. I had videos of him at home and couldn't believe I was there talking to him. Blackburn offered to take me on after the trail. The Youth coach was Alan Irvine. He was good to learn from and a nice man as well.*

First Favourite movie star? *Robert De Niro. I suppose a lot of people would choose him but it's not surprising. He's really good in all of his films?*

First record bought? *I'm going to put myself on the line here and admit that it was a song by MC Hammer. I think it was 'Can't Touch This' but it might have been the other one he had out at that time, 'Pray'. Back then he was quite respectable. I didn't go the whole way and have those baggy silk trousers he used to wear, though.*

First favourite singer or band? *Stone Roses. A great band who write great songs.*

First girlfriend? *Claire O'Kane, when I was at school. I was about 12 or 13 and you know what it was like when you were that young – your romances would last only a couple of weeks. I don't know what she is doing now.*

First Car? *A Peugeot 306. I bought it second-hand when I was at Blackburn.*

First House? *A three bedroomed semi-detached in Clitheroe, Lancashire. It cost me about £75,000 and I've still got it now. Blackburn is not a particularly pretty town and a lot of the lads tended to live further out, in scenic parts of the countryside.*

First Pet? *I've never had a pet and I don't intend to have one, either. Not a great fan of animals.*

First Wage? *It was at Blackburn, earning £40-a-week as an apprentice. We used to get a bonus of £1 a draw and £2 a win. I can tell you, it really mattered to us.*

First Professional Match? *For Blackburn against Preston in the Coca-Cola Cup. I played wide on the right. It was a bit of a nightmare really. We were on a hiding to nothing because we'd won the first leg 6–0 at Ewood Park. The manager changed the team around and gave a few of us a chance. We lost 1–0.*

First goal as a professional? *Against Arsenal for Blackburn. We were losing 2–0 and I got on the end of a cross by Damien Duff and beat David Seaman with a header. I sneaked up unnoticed at the back post.*

Most memorable match for Blues? *3–0 against Aston Villa at home, first derby in the Premiership.*

Superstitions? *None really.*

First Sending Off? *I've never been sent off in a domestic game but I got a red card for Northern Ireland Under-21 against the Republic of Ireland in an Under-21 tournament. The first yellow card was for a tackle, the second for mouthing at the referee. It was a bit of a needle match. I'm always being told about my backchat.*

How many autographs have you signed this week? *Not many.*

Funniest moment at Blues? *Dunny's trick against Aston Villa last season (2003-04).*

Funniest player at Blues? *Benno or Dunny.*

Worst dress sense? *Benno or Dunny (Benno – Ian Bennett and Dunny – David Dunn).*

Favourite TV Programme? *The Sopranos.*

Favourite Stadium? *Celtic Park.*

Favourite Sports Commentator? *Ian Crocker.*

Favourite Newspaper? *Belfast Telegraph.*

Favourite Food? *Steak.*

Favourite Restaurant? *Teppen Yaki –Shogun.*

Favourite Drink? *Lilt.*

Favourite Film? *Usual Suspects.*

Favourite Holiday Destination? *Rome.*

Favourite Pizza Topping? *Pepperoni.*

Favourite Sport apart from football? *Gaelic Football.*

Favourite City apart from Birmingham? *Lisburn.*

JANUARY 2004

If you could have anyone bring you breakfast in bed, who would it be and what would you have for breakfast? *Kelly Brook with a bowl of Tiger's Frosties. That would be a very nice way to start the day.*

What was the last household chore you undertook and when was it? *I made my own bed this morning. I live on my own in a flat in Birmingham, so I tend to do all my own stuff anyway. I'm quite tidy, not too messy.*

What CD is playing on your stereo at this moment? *The Strokes, 'Room on Fire' it's called. I like them. I'm not really into R n B and that stuff. I like guitar, rocky music.*

If you could choose to be any animal, what would it be? *I suppose everyone goes for either a lion or a leopard, something strong and quick. I can't really answer this question without sounding a bit cheesy.*

What materialistic possession would you most want to save if your house burnt down? *I would go for my television, that's all I'd want. Why? That's all I tend to do. I'm a telly addict.*

You are stranded on a desert island. What three luxuries would you choose to have with you? *A book, a pillow and some sun block. You'd have to get comfortable while you waited for someone to come and rescue you.*

JEFF KENNA

September 2001

If you could have anyone bring you breakfast in bed, who would it be and what would you have for breakfast? *That would have to be my wife, because she never, ever does it. And the food would be a full English breakfast, as she never cooks that either. Of course, it would be on a Sunday, after a match, not before.*

What was the last household chore you undertook and when was it? *I loaded up the dishwasher. I do my fair share around the house – a new man and all that.*

What CD is playing on your stereo at this moment? *It's one of those compilations, 'Summer Vibes' or something like that. It has a bit of everything on it. My musical tastes are quite broad, whatever catches my ear. My favourite has to be U2.*

Who has got the worst dress sense in the Blues first team squad, and what is the most ridiculous item of clothing you have seen him wear? *Benno. His worst gear is his underwear. His collection has to be seen to be believed. I think he gets it off a market stall. It's not very flattering at all.*

If you could choose to be any animal, what would it be? *I won't be doing the macho thing and going for a lion, king of the jungle and all that. I'd say an eagle. There's just something about them when they soar in the sky, they're so regal.*

What materialistic possession would you most want to save if your house burnt down? *I'm not very materialistic so, on a nice memorable note, it would probably be the man-of-the-match champagne from the Aston Villa game last season.*

You are stranded on a desert island. What three luxuries would you choose to have with you? *A chef, for obvious reasons, sun tan lotion, because I presume it would be red hot, and a helicopter so I could leave whenever I wanted.*

What is your favourite and worst holiday destinations? *We stayed on an island, Ko Sunai, just south of Thailand. It was absolutely gorgeous, a wonderful place. It was quite funny as the missus fell pregnant and it was around the same time as Posh and Becks went away and then named their son Brooklyn after where he was conceived. Ko Sunai Kenna? It doesn't quite work does it? Mallorca would be next as we've just bought property out there. Worst would be anywhere in Greece or Turkey.*

What would be your specialist subject on Mastermind? *Guinness and hangovers – and I'm not going to elaborate!*

In 2002
Favourite Player? *Zinedine Zidane.*

Favourite Foreign Team? *Real Madrid.*

Favourite Football Pundit? *Andy Gray.*

Favourite Away Ground? *Old Trafford.*

Favourite Film? *Training Day.*

Favourite CD? *Anything by U2.*

Favourite TV Programme? *Frasier.*

Favourite Book? *Anything by John Grisham.*

Favourite Newspaper? *The Sun.*

Favourite Magazine? *FHM.*

Favourite City? *Palma.*

Favourite Woman? *My Wife.*

Favourite Footballing Moment? *Winning the Premier League with Blackburn at Anfield.*

STEPHEN CLEMENCE

In December 2004 – BLUES MAGAZINE – '6 1/2 MINUTES WITH CLEM'

Which sporting event would you most like to attend? *The Masters (Golf).*

Which Football stadium you would love to play in? *Nou Camp or Bernabeu.*

Favourite Sports Programme? *Match of the Day.*

Favourite Sporting Hero? *Paul Gascoigne.*

Best Player played against? *Steven Gerrard.*

First pair of football boots? *They were a pair called Laudrups by Patrick.*

First team played for? *Broxbourne Saints.*

First Team supported as a boy? *Tottenham Hotspur.*

First match seen live? *FA Cup Final Spurs v Coventry City in 1987.*

Most memorable match for Blues? *Beating Liverpool and scoring in my first season.*

Superstitions? *Same routine from waking up on a matchday every match.*

First Sending Off? *Against Barnsley FA Cup Fourth Round (two yellows.)*

How many autographs have you signed this week? *Not many.*

Funniest moment at Blues? *Too many too mention.*

Funniest player at Blues? *Stan Lazaridis had some funny stories.*

Worst dress sense? *Matty Upson could do better.*

Any football rules you'd like to change? *Cameras on the goalline.*

Favourite TV Programme? *24.*

Favourite Stadium? *Old Trafford.*

Favourite Sports Commentator? *Martin Tyler.*

Favourite Newspaper? *The Sun.*

Favourite Food? *Chicken Pasta.*

Favourite Restaurant? *Any Japanese.*

Favourite Drink? *Coke.*

Favourite Film? *Gladiator.*

Favourite Holiday Destination? *Anywhere hot with a pool and a beach.*

Favourite Pizza Topping? *Ham and Mushroom.*

Favourite Sport apart from football? *Golf.*

Favourite City apart from Birmingham? *London.*

May 2003

MICHAEL JOHNSON

If you could have anyone bring you breakfast in bed, who would it be and what would you have for breakfast? *It has to be Halle Berry, she's quality. I'd ask her to bring soft boiled eggs with soldiers, so then I could dip them in…*

What was the last household chore you undertook and when was it? *Living on my own, I do all the stuff around the house. I can't stand mess. I'm the sort that if I eat at 6.45pm, by 7pm the plates are washed and put away. Otherwise I'd go to bed still thinking about having to clear up.*

What CD is playing on your stereo at this moment? *I'm playing quite a few at the moment, mainly Busta Rhymes, Snoop Dogg and Bounty Killer – a*

Jamaican Reggae start. I tend to go for Reggae, rap, R n B. I'm not into guitar stuff.

Who has got the worst dress sense in the Blues first team squad, and what is the most ridiculous item of clothing you have seen him wear? *Paul Devlin's gear is appalling. He came to training once in a bright luminous green T-shirt. I thought it was a guy off the M42 who had got lost until Devs came closer to me.*

If you could choose to be any animal, what would it be? *Got to be a lion, King of the Jungle, no-one messes with him, and fearless – a bit like me!*

What materialistic possession would you most want to save if your house burnt down? *My stereo. I've got a couple of Panasonics in the house, complete with sub-woofers and stuff like that – the works. When I play music it has got to be loud. The neighbours aren't too keen though. I've had a few problems with them.*

You are stranded on a desert island. What three luxuries would you choose to have with you? *My stereo, my dog, Simba, a German Shepherd, and Halle Berry for those lonely nights...*

What is your favourite and worst holiday destinations? *The best is Ontario, Canada, where my dad lives. I go out there every summer and have a great time. There are people from all over the world living in Canada, it's not a case of 'this is our country' so, as a result, everyone gets along with each other. The worst is Tenerife. Last time I went it was full of 'tea leaves' (thieves) and it was all dirty.*

What would be your specialist subject on Mastermind? *Basketball, I love it. I'm a big fan of the Toronto Raptors and try to follow them.*

Who is the funniest footballer you have ever met and what is your funniest recollection of him? *Got to be Sav. The other day he got absolutely hammered by the gaffer and the lads after a stunt he tried to pull on the PFA website, where they were asking for votes for March's player of the month. Apparently he was in the running, so he got the guys who look after the club website to send out e-mails to fans begging them to vote for him. Next thing we know he's got 15,000 votes in one day and suddenly goes to the top of the list ahead of Henry, Vieria and Shearer! The PFA smelled a rat and ruled out all the multiple votes on his behalf. We had him up in front of a Kangaroo Court we hold every Friday before training but he kept denying it. He was bang to rights though and speechless, which was a first. Running him close is Benno. I've travelled with him for nine years and one thing that hasn't changed is his undies. They're like your granny's tablecloth, all cotton and stitched together. Going with his Mr Universe physique, he's quite a sight to behold in the dressing room.*

19.

PAUL ROBINSON

For me it would have been impossible not to include the current Blues skipper in this celebration of successful captains.

I include an extract from our book *ROBBO – UNSUNG HERO,* which is Chapter One 'What's it all about?'

Whilst ROBBO has not lead Birmingham City to any honours (yet!) he played a vital role at the end of season 2013–14 in keeping Blues in the Championship. Most Bluenoses feel that if the club had descended into League One then that could have meant the end of the club as we know it.

After the extract from *ROBBO – UNSUNG HERO* I include a report on the final match of the 2013–14 season against Bolton Wanderers.

CHAPTER ONE

WHAT'S IT ALL ABOUT?

Paul recalls: I had been approached previously about writing my life story but it had never really appealed, I guess I thought I was not that type of personality. When I met Keith for the first time it was to discuss my contributing the Foreword to his book *THE LEADERS – BIRMINGHAM CITY* – a task which I have achieved successfully. During discussion he suggested that writing my Biography would be something worth doing if only for my four sons to be able to say to their children 'this is what your Grandad did!' So here we are!

As I think all the subjects of a biography or autobiography say, the process has been 'interesting' – re-living your life's experiences from a different age gives you a unique opportunity to analyse your actions. Whilst you cannot change the circumstances it does allow you to put things into context and justify what happened. I have had the opportunity to review my career from a different perspective and for that I am grateful.

In this book I will be giving my opinion and answering a few questions on subjects as diverse as:

- Can I pick a team made up of the best players with whom I played? (See Chapter Seven.)
- Can I pick a team made up of the best players I played against? (See Chapter Seven.)
- Who are the Top Ten players in my position? (See Chapter Seven.)
- Who do I admire outside of football? (See Chapters Seven and Eight.)
- Foreign Players – How have they influenced and changed the English game? (See Chapter Eight.)
- What happens on a match day? (See Chapter Ten.)
- How is training conducted? (See Chapter Ten.)
- Video technology? (See Chapter Eight.)
- What career would I have had if I had not been a footballer? (See Chapter Seven.)

As always, when I have been asked a question my responses have always been honest. I hope you enjoy my answers.

To have played against some of the world's best players like Cristiano Ronaldo, Wayne Rooney and David Beckham, is not something that every footballer can say. But I have been incredibly fortunate to have had the opportunity to play against some of the most talented players ever to grace a football pitch whilst wearing the shirts of Watford, West Bromwich Albion and Bolton Wanderer's in England's Premier League.

And here I am in my thirty-seventh year and still people who are important to me are being respectful of the job I do:

In the Official Match Day programme for the Birmingham City Home fixture with Reading on 13 December 2014, Michael Morrison was the featured player for interview by Peter Lewis the *Blues News* editor. Peter asked the question 'Do you feel as though you're building up a good understanding and partnership with Paul Robinson in the centre of defence?' Michael replied: 'Yes. I think it works well with him being a left-sider and me coming in and playing the right. He's very experienced and vocal. You know exactly where he's going to be because we're both talking and that's a big part of any position in football, especially at centre-half. If you can get that good relationship then it makes a massive difference.' (Note: Match Result – Birmingham 6 Reading 1.)

In the *Birmingham Mail* Friday 12 December 2014 under the headline 'ROBBO GIVEN TIME TO GET OVER INJURY' The Blues Manager Gary Rowett was reported as saying, 'I am giving Birmingham City captain Paul Robinson every chance to prove his fitness before tomorrow's game with Reading.' The Blues manager revealed today the veteran defender needed several stitches in his foot during half-time of the defeat at Blackpool the previous Saturday. The injury was sustained in a tackle with Seasiders' striker Steve Davies, a challenge Rowett felt was worthy of a caution which resulted in Robinson being restricted in training this week. However it went unpunished – despite the fact that David Coote showed seven yellow cards. Rowett said, 'Davies just caught him early on in the game. I actually spoke to the referee about it afterwards and felt that it was probably a worse tackle which didn't get booked other than lots of other tackles which got booked and were nowhere near as bad as that. Paul ended up with five or six stitches in his foot at half time. I think even Robbo said he should have come off if the truth be known, if he was being really honest. But the type of pro and character he is, that's not an option for him. He soldiered through. This week it has been tight and sore as is often the case, it's right on the bone of his left foot. I don't see it as too much of an issue but we've not wanted him to train and open it up early in the week so we are trying to leave it as late as we can.' (Robbo passed a fitness test and lead his team to a 6–1 home win)

Born and bred in Watford, I came through the ranks at Watford FC, making over 200 appearances for my local team during a seven-season stint at the club. I was part of the team that achieved promotion to the Premier League and I am lead to believe in all humility that I am regarded as one of the best left-backs that the Hornets have ever had to date.

I then moved to West Bromwich Albion in October 2003, and never made less than 32 appearances in a season for the Baggies, during a six-season spell at the club. I helped the team achieve promotion to the Premier League and was part of the Baggies squad that made the 'great escape' from relegation in 2005.

Moving to Bolton Wanderers before the start of the 2009–10 season, initially on loan, I linked up with former West Bromwich Albion manager Gary Megson. My move was made permanent at the end of the season and I went on to enjoy two more successful seasons with the Trotters in the Premier League.

After a loan spell at Leeds, I joined my present club, Birmingham City in September 2012 on a one-month contract. My performances for the Blues were good enough for me to be rewarded with a contract extension till the end of the season.

At the end of the 2012–13 season, I got a further one-year contract and was handed the captain's armband for the 2013–14 Championship season.

Obviously I learnt the game from a young age. I watched it on the TV. Watching FA Cup Finals, World Cup Finals and I just wanted to play football on the biggest stage I could, as often as I could and that drove me to, sort of, decide that I wanted to be a footballer and I wanted to achieve great things in life.

Initially I started off up front when I was younger and then I progressively made my way back as I got older. I went from up front to left wing and then to left-back.

My current personal highlight, is obviously, my Great Escape two with Birmingham City. Obviously at the moment (July 2014) that stands out for me. I mean I did it with West Bromwich Albion whilst I was there but the Birmingham one was just an unbelievable feeling knowing that it was going down to the last game and what it all meant to everyone.

I love being the captain here at Birmingham City and it is a new experience towards the end of my career as I have never been an appointed captain at any of my previous clubs. It gives me great responsibility. I mean, if the players want to talk to me about certain things, they can, because they know I'm always there to listen. I really love working with the young lads and trying to help them improve and it works because they are so keen to learn – just me listening to them helps them. It gives me that responsibility that I want, because obviously, when I decide to hang up my boots, I want to go into coaching or management. As I want to go that route, my role as captain has set me on a great learning curve. I have always tried to set a good example both on and off the pitch – both as a professional footballer and a person. My family, who are the most important thing to me, expect me to set a good example for my family and in my work. So to set a good example to my kids off the pitch is the most important thing.

The Premier League is fantastic. It's the best league in the world, so you want to play in it. You get all the world-class players playing in it and to play against those players is incredible. Imagine when my sons have grown up and they will be able to watch me playing against the likes of Ronaldo, Rooney and all the other top quality players that I have played against, it will be a surreal moment for them. You have to pinch yourself sometimes that you've actually played against that player, in that week. So, it's something that you can dream of. I mean, you always dream of playing at the highest level and playing against the best clubs in the world and I've been lucky enough to do that.

Fans often ask me who is the best player I have played against and the answer is so tough because there have been so many. But I would say (Cristiano) Ronaldo, although, Beckham when I first played against him, he was probably one of the hardest players to mark because you couldn't mark him. You never knew where he was positionally. But Ronaldo was on another planet, he was so strong, quick and physically he could blow you away in a space of a couple of seconds just with his movement and skill. Ronaldo without a shadow of a doubt is the best player that I have played against.

Being a professional footballer is a job that I love doing, but it takes a lot of dedication, a lot of drive and a lot of passion. I have dedicated my life to it. So for me, the advantages of it, is just loving the job that I do. It's going out every time with a smile on my face and enjoying my football as much as possible. There are some disadvantages; you're always going to get the negative press that is around and certain things that go out about you. But that's just part and parcel of life and part and parcel of the game. You're always going to get negatives with the positives. Sometimes it can go over the top a little bit with fans, with their reactions and the way that they can personally come for you. But as they say, it is how you deal with it that shows your own personal qualities, what I try to do is block out as much as I can, however, with social media these days, it is very easy for your family and friends to read things about you which are negative opinions. For your children to read or hear things that people have said about their dad is not a nice thing for them to experience. Here's an example when I was at The Albion four of us used to play head tennis after training; Geoff Horsfield, Neil Clement, Russell Hoult. It was just a bit of fun, but it got reported that we were playing for £60 per point – which was not only inaccurate but what impression did it give to the Baggies' supporters!

My approach to the game is relatively simple, I work on what I believe I am good at and continue to strive to be better in each training session/ game, there is always room for improving your game. Obviously my main aim is to go out and enjoy myself as well, because that's what I also believe is important. Enjoy it and make the most of it as much as I can. I watch and study opposition players, the ones that I am going to come up against and studying their movements and qualities, what positions you can get yourself in to and work on that in my head and work on that on the training pitch. That's one of the most important things, preparation on the training pitch, working hard to be the best defender I can be, knowing what player I am coming up against at the weekend and that I am going to get the better of him.

I think I have made the most of the opportunities I have been given. It's such a driven sport. You know you've got to have that drive, you've got to have that passion and you've got to have that desire to become the best player you can be. Technically I may not be the most skilful, but what I do have is the heart and drive to want to be the best at what I do and I want to prove people wrong who said to me that I wasn't good enough.

THE BLUES GREAT ESCAPE

If Blues fans were asked to vote for the most important game in the club's current history then their choice is influenced by a day In May 2014 when Blues travelled to Bolton Wanderers for the last match of the season. Paul was back in the team after a three-match suspension following a 13th booking for what I believe was the only 'real' tackle at the City Ground, Nottingham.

Booked at Nottingham Forest so miss the next three games

Although the plaudits for the remarkable escape go quite rightly to Paul Caddis the influence of Robbo cannot go unrecognised. The day was recorded in a *Birmingham Mail* 16-page souvenir entitled 'THE GREAT ESCAPE', Colin Tattum writes; 'Blues came, Blues conquered and how they roared. Against all odds they somehow managed to pull off The Great Escape and stop the club from plunging into oblivion. Championship survival on the last day of the season will go down as a watershed moment in the history of Birmingham City FC. Had they dropped down to League One – and at one time it looked a nailed-on certainty – one can only imagine the consequences. The supporters were only too aware of the precarious state of their beloved club. They've seen so much heartache over the years – last day relegations, cup final defeats, play-off misery, the list goes on.

But with their brave faces, slick suits, waistcoats and flat caps, the Peaky Blinders travelled to Bolton in their droves. By 11.45am the away end was almost full voice. *Keep Right On* echoed around the stands as the Blues players warmed up – but what followed wasn't pretty. Their brief of not losing at the Reebok Stadium and then bettering the Doncaster Rover's result against Champions Leicester City looked like too much to ask. Even when news filtered through to the 3,800 travelling fans that the Foxes had taken the lead, Blues conceded later and were 2–0 down with 14 minutes to save their season.

Something quite incredible happened next.

Backed by one of the most passionate set of supporters, that ground will ever see, Blues fought back with goals from Nikola Zigic (Note: we thought this was his last game for BCFC) and a 93rd minute equaliser from Paul Caddis. And so they staved off the drop…on goal difference!

For many the rest is a blur. For others there are unanswered questions – where did the six minutes of injury time come from? How did Neil Danns (Note: ex-Blues player) miss that one-on-one for Bolton? Did that just happen?

Of course it's all history now, but certainly not forgotten. The echoes of Blues' famous and fitting terrace chant are still ringing out in supporters ears. Replays of Lee Clark's passionate sprint and leap into the crowd continue to circulate around social networking sites. And now the dust has finally settled those who witnessed the drama unfold can look back on the momentous occasion and proudly say, 'I was there.' (*Birmingham Mail* – Saturday 10 May 2014.)

MATCH REPORT:
BLUES CLINCHED SURVIVAL IN THE MOST DRAMATIC FASHION AS PAUL CADDIS' HEADER THREE MINUTES INTO STOPPAGE TIME PREVENTED THE 2011 LEAGUE CUP WINNERS FROM DROPPING INTO THE THIRD TIER OF ENGLISH FOOTBALL FOR THE FIRST TIME IN 20 YEARS. WITH 14 MINUTES REMAINING, SECOND-HALF STRIKES FROM BOLTON'S LEE CHUNG-YONG AND LUKAS JUT-KIEWICZ HAD LEFT LEE CLARK'S MEN STARING DOWN THE ABYSS.

Yet late goals from Nikola Zigic and Caddis earned them a 2–2 draw, and Leicester's win over Doncaster therefore meant Blues, who only dropped into the bottom three for the first time this season a week ago, stayed up at the expense of Doncaster. It meant Clark's men, who were playing in the top flight just three seasons ago, can now look to rebuild.

The club is reportedly up for sale after former owner Carson Yeung was sentenced to six years in prison for money laundering, while Clark and the future of many of his players, a handful of whom are on loan deals, remains murky.

Captain Paul Robinson was back in the Blues starting line-up following suspension and Clark recalled big-earning Zigic, probably for the final time before he is released this summer.

He was involved in a bright opening patch for the visitors too with both him and Emyr Huws, the only loanee selected in Clark's XI, seeing shots blocked while Lee Novak was inches away from turning Caddis' driven cross home.

However, Birmingham failed to build on that spell and Wanderers came close with both Lee and Rob Hall narrowly missed the target with decent efforts.

Clark's men would find a second wind before the break, though, and they kept Bolton's back-up goalkeeper Andy Lonergan busy.

Twice he denied Novak with fingertip saves, the first in particular was a fine stop down to his left, and although the ex-Huddersfield forward eventually found a way past Lonergan, the whistle had already blown for Zigic's foul on David Wheater.

While Birmingham's need for victory was evident in their hurried play, the hosts were, perhaps understandably, far more ponderous with visiting goalkeeper Darren Randolph having little to do.

As the two sides headed into the tunnel at half-time, Blues knew they were going down with Doncaster drawing and Millwall winning. Yet they were surprisingly slow out of the blocks and were punished for it 12 minutes after the restart.

David Wheater was given plenty of time to pick his pass into the box and Lee span before rifling a finish into the far corner from the right-hand side of the area.

Clark responded by introducing Jordan Ibe and Federico Macheda, both part of the second batch of Birmingham loanees who had come under fire from captain Robinson for a perceived lack of effort.

Ibe at least gave them more directness out wide and Lonergan flipped the Liverpool winger's cross into Novak's path, but he could not bring the ball under his spell quickly and eventually smashed a low shot past the post.

Birmingham's attacking play got increasingly desperate and scrappy but their fans were heartened by news of a Leicester goal against Doncaster. They relayed the message that they now only needed one goal to their players but, as those chants sounded out, substitute Jutkiewicz doubled the hosts' advantage.

The Middlesbrough loanee picked up the ball on the left channel and somehow skewed a shot under Randolph's near post 14 minutes from time.

However, two minutes later, Zigic gave the travelling support hope once more when he bundled the ball over the line after a cross from the left ended up in his path.

Neil Danns should have restored Bolton's two-goal lead but blazed over the bar and with six additional minutes signalled, Birmingham had a chance.

And it was another mad sequence of events, which led to their all-important equaliser in the third of those half-a-dozen minutes added on.

Zigic's header was cleared off the line by Tim Ream and the ball fell kindly for Caddis to nod in from barely a yard out and spark jubilant scenes in the stands and along on the touchline.

Birmingham's Paul Robinson interrupted an interview
to scream 'Who gives a f*ck! We are staying up!'

EPILOGUE

Whilst this book was never intended to be a definitive record of all Birmingham City captains I feel there are a number of captains that should be recognised in this book because as well as being captains they were great servants to the club and held in high esteem by the majority of Bluenoses. As author I have chosen to include in *THE LEADERS – BIRMINGHAM CITY* - Howard Kendall, Darren Purse, Kenny Cunningham, Stephen Clemence and Michael Johnson.

HOWARD KENDALL

FULL NAME: Howard Kendall.
DATE OF BIRTH: 22 May 1946
PLACE OF BIRTH: Ryton-on-Tyne, Nr. Blaydon Co.Durham.

Playing Career:

Youth Career:
1961–63 Preston North End.

Senior Career:

1963–67 Preston North End 104 appearances 13 goals, 1967–74 Everton 229 appearances 21 goals, 1974–77 Blues 115 appearances 16 goals, 1977–79 Stoke City 82 appearances 9 goals, 1979–81 Blackburn Rovers 79 appearances 6 goals, 1981 Everton 4 appearances 0 goals. TOTAL 613 appearances 65 goals.

International Career:

He never played for England at senior level, but won caps at Schoolboy, Youth and Under-23 level, captaining the England Youth side to victory in the 1964 Little World Cup Final.

Management Career:

1979–81 Blackburn Rovers, 1981–87 Everton, 1987–89 Athletico Bilbao, 1989–90 Manchester City, 1990–93 Everton, 1994 Xanthi, 1995 Notts County, 1995–97 Sheffield United, 1997–98 Everton, 1998–99 Ethnikos Piraeus.

BLUES CAREER:

He was sold to Blues in February 1974 and he spent four seasons at St Andrew's helping Birmingham survive in the First Division. The transfer was a complicated one with Howard and Archie Styles plus cash coming to St Andrew's whilst Bob Latchford went to Goodison Park His debut was on 16 February 1974 away at Wolverhampton Wanderers a game Blues lost 1–0 in front of a crowd of 33,821. He scored his first Blues goal at St Andrew's on 23 April 1974 against Queen's Park Rangers a game Blues won 4–0 in front of a crowd of 39,160 the other scorers were Gordon Taylor and Trevor Francis got two. His final appearance in Royal Blue was away at Queen's Park Rangers on 23 May 1977. Blues drew 2–2 in front of a crowd of 14,976. He scored along with Roy McDonough. He left Blues for a fee of £40,000 in August 2007 to join Stoke City.

I was fortunate to have the opportunity to interview Howard and here are the answers to my questions:

How did your move to Blues come about?

I had been at Everton seven years and Billy Bingham was the manager, he decided that the club needed a centre-forward and that he could progress the club without me. He had targeted Bob Latchford and Denis Tueart of Sunderland. In fact I was expecting to move to Sunderland before I met Freddie Goodwin at Knutsford Services on the M6. It was a really complicated deal, in exchange for Bob, Everton gave Blues £350,000, me and Archie Styles. The deal nearly stalled over a loyalty bonus I felt I was due, it was only £5,000 but that was a lot of money in 1974. Freddie was very helpful and supported me saying that I should hold out for the payment as they had already introduced Bob at Goodison Park therefore the deal was done.

What were your initial thoughts of the Blues?

When I turned up at the Elmdon training ground it was like an air raid shelter compared to what I had been used to at Everton. My value in the transfer deal was estimated at £180,000 that was the biggest transfer fee Blues had paid, a fact that John Roberts used against me on my first day. At Elmdon there was no washing facility so training tops that were dirty were simply dried and then worn the next day. The lads' tops were covered in mud and John said to me, 'Come on you're the most expensive player ever, go and complain about the condition of our tops!' I looked at Archie who like me had been issued with a brand new top and said 'Nothing wrong with mine' and I walked out leaving John open-mouthed and the rest of the lads in stitches.

Freddie had bought me to ensure that we stayed in Division One and immediately made me Captain, a job I had performed at Everton.

What was your proudest moment at Blues?

That has to be the avoidance of relegation at the end of my first season 1973–74. We finished 19th and played the last game at home against Norwich which we won 2–1. After the game I was in the bath (individual ones in those days) along with the rest of the team, when Freddie came in and said, 'They're still out there, they won't go until you go out and do a lap of honour.' So as Captain I had to organise the lads to get dry, get back into their kit and do a lap of honour for the fans, I couldn't believe it – a lap of honour for avoiding relegation. I had done the job Freddie had bought me for!

What do you remember of your debut?

I always got nervous on debuts, I had a real nightmare on my Everton debut and my performance against the Wolves for Blues was only average. It was a really heavy pitch and we lost 1–0 on 10 February in front of a crowd of 33,821. We had some real personalities in my debut team: Gary Sprake (what a character!), Ray Martin, Joe Gallagher, Roger Hynd, Garry Pendrey, Trevor Francis, Kenny Burns, Bobby Hope and Gordon Taylor. We were very close to being a really good side.

I felt sorry for Gary because he had the reputation for making mistakes and when he was at Leeds he had a team in front of him that could make up for his errors, at Blues he never had that luxury, so his mistakes on occasions cost us dear. He was replaced by Dave Latchford after my debut game and only played a further two games for the Blues first team. There was real competition between the sticks as Paul Cooper was third choice!

What was your unhappiest experience at Blues?

April 9 1974 at Maine Road in the FA Cup semi-final replay against Fulham, which we lost with the last kick of extra-time having played them off the park. Their 'keeper Peter Mellor was unbelievable. That was without doubt the hardest night in my football career. The players were just stunned and we went off to our hotel in Buxton where we had planned to celebrate going to Wembley. As skipper I had missed the chance to lead out a team in an FA Cup Final. The lads had a few beers and went to bed the atmosphere was very sombre. At five o'clock in the morning, Freddie said to me get the lads up we're going home. We were devastated.

Viv Busby played for Fulham that night. We met up later at Stoke and he became a friend and a colleague later in my career.

What was your opinion of Freddie Goodwin?

Although Willie Bell was his assistant they weren't very close, so Freddie used to talk to me in my capacity as Captain to gain my thoughts on a number of topics. He was always the boss and made the final decision on his own but he valued my opinion. The way he was with me had a positive influence on my decision to stay in the game as a manager in fact I started to gain my coaching qualifications at Lilleshall whilst at Blues. Thank you Freddie.

How did you career end at Blues?

Freddie had left and in September 1975 Willie Bell was appointed as Caretaker Manager. On October 11 we were due to play away at Liverpool and he dropped me, it was only the second time in my career and I was not best pleased, it was as if he wanted to assert himself as being his own man and dropping me was a way of showing this to the Board. We lost 3–1 and I was re-instated for the following match. Whilst I didn't leave until the end of 1976–77 season things were never the same after that and he left the month after my move to Stoke City for £40,000. George Eastham was the Stoke manager then and he had been my boyhood hero. Not long after my signing he was replaced by Alan Durban who offered me the Player/Coach role and I was on the managerial ladder.

How do you rate the Blues v Villa derbies against the Liverpool v Everton games?

I've played in both and believe me the Blues v Villa games are unbeliev-able in terms of passion and equal to that of the Merseyside derbies. I played in four games against the Villa and won three of them!

What else do you remember about your time at Blues?

I got on really well with Jimmy Calderwood, now Manager at Aberdeen. When he was at Dunfermline I met him on a beach in Majorca walking with his Chairman. He was on the phone to Aberdeen about a possible move whilst obviously not wishing to alert the Chairman of his intentions. I shouted out that if Jimmy ever left I could be his replacement. I thought it was really funny but Jimmy was not best pleased. Thankfully it didn't affect our friendship long-term and when he was playing in Holland he would feed me information about the game over there.

What was your opinion of Trevor Francis?

I rate TF as one of the two best players I have seen in the English league, he had everything! The fact that the other player to match him was Alan Ball is testament to how highly I rated Trevor.

You had a decent ratio of goals at Blues can you remember any?

I can remember my first goal for Blues in a 4–0 win over Queens Park Rangers on 23 April 1974. Phil Parkes was the 'keeper and he paid me the compliment of acknowledging that it was one of the best goals he ever conceded. It was a strike from outside the box with my left peg!

SEASON BY SEASON

SEASON	LEAGUE APPEARANCES/ GOALS	FA CUP APPEARANCES/ GOALS	LEAGUE CUP APPEARANCES/ GOALS	OTHER APPEARANCES/ GOALS
1973–74	15 (1)	0 (0)	0 (0)	0 (0)
1974–75	39 (4)	6 (1)	1 (0)	6 (0)
1975–76	36 (8)	1 (0)	2 (0)	0 (0)
1976–77	25 (3)	2 (1)	1 (0)	0 (0)
TOTAL	115 (16)	9 (2)	4 (0)	6 (0)

HONOURS

As a Player:

- Preston North End – FA Cup runners-up: 1964.
- Everton – First Division champions: 1969–70, FA Charity Shield winner: 1970, FA Cup runner-up: 1968.
- Stoke City – Second Division third-place promotion: 1978–79.

As a Manager:

- Blackburn Rovers – Football League Third Division runner-up: 1979–80.
- Everton – First Division champions: 1984–85, 1986–87, First Division runner-up: 1985–86, FA Cup winner: 1983–84, FA Cup runner-up: 1984–85, 1985–86, FA Charity Shield winner: 1984–85, 1985–86, 1986–87, European Cup Winners' Cup winner: 1984–85, Football League Cup runner-up: 1983–84, Screen Sport Super Cup runner-up: 1985–86, Full Members Cup runner-up: 1990–91.
- Notts County – Anglo-Italian Cup winner: 1994–95.
- Sheffield United – First Division play-offs runner-up: 1996–97.

Individual:

- Stoke City player of the season: 1978.
- English Manager of the Year 1985.
- English Manager of the Year 1987.

DARREN PURSE

FULL NAME: Darren John Purse.
DATE OF BIRTH: 14 February 1977.
PLACE OF BIRTH: Stepney, London.

Playing Career:

1994–96 Leyton Orient 55 appearances 3 goals.

1996 BK-IFK (loan).

1996–98 Oxford United 59 appearances 5 goals.

1998–2004 Blues 168 appearances 9 goals.

2004–05 West Bromwich Albion 22 appearances 0 goals.

2005–09 Cardiff City 111 appearances 10 goals.

2009–11 Sheffield Wednesday 61 appearances 2 goals.

2011–12 Millwall 13 appearances 1 goal.

2011 Yeovil Town (loan) 5 appearances 0 goals.

2011–12 Plymouth Argyle (loan) 3 appearances 0 goals.

2012–23 Plymouth Argyle 42 appearances 2 goals.

2013 Port Vale 17 appearances 2 goals.

2013 IFK Mariehamn 6 appearances 0 goals.

2014 – 2015 Chesham United 11 appearances 0 goals.

Currently Welling United.

International:

1998 England Under 21 2 appearances 0 goals.

He joined Blues for £600,000 plus Kevin Francis (valued at £100,000) in February 1998. His debut as a substitute was on 17 February 1998 away at Crewe Alexandra a game Blues won 2–0 in front of a crowd of 5,559. The scorers that day were: Bryan Hughes and Dele Adebola. His first full debut was on 29 February 1998 at St Andrew's against Bury, Blues lost 3–1 in front of crowd of 20,021 with Michael Johnson scoring the consolation goal. He scored his first Blues goal at St Andrew's on 16 October 1999 against Crystal Palace a game Blues won 2–0 in front of a crowd of 21,582 the other scorer was Jon McCarthy. His final appearance in Royal Blue was away at Aston Villa on 27 February 2004. Blues drew 2–2 in front of a crowd of 40,061 with Stern John and Mikael Forssell scoring. He left Blues for a fee of £750,000 in June 2004 to join West Bromwich Albion.

He started just two First Division games at the end of the 1997–98 season. He made 11 league starts and nine substitute appearances in the 1998–99 campaign, and also appeared at St Andrew's as a substitute in the play-off defeat to Watford after David Holdsworth was sent off – he converted a penalty in the shoot-out, which ended in a 7–6 victory for Watford.

Purse established himself in the Blues first team in the 1999–2000 season, making 41 starts in league and cup competitions. He played at the Millennium Stadium, in the 2001 Worthington League Cup Final, and scored a 90th minute penalty to take the game into extra-time. He also converted his penalty in the shoot-out, which was won by Liverpool 5–4. With four goals in 49 appearances in the 2000–01 season, Purse won the vote to be named as the club's player of the season. This represented a significant turnaround for a young defender who was barracked by City supporters at the start of the campaign.

He missed the start of the 2001–02 season after a training ground shot from manager Trevor Francis broke his wrist. Francis was sacked just after Purse returned to full fitness, though the defender managed to keep his first team place under new boss Steve Bruce, and started 40 matches in the 2001–02 season.

In August 2002, Purse 'ended months of speculation' by signing a three-year deal (with an option for a fourth year). Having been courted by Arsenal, Charlton Athletic and Everton, he had previously been stripped of the club captaincy after twice rejecting Birmingham's offer of a £10,000 per week five-year contract. The protracted negotiations were put down to his ambitions for top-flight football, which were secured with victory in the 2002 play-off Final (Purse did not feature in the matchday squad). However he missed a large chunk of the 2002–03 season after his ankle became infected following surgery.

Purse had a quiet 2003–04 campaign, making only nine Premier League appearances. He did, however, hit the headlines after elbowing Chelsea striker Adrian Mutu; the Romanian reportedly launched a 'volley of expletives' at Purse in a post-match dressing room incident.

SEASON BY SEASON

SEASON	LEAGUE APPEARANCES/ GOALS	FA CUP APPEARANCES/ GOALS	LEAGUE CUP APPEARANCES GOALS	OTHER APPEARANCES/ GOALS
1997–98	8 (0)	0 (0)	0 (0)	0 (0)
1998–99	20 (0)	0 (0)	3 (0)	1 (0)
1999–2000	38 (2)	1 (0)	5 (1)	2 (0)
2000–01	37 (3)	1 (0)	9 (1)	2 (0)
2001–02	36 (3)	1 (0)	1 (0)	2 (0)
2002–03	20 (1)	0 (0)	1 (0)	0 (0)
2003–04	9 (0)	3 (0)	0 (0)	0 (0)

Senior Career Total: 562 league appearances 34 goals, 20 FA Cup appearance 0 goals, 44 League Cup appearances 6 goals, 19 Other appearances 3 goals. TOTAL 645 appearances 43 goals.

HONOURS

- Birmingham City – Football League Cup runners-up 2000–01, Player of the season 2000–01.
- Cardiff City – Football League Cup runners-up 2001, FA Cup runners-up 2008.
- Port Vale – Football League Two third-place promotion 2012–13.

KENNY CUNNINGHAM

FULL NAME: Kenneth Edward Cunningham.

DATE OF BIRTH: 28 June 1971.

PLACE OF BIRTH: Dublin, Ireland.

Playing Career:

Youth Career:

Home Farm.

Senior Career:

1988–89 Tolka Rovers, 1989–94 Millwall 136 appearances 1 goal, 1994–2002 Wimbledon 250 appearances 0 goals, 2002–2006 Blues 134 appearances 0 goals, 2006–07 Sunderland 11 appearances 0 goals. TOTAL 531 appearances 1 goal.

International:

1994 Republic of Ireland 'B' 1 appearance 0 goals, 1996–2005 Republic of Ireland Full 72 appearances 0 goals.

Cunningham moved to Blues, newly promoted to the Premier League, in 2002 for a £600,000 fee from Wimbledon. His debut was on 18 August 2002 away at Arsenal a game Blues lost 2–0 in front of a crowd of 38,018. He never scored for Blues in any competition. His final appearance in Royal Blue was at home against Newcastle United on 29 April 2006. Blues drew 0–0 in front of a crowd of 28,331. However after the club's relegation at the end of the 2005–06 season, Cunningham was released along with seven other first team players. On 11 May 2006, Cunningham launched a scathing attack in the press on Bruce and the board, blaming the club's relegation on a lack of preparation throughout the season and likening the club to a 'stiff corpse' that has 'no heartbeat and, more worryingly, no soul'. While fans were in the main supportive of Cunningham's views, the club reacted furiously, and chairman David Gold wondered, 'if Kenny would have said the same things if we'd stayed up, Portsmouth had gone down and he'd been given a lucrative new contract'.

Cunningham signed for Sunderland on 19 July.

Cunningham won a total of 72 caps for the Republic of Ireland. Cunningham was named team captain after the 2002 FIFA World Cup. According to manager Mick McCarthy: 'Kenny's qualities as a player are easy to see. From day one he has been a great influence. He is a talker on the pitch, he organises the players around him, and off the pitch he is a calm influence.'

He retired from international football at the age of 34 on 12 October

2005, following Ireland's draw with Switzerland at Lansdowne Road which resulted in his team's failure to qualify for the 2006 FIFA World Cup.

HONOURS

- Sunderland – Football League Championship 2006–07.
- First Blues' captain in The Premiership.

18 August 2002 v Arsenal (away) Attendance 36,018 of which 2,700 were Bluenoses Lost 2–0 to goals from Henry after 8 minutes and Wiltord on 24 minutes.

> **The team that day was:** Vaesen, Kenna, Grainger, Tebily, Cunningham, Purse, Johnson D, Cisse, Hughes, John, Horsfield Substitutes: Carter for Tebily (60 minutes) Lazaridis for Horsfield (71 minutes) Unused Substitutes: Mooney, Johnson M, Bennett.

Purse was booked and Cisse sent off.

STEPHEN CLEMENCE

reviewing the action
STEPHEN CLEMENCE

"Sav swung his free kick in and I managed to nick in front of Jamie Carragher and nod it in the corner, although a lot of the lads might tell you it was off my ear!"

Liverpool-born Stephen Clemence scored his first goal for Blues in a crucial 2-1 victory over his hometown club.

"I was delighted to get my first goal, because I don't get that many," said Clem.

"Obviously it was a big game for us coming on the back of a bad run.

"I didn't care who scored the goal as long as we won, but it was nice to score and come out of that bad spell.

"Sav swung his free kick in and I managed to nick in front of Jamie Carragher and nod it in the corner, although a lot of the lads might tell you it was off my ear!

"When Owen came on and nicked a goal it made it a bit tense for us, but if we hadn't have gone on to win the game it would have been a big injustice, particularly with the amount of effort we put in.

"At the time Liverpool were getting a lot of bad press because of their results but since then they have shown what a very good team they are with their performances."

Following on from the great win over Gerard Houllier's side, Clem was an integral part of the Blues team which gloriously turned over Villa on their own doorstep.

"The Liverpool win gave us confidence going into the Villa game," he said.

"It made the training ground a happier place to be around and certainly lifted our spirits.

"Having played in North London derbies I know that form often goes out of the window.

"Goals usually come about as a result of either somebody making a mistake or a moment of really good play.

"After Dublin was sent off we had a bad ten or 15 minutes and we didn't really take advantage of it.

"Then Jeff Kenna put a great cross in and Stan was there to meet it with a good header at the back post."

Following Dublin's dismissal and Lazaridis's goal, the atmosphere inside Villa Park intensified but Clem says the Blues players were determined not to let it affect their own game.

"The sending off and the goals flared things up a bit, but our only concern at that moment was to make sure that our fans behaved themselves, which I am delighted to say they did.

"We thought that if the Villa fans carried on and tried to get the game called off it was more than likely that we would have got the three points anyway.

"The one really disappointing thing to come out of the night was Nico's injury.

"It's a bad injury and we were all devastated for him but he's a strong lad and a great character and I'm sure he'll bounce back stronger than before."

After picking up their first back-to-back Premiership victories this season, Blues made the trip up the M6 to face what is fast becoming their number one bogey team, Manchester City. And sure to recent form against Keegan's men, Blues were disappointingly beaten by a single goal.

"We didn't go there for a draw, we went there believing we could win the game," said Clem.

"It turned out that we had to defend for large parts of the game and we did a good job of that, but then Robbie Fowler nicked in and scored with a great finish.

"Personally I felt that in the second half, when people were beginning to get tired, we could have played better than we did and I was quite disappointed.

"We didn't really threaten them much.

"We had a good chance to pick up a draw at the end, but unfortunately Geoff mis-kicked the ball.

"It was just one of those things, because 99 times out of 100 he would have scored it."

By Paul Leedham.

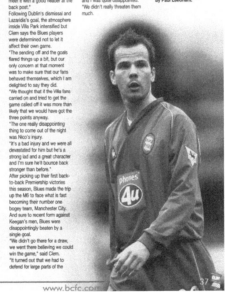

www.bcfc.com

FULL NAME: Stephen Neal Clemence.
DATE OF BIRTH: 31 March 1978.
PLACE OF BIRTH: Liverpool.

Playing Career:

Youth:

1994–97 Tottenham Hotspur.

Senior:

1997–2003 Tottenham Hotspur 91 appearances 2 goals; 2003–2007 Blues 121 appearances 8 goals, 2007–08 Leicester City 31 appearances 2 goals. TOTAL 243 appearances 12 goals.

International:

1998 England Under 21 1 appearance 0 goals.

He scored his first senior Blues goal at St Andrew's on 23 February 2003 against Liverpool a game Blues won 2–1 in front of a crowd of 29,449 the other scorer was Clinton Morrison. His final appearance in Royal Blue was away at Preston North End on 6 May 2007. Blues lost 1–0 in front of a crowd of 16,837.

In the summer of 2007 he joined Leicester City in a three-year £750,000 deal.

When the transfer window opened in January 2003, Birmingham City agreed a fee believed to be in the region of £1.3 million for Clemence. He joined Birmingham City for a fee of £900,000 on 10 January, signing a three-and-a-half-year contract. He made his debut in a 4–0 defeat to Arsenal at St Andrew's on 12 January 2003 in front of a crowd of 29,505. In July 2003, Birmingham City participated in the Premier League Asia Trophy in Kuala Lupur losing out in the final but beating Malaysia 4–0 for third place, with Clemence scoring the third goal. Injury struck again in the 2003–04 season, meaning that once again he had to sit several games out. Nonetheless, he finished the season by making his 50th appearance for the club.

In the 2005–06 season, the club opened talks with Clemence in May 2005, and he signed a new three-year contract on 14 October. He was injury prone suffering a calf problem in a 1–0 defeat to Aston Villa on 16 October 2005, a torn hamstring on 4 April 2006,in a 1–0 win over Bolton Wanderers which sidelined him for the remainder of the season while Birmingham were relegated from the Premier League

He contemplated leaving the club after being dropped twice in 2006–07, but later became an integral part of the team helping the club win promotion back to the Premier League. For his contributions, Clemence was named the club's player of the year and players' player of the year that season.

His crucial goal at Derby County in October re-ignited the promotion push when boss Steve Bruce was under pressure and he left with Bruce declaring 'I will never get a better professional or meet a nicer person than Clem.'

On 21 November 2004, Clemence and Birmingham City teammate Dwight Yorke had two Blackburn Rovers supporters arrested by police for racist abuse in a 3–3 draw at Ewood Park, before pressing charges against them.

HONOURS

- Tottenham Hotspur – Football League Cup winners 1998–99.
- Birmingham City – Championship runners-Up 2006–07.

SEASON BY SEASON

SEASON	LEAGUE APPEARANCES/ GOALS	FA CUP APPEARANCES/ GOALS	LEAGUE CUP APPEARANCES/ GOALS	OTHER APPEARANCES/ GOALS
2002–03	15 (2)	0 (0)	0 (0)	0 (0)
2003–04	35 (2)	2 (1)	1 (0)	0 (0)
2004–05	22 (0)	2 (0)	2 (0)	0 (0)
2005–06	15 (0)	4 (0)	2 (0)	0 (0)
2006–07	34 (4)	0 (0)	1 (0)	0 (0)

Career Total: 278 appearances 15 goals

MICHAEL JOHNSON

FULL NAME: Michael Owen Johnson.
DATE OF BIRTH: 4 July 1973.
PLACE OF BIRTH: Nottingham.

Playing Career:

1991–1995 Notts County 107 appearances No goals.

1995–2003 Birmingham City 262 appearances 12 goals.

2003–2008 Derby County 138 appearances 4 goals.

2007 Sheffield Wednesday (Loan) 13 appearances No goals.

2008 Notts County (Loan) 29 appearances 2 goals.

Total 561 appearances 19 goals.

International Career:

Jamaica – 12 full international appearances.

Management Career:

13 October to 27 October 2009 Notts County (caretaker) 2 games, 1 win, 1 draw.

BLUES CAREER:

He joined Blues, who had just been promoted back to the First Division for £230,000 at the end of that relegation season. 'Johnno' played 33 league games in his first season for Blues helping them to consolidate in the league with a mid-table finish. His debut was on 2 September 1995 away at Barnsley a game Blues won 5–0 in front of a crowd of 11,121. The scorers that day were: Hunt (pen) Claridge, Forsyth, Doherty, Charlery. He scored his first Blues goal at St Andrew's on 22 February 1998 against Sheffield United a game Blues won 2–0 in front of a crowd of 17,965 the other scorer was Grainger. His final appearance in Royal Blue was as a substitute, away at Newcastle United on 3 May 2003. Blues lost 1–0 in front of a crowd of 52,146. He left Blues on a free transfer in August 2003 to join Derby County.

SEASON BY SEASON

SEASON	LEAGUE APPEARANCES/ GOALS	FA CUP APPEARANCES/ GOALS	LEAGUE CUP APPEARANCES/ GOALS
1995–96	31+2 (0)	1 (0)	5 (0)
1996–97	28 +7 (0)	1+2 (0)	0+2 (0)
1997–98	22+16 (3)	0+2 (0)	1+4 (0)
1998–99	45+2 (5)	1 (0)	4 (2)
1999–2000	31+5 (2)	2 (0)	4 (0)
2000–2001	41 (2)	1 (0)	8 (2)
2001–2002	31+2 (1)	0 (0)	3 (1)
2002–2003	5+1 (0)	0 (0)	0 (0)

HONOURS

- Notts County: 1990–1991 Division Three Play-off winners promoted to the old second division, Voted Young Player of the Year – 1991–1992 Division Two Play-off winners promoted to the old first division, 1993–1994 Anglo Italian Cup Runners-up, 1994–1995 Anglo Italian Winners.
- Blues: 1998–1999 Division One Play-off semi-finalist, Voted Player of the Year, 1999–2000 Division One Play-off semi-finalist, 2000–2001 Division One Play-off semi-finalist, Voted Player of the Year, 2001–2002 Division One Play-off winners promoted to the Premier League, 2000–2001 Worthington Cup Runners-up, Team Captain.
- Derby County: 2004–2005 Championship Play-off semi-finalist, 2005–2006 Championship Play-off winners, promoted to the Premier League – Club Captain.

OTHER NOTABLES

Billy Edmunds was the first-ever Blues' captain, he was also the first Honorary Secretary from 1875–1884.

Pre-1900 captains included: Arthur James, Harry Morris (later a Director of BCFC), Caesar Jenkyns.

Alec Leake – Captained Promotion team to Division One in season 1900–01.

Billy Beer – Captained Promotion team to Division One in season 1902–03.

Alex McClure – Captained Division Two Champions side in season 1920–21.

Pre-World War II skippers included: Alec Leslie, Lew Stoker, Cyril Trigg.

Frank Womack – Longest serving Captain, 1908 to 1928.

In the 60s Roy Warhurst, Dick Neal, Terry Hennessey, Ron Wylie and Ray Martin took on the role for limited periods of time.

In the 70s Joe Gallagher, Malcolm Page and Tony Towers skippered the team.

In the noughties Barry Ferguson held the office and in recent times, Steven Caldwell, Chris Burke and Paul Caddis have worn the armband.

ND - #0192 - 270225 - C0 - 234/156/14 - PB - 9781780914534 - Gloss Lamination